IMAGINARY LINE

Also by Jacques Poitras

Beaverbrook: A Shattered Legacy (2007, 2008)
The Right Fight: Bernard Lord and the Conservative Dilemma (2004)

IMAGINARY LINE

Life on an Unfinished Border

JACQUES POITRAS

The poem "Driving to Fort Kent in a Mid-Spring Snowfall" is © Laurence Hutchman and Guernica Editions, 2007. Reprinted by permission of the copyright holders and of Broken Jaw Press. Quotations from Samuel Leonard Tilley's correspondence reprinted by permission of Archives and Special Collections, Harriet Irving Library, University of New Brunswick. Quotations from William Odell's correspondence reprinted by permission of the New Brunswick Museum.

Unless otherwise identified, all photographs are by the author.

Edited by John Sweet.
Cover and page design by Jaye Haworth.
Maps by Peter Manchester.
Printed in Canada.
10 9 8 7 6 5 4 3 2 1

Library and Archives Canada Cataloguing in Publication

Poitras, Jacques, 1968-
  Imaginary line: life on an unfinished border / Jacques Poitras.

Includes bibliographical references and index.
Also issued in electronic format.
ISBN 978-0-86492-650-0

  1. New Brunswick — Boundaries — Maine. 2. Maine — Boundaries — New Brunswick.
3. New Brunswick — Relations — Maine. 4. Maine — Relations — New Brunswick. I. Title.

FC182.P64 2011   971.5'1   C2011-902887-5

Goose Lane Editions acknowledges the financial support of the Canada Council for the Arts, the Government of Canada through the Canada Book Fund (CBF), and the government of New Brunswick through the Department of Wellness, Culture, and Sport. The author acknowledges the financial support of the Canada Council for the Arts under the Creative Writing Program.

Goose Lane Editions
Suite 330, 500 Beaverbrook Court
Fredericton, New Brunswick
CANADA E3B 5X4
www.gooselane.com

For Giselle, Sophie, and Zachary

From this hour I ordain myself loos'd of limits and imaginary lines,
Going where I list, my own master total and absolute,
Listening to others, considering well what they say,
Pausing, searching, receiving, contemplating,
Gently, but with undeniable will, divesting myself of the holds that
would hold me.

I inhale great draughts of space,
The east and the west are mine, and the north and the south are mine.

— Walt Whitman, "Song of the Open Road"

The boundary between Canada and the United States is a typically
human creation; it is physically invisible, geographically illogical,
militarily indefensible, and emotionally inescapable.

— Hugh L. Keenleyside, Canadian diplomat, 1929

CONTENTS

LIST OF MAPS

INTRODUCTION
GATEWAYS

IN JANUARY 2010, STEPHEN HARPER, the prime minister of Canada, travelled to New Brunswick to cut the ribbon at a new border crossing with the United States. The ceremony was a mere formality. For two months already, eighteen-wheeler operators, commuters, and tourists had been driving across the new black asphalt spanning the St. Croix River in barely the amount of time it took to take their passports out of their pockets.

So the bridge, the third to connect St. Stephen, New Brunswick, with Calais, Maine, was already achieving the objective for which it had been designed. As Harper himself pointed out in his speech, in eight short weeks, commercial traffic crossing the border between the two communities had increased by twenty percent. The bridge was also fulfilling a secondary purpose: the historic downtown of St. Stephen, linked to Calais since the nineteenth century, was no longer choked by long lineups of transport trucks stretching to the edge of town. And local residents, many with relatives on the other side of the border, were no longer subjected to long waits when crossing for a visit or to buy inexpensive milk or gas. Traffic was moving more efficiently on the two older bridges as trucks diverted to the new one.

By January, when Harper arrived, people on both sides of the St. Croix were already wondering how they had ever managed to function without it.

Still, politicians and their communications advisors love a good ribbon-cutting, and they positively adore them when the facility to be "opened" offers an apparent solution to a complex problem.

And no problem has been more complex for Canadian prime ministers than relations with the United States, particularly following September 11, 2001. The new bridge may have made it easier for folks in St. Stephen or Calais to visit their American aunts or Canadian cousins, but what really needed to keep moving across the border was money. The modern checkpoints at each end of the new bridge featured the very latest in high-tech equipment — weights, scanners, digital imaging, and a myriad of other tools — to ensure that commerce was not impeded by tighter security.

For Harper and his government, the bridge was part of the so-called "Atlantic Gateway," the latest in a long series of slogans used by various governments to give a visionary sheen to a new round of spending on highways, bridges, and other transportation infrastructure. This one, at least, had some basis in history: the idea was to strengthen Atlantic Canada's ties to one of the most lucrative markets on earth, the densely populated eastern seaboard of the United States. Merchants and their goods had been crossing the St. Croix for more than a century before the border had even been drawn there. The priority now was to ensure that trade continued.

And so Harper opened a bridge that had been open for two months. At his side were his senior cabinet minister for New Brunswick, Greg Thompson — who happened to be the member of parliament for St. Stephen — and the premier of New Brunswick, Shawn Graham. They briefly toured the inspection booths and greeted the Canada Border Services Agency officers, then entered the vast, grey, antiseptic building where more than a hundred local officials, dignitaries, and Conservative Party supporters had gathered.

Early in his tenure, Harper's public pronouncements about the United States had been closely watched by his political enemies, who routinely accused him of being too pro-American and thus too likely to surrender Canada's interests to the superpower to the south. As opposition leader, Harper had appeared on Fox News, where he reinforced American alarmism when he described Canada's "porous borders and immigration system." As if to counter the perception, within days of taking office in

Prime Minister Stephen Harper, New Brunswick Premier Shawn Graham and MP Greg Thompson meet Canadian Border Services officers during the official opening of a new customs building at St. Stephen, New Brunswick, January 8, 2010.
(Province of New Brunswick photo)

2006, Harper made bullish comments about Canada's sovereignty over Arctic waters, in defiance of American claims that the U.S. did not need Canadian permission to sail through what it considered international passages.

On the banks of the St. Croix River, however, there was no need for the prime minister to calibrate his views and no political risk in embracing America. Here, the United States was such a facet of daily life that one of the leading scholars of the area, Harold Davis, had labelled it "an international community." Harper echoed that idea in his speech. "One does not build a border crossing like this one to exclude neighbours," he said in his flat, even-speaking style. "It is the kind of border crossing you build to welcome friends and to foster greater trade between them. For friends we are, and friends our two peoples will always be."

The prime minister's speechwriters had done their homework, building the remarks around the notion that St. Stephen and Calais were a microcosm of the Canada-U.S. relationship: forced together by geography yet living together in harmony most of the time, despite occasional complications. All the requisite rhetoric was there, including the words of an American president who had summered just an hour away on the New Brunswick island of Campobello. Franklin Delano Roosevelt, Harper recounted, had bristled at a news account of his 1936 state visit to Canada that reported he had been welcomed "with all the honours customarily accorded to a foreign ruler." Roosevelt, Harper recounted, had responded, "I've never heard a Canadian refer to an American as a foreigner. He is just an American. And in the same way, in the United States, Canadians are not foreigners. They are Canadians."

The normally taciturn Harper chuckled as he reached further back in time for an even better anecdote. "I love this story," he smiled, recounting what had happened when British officials prepared for invasion along the St. Croix at the outbreak of the War of 1812. Despite the hostilities elsewhere, "St. Stephen actually gave Calais gunpowder to bolster its Independence Day celebrations," he said, as the crowd issued a knowing murmur of approval.

Thompson, the local MP, may have been engaging in hyperbole when he predicted, during his turn at the podium, that "historians will look back on this as a very defining moment, a turning point for Atlantic Canada and the northeastern seaboard of the United States." But Thompson, who knew his local history, could not help but see Harper's photo-op as part of a much larger story. It swept back to 1604, when Samuel de Champlain landed on a small island just eight miles downriver from the new bridge. Though the settlement lasted only a single winter, it left behind a landmark that eighteenth-century negotiators would use to mark the boundary between the United States and the British colonies.

Even closer to the new bridge was a glimpse of the future of that imaginary line. Just a mile away, hanging about a hundred feet above the river's current, a set of three ordinary-looking power transmission cables connect to a small dam across the St. Croix. They allow this small corner of Maine, isolated from New England's vast electricity transmission network, to plug into New Brunswick's grid — a physical manifestation of a growing trade in energy that is likely to define the next century of Canada-U.S. relations on the eastern half of the continent.

The two countries, and New Brunswick and Maine in particular, were so deeply linked by history, blood, and trade that they would not be able to extricate themselves from the relationship if they wanted to. This was, Harper suggested, an example to the world. "No two nations on earth," he told the crowd, "have worried less about the line on the map that divides them and more about how to build good will across it."

For years, the only apprehension most New Brunswickers had experienced at the border was during the return to Canada, when they had to decide whether to declare the American goods they had purchased and pay the tax and duties or to stuff some of the items beneath a seat or a coat and play the odds that Customs officers would not search the car. Beyond that, the border was not to be feared. It was merely an administrative marker where one country gave way to another.

Yet in other ways it was a powerful symbol. During the existential debate over free trade in the 1988 Canadian election, the Liberals jolted the campaign with a television ad showing fictitious U.S. and Canadian negotiators finalizing the agreement. "There's one line I'd like to change," the American said, using an eraser to remove the border from a map of the two countries.

Borders have captured my imagination, and have been a subtext of my journalism, for more than two decades. A year after that free-trade election came the first great defining geopolitical moment of my generation: the Berlin Wall fell and, across the middle of Europe, checkpoints opened, barbed-wire fences came down, and people streamed across previously forbidden frontiers. I was one of them: on a January night in 1993, I was on a night train from Frankfurt to Prague, unable to sleep, when it halted just inside what had once been the Iron Curtain. A vestigial ritual of the Cold War played out: surly young men speaking in indecipherable Slavic tones moved through the compartments, looking suspiciously at Western passports before grudgingly stamping them. It felt like I was leaving the West behind; in fact, the West was following me across the border. By the end of the 1990s, the region was integrating rapidly into NATO and the European Union. On a return visit in the summer of 2001, I marvelled not only at the robust democracy and the consumerist culture but also at the new generation of relaxed, smiling Czech border guards. In one corner of the globe, at least, the promise of a world without borders seemed tantalizingly close to being fulfilled.

Prague made me a believer in vanishing borders. The American journalist and author Robert Kaplan, one of the leading chroniclers of the idea, perceived a darker side to the trend. The evaporation of arbitrary, politically imposed boundaries was allowing ancient impulses — long-contained ethnic grievances, trading patterns, and rivalries over natural resources — to re-emerge, often violently. In 1998, Kaplan, who had written on Afghanistan, the Balkans, and the developing world, turned his apocalyptic lens on his own country. In a journey across the United States, chronicled in his book *An Empire Wilderness*, he observed hardening race and class divisions, hollowed-out inner cities, and pressures of geography, climate, and history, all of them threatening to splinter the country.

Given what he considered the inevitable collapse of Canada — a popular prediction at the time, given Québec had come close to voting to separate in 1995 — Kaplan presumed that natural north-south links between American border states and their neighbouring Canadian provinces would soon reassert themselves and "unleash cross-border energies everywhere on the continent." Though his forecast of Canada's demise and the emergence of a Swiss-style North American confederacy of regions has not come to pass, the idea of a regional trading bloc melding New England and the Maritimes, with the New Brunswick-Maine border as its fulcrum, has gained favour among the political and business élite. A 2006 roundtable convened by the Canadian government to discuss "cross-border regions" found the Maritime-New England dynamic distinguished by the "importance of history and geography" and a "strong sense of regional identity," two favourite Kaplan themes.

The second great defining moment of my generation was September 11, 2001, which effectively shattered the vanishing-border era. Like many other journalists, my first instinct that day was to get to the border as quickly as possible to see what was happening. The morning after the attacks, I drove from Fredericton, the capital of New Brunswick, to the land crossing at Houlton, Maine, the northeastern terminus of Interstate 95. After submitting to a thorough security sweep of the CBC vehicle, I headed to the Houlton hospital, where Tammy Chase, one of the many Canadian nurses who commuted across the border to Maine every day, told me her family had asked her to stay home. "The sense was there yesterday, 'Why are you going into that country where everything is happening?'"

Despite the attacks, Tom Moakler, the American hospital administrator, had been over to Florenceville, New Brunswick, the night before for his regular indoor tennis game with his daughter. "I was debating whether to go over because I thought there might be a long line, but there wasn't," he said, visibly relieved. Both Chase and Moakler were hopeful the border would not change, but in the main waiting room, George Solesky of Monticello, Maine, a regular visitor to New Brunswick, was less optimistic. "I don't want it to affect us," he told me. "Usually this is what happens. We get inconvenienced because of the crooked people. I mean, why are we always inconvenienced to solve these problems? And it still doesn't solve the problem."

Solesky was prescient. The border was changing. Before 2001, the stories I filed from Maine reflected a porous boundary: there were the American school kids attending French immersion classes as part of an effort, inspired by bilingual New Brunswick next door, to salvage their francophone culture. Or the merchants and industries in New Brunswick and Maine who watched as a fluctuating exchange rate sent bargain-hungry shoppers stampeding first in one direction across the line, then the other. Late in 2001, though, my border stories began to reflect a harder edge. A month after 9/11, I was in Lubec, Maine, the easternmost town in the United States and the closest piece of mainland for the residents of Campobello Island, New Brunswick. "The border tightened up that day,"

Terri Greene told me as we sat in a local coffee shop and watched the international bridge vanish in a thick fog, then reappear. "There were more officers on both sides, and they were asking more questions, and they were going through everything that was in each vehicle that came across, and being very, very careful of what, and who, came across the border. If anyone was any question at all, they were sent back, or sometimes they were detained and questioned."

Greene was born in Lubec, but she and her husband Afton lived on Campobello, where he had been raised. Their story was typical of a more idyllic time on the border. They began dating before the international bridge was built in 1962. "There was a car ferry," Terri told me, "but in the evening the car ferry didn't run, and if anyone wanted to come from Campobello to Lubec, they had to come by rowboat." Afton picked up the story: "Most island guys certainly thought the American girls were much prettier, and there was more going on in the town of Lubec, so the only way we had to get across was to get a dory and row across. There was a lot of tide here in the narrows. Lot of wind came in. Snow, sleet. But I always got through. I look back on it today and I wonder. I must have been crazy. But I guess maybe that's what girls will do to you." Now they feared how increased security would affect the relationship between Lubec and Campobello. "We feel the same toward each other as we always have, yet there's just that little bit of difference on the border," Terri said. "There is an undercurrent that wasn't there before."

Canadian author James Laxer was researching his book *The Border* when the 9/11 attacks took place. Laxer lamented the increase in U.S. border security, but only in passing. His book was more of a lament for American foreign policy in general, and a recap of standard left-wing tropes about the United States. Laxer rejected Kaplan's notion of a north-south axis defining the cross-border relationship, citing instead Canadian political economist Harold Innis and historian Donald Creighton, who had argued that Canada was defined by the east-west commercial-communications path of its waterways, most notably the Great Lakes and the St. Lawrence River. "Understood this way, the logic of a Canada that was separate from the United States jumped out at them," Laxer writes. Left unsaid was where New Brunswick and the Maritimes, a geographical and geological extension of New England, fit into this St. Lawrence-centred vision.

No matter: the border, Laxer argued, is a protective barrier against the United States. He called for Canada to strengthen its own border security to keep America, and everything it represented, at bay. His view appeared to prevail: between 2005 and 2009, the number of passenger vehicles travelling between St. Stephen and Calais, the busiest crossing between the Maritimes and New England, dropped by twenty-two percent. The relationship appeared to have changed forever.

After Harper finished his remarks, the U.S. ambassador to Canada, David Jacobson, stepped to the podium. "I can assure you that feeling of brotherhood and camaraderie is felt by people on my side of the border as well," said Jacobson, a Chicago lawyer and a top fundraiser for Barack Obama in the 2008 presidential campaign. Like Harper, the ambassador sprinkled local references into his speech, mentioning how delighted he was to return to St. Stephen for more of the town's famous Ganong chocolates. This was another reminder that the ceremony was marking something that had actually occurred two months earlier: Jacobson had scored his first batch of chocolates when he had come to cut the ribbon at the Calais end of the bridge in November 2009. "Some things are important enough that you do them twice," he joked, turning the lack of coordination among governments into a crowd-pleasing punchline.

When Harper returned to the podium to take questions from reporters, however, it became apparent that the ribbon-cuttings weren't the only thing out of sync in the international community of the St. Croix. Despite the professions of long-standing friendship, there were still two countries here, and two definitions of the national interest. A reporter from a local New Brunswick weekly newspaper was the first to raise an issue that, like the new bridge itself, was both international and profoundly local: a dispute between Canada and the United States over liquefied natural gas terminals that developers wanted to build on the American side of Passamaquoddy Bay and the St. Croix. "I think you know our position on this," Harper told the reporter. "There are things from time to time on which we don't agree with our American friends. Our position is that those are sovereign Canadian waters. We oppose the tanker traffic through this passage and we continue to make representations to the highest level of the American government." A second journalist pressed the matter: would the Canadian government pass a regulation to explicitly ban the tankers? "The government will examine all of its options," the prime minister said. "Obviously our preference is to work with our American friends to try and find a resolution to this issue."

The Canadians in the room, most of whom opposed the Maine LNG proposals because of their potential impact on the environment and tourism in the area, were heartened. Despite the caricatures of the prime minister as an American lackey, his opposition seemed genuine and firm. The American mayors and business leaders, however, were dismayed. For them, the LNG proposals meant badly needed jobs in an isolated, economically depressed coastal area at the easternmost edge of the United States. But the border gave Canada leverage, and Harper seemed inclined to use it.

Borders are crucibles, places where populations and countries collide: how they manage that collision says much about them. In the twenty-first century, Canada and the United States seem once again to face a choice between Kaplan's vision of a north-south axis and Laxer's concept of east-west fortresses.

In my travels I have crossed borders that barely mattered, in the European Union; that were frighteningly militarized, between China and Mongolia; and that were seethingly, ethnically ambiguous, in the former Yugoslavia. The New Brunswick-Maine border, an accident of history, has been like all of those borders at different times. "In places, the border feels arbitrary," James Laxer writes. It felt arbitrary because it was — and it still is. It began as a boundary of the imagination, a line drawn by politicians and diplomats, and then it became quite real. Yet even today it feels unresolved.

That is why it tells us such a compelling story about ourselves.

PART ONE
DRAWING THE LINE

C'est la langue des ancêtres du Maine.
C'est comme un rêve, ces mots étranges
qui chantent comme les flocons...

— Laurence Hutchman, "Driving to Fort Kent in a Mid-Spring Snowfall"

I thought that if the commissioners themselves, and the King of Holland with them, had spent a few days here, with their packs upon their backs, looking for that 'highland,' they would have had an interesting time, and perhaps it would have modified their view of the question somewhat.

— Henry David Thoreau, *The Maine Woods*, 1864

1. WICKED CLOSE

THE LOON'S CRIES HAVE FADED somewhere behind us as our canoe moves up the narrow channel. The river widens, opening up into the bottom of a wide, long body of water called Beau Lac. Ahead, a young eagle skims the treetops, following the edge of the water. The bird carves a long arc in the blue sky, then flies away in a straight line up the middle of the lake. There is silence as the engine stops. The treetops of a distant hill appear to slide behind a closer hill, an illusion created as the boat, seemingly still, drifts in the current beneath the noontime sun.

The borders of Québec, Maine, and New Brunswick
meet at the bottom of Beau Lac.

It feels as if nothing here has changed for centuries: loons, eagles, and beaver dams. The water, flowing south. And the trees. There is no sign whatsoever of what we call civilization.

Earlier, downstream, on Glazier Lake and Grew Pond, we saw a scattering of small boats, each of them holding one or two people fishing close to the western or eastern shore. They were all locals: the Saint-François waterway is largely unknown except to a small number of serious fishermen and to residents of nearby towns, of which there are few. Even they rarely venture to where we are now. There are no good roads leading this far, and the trip by boat took about forty-five minutes — and that was after getting to the lakeshore in the first place.

We also glimpsed markers on each shore, white reference monuments used to measure the precise location of the invisible line we followed up the Saint-François waterway. It is this line, an artificial, invisible construct, that I have come to "see." I am right on top of it now: it runs from bow to stern below the canoe. And there is another line cutting across the lake to meet it. It, too, exists only in treaties and on maps, so I do not immediately realize, as we sit here in the current, that we have reached our destination.

A voice behind me breaks the silence. "Maine is there," says the other man in the canoe, and I glance to the left, to the western shore, perhaps twenty feet away. "And New Brunswick is here," he adds as I look to the right, to thick trees at land's edge, twenty feet in the other direction.

I turn in time to see Dr. Yves Carrier point a few feet farther up the same eastern shore. "And Québec is there," he says at last. "So this is the spot."

Depending on your perspective — and here, I am learning, much depends on your perspective — this is where New Brunswick's Madawaska panhandle thrusts itself between the hinterlands of Québec and the United States, or where the northern tip of Maine is wedged into the narrow meeting place of two Canadian provinces. Either way, this is where the international boundary between New Brunswick and Maine begins. Any exploration of that boundary has to begin here as well. And when I asked around for someone to bring me to this starting point so I could see the exact location with my own eyes, I was told to contact Yves Carrier:

physician, community activist, environmentalist, and forceful defender of the Rivière Saint-François.

From behind the sunglasses perched on his impish face, Carrier watches and waits a good long time to let me take in the moment. Only when I signal that I have absorbed it does he fire up the motor, turn us around, and point the nose of the canoe straight down the Saint-François. We ease up to cruising speed, following the current, and the border, back towards the Saint John River.

The Saint-François flows down from a line of hills in Québec that separates the St. Lawrence watershed from that of the Saint John, which is why Carrier is among those who believe the United States got a raw deal in the Treaty of Washington, the document which, in 1842, drew the international boundary along our path. The debate over the border, which almost led to a war, was based on a single word, "highlands," in an earlier treaty of 1783. The American interpretation — that the drafters of that previous agreement clearly meant the line of hills Carrier referred to — would have given the United States everything below those highlands, including both shores of the Saint-François and of the Saint John.

But London, Carrier says, played a clever game by muddying the waters. "The British always interpreted it like it was confusing, but it wasn't confusing at all," he calls to me over the hum of the little motor at the back of the canoe. "Everyone knew the highlands because of the portages. You rowed up the streams of the St. Lawrence, you got out, you did your portage and you got back in. Those were the highlands. Everyone who'd been through this area, from Champlain on down, knew that area as the highlands. It was a good way to draw a border. It was logical, because whoever controlled the watershed controlled the territory. Champlain met natives around what's now Saint John, whom he'd met at Tadoussac, and they told him about the Madawaska portage. But when it came time to interpret the treaty, the British said it was a mess. It was 'confusing.'" He pauses for effect. "Everyone knew where they were. No contest. But it created a fight that went on for decades."

Other than as an obvious physical barrier — though in some narrow sections, it is barely that — there is nothing about the Saint-François

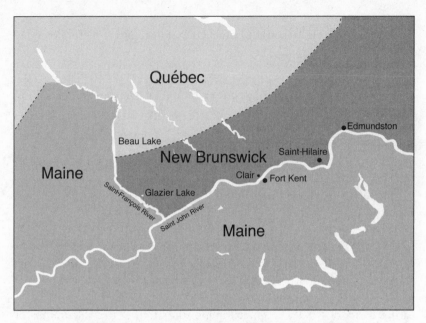

The Saint-François River and the Upper Saint John River Valley.

that makes sense as a border. It is so arbitrary that a local legend holds that it was an accident, or worse. One story has it that when surveyors arrived in Clair, New Brunswick, on the Saint John River, to mark the line in the 1842 treaty, they spent too much time drinking at a local inn before continuing on their intended course southwest up the Saint John. And whether by mistake, or encouraged by crafty Americans who saw a chance to snatch some extra territory, they found themselves staggering northwest, surveying the Saint-François, believing it to be the Saint John. "Now this is a story and I will not vouch for it," Jim Connors, a descendant of some of the early settlers to the area, recalled once in an oral history interview with researchers from the University of Maine.

The story is, in fact, fiction. The Treaty of Washington specifies that the border runs up the Saint John to the mouth of the Saint-François, then veers northwest to follow that river. The line is where it was supposed to be, and is not the result of insidious motives. But the folklore surrounding it is a measure of its illogical configuration and the chicanery that went into its creation.

Dr. Yves Carrier keeps to the Canadian side on the Saint-François River.

Carrier keeps the canoe to the left, close to the Canadian shore, as we continue downstream, though at times he uses a flick of his paddle to steer us into American territory when he needs to avoid shallows or navigate rapids. There is a risk of arrest, though if U.S. border officers suddenly come crashing out of the woods, it will take only a moment to nose back into Canadian territory. On our way up the river, Carrier points out the mouth of a stream on the American side. In the years after Prohibition, a local Canadian set up a floating cottage there to cater to lumbermen from Allagash, a Maine logging town that remained dry. They would travel up a logging trail to the lake and take a small boat out to the cottage. "They played cards and had a few drinks," Carrier says. "And when U.S. Customs were around, they anchored themselves across the line so that U.S. Customs had no jurisdiction. And when the RCMP were around, they'd go back across to the other side of the line."

I met Carrier earlier in the day at his house near the village of Clair, and we followed Route 205 along the north bank of the Saint John River, deeper into the panhandle, towards the mouth of the Saint-François.

Across the river, Maine's Highway 161 followed the south bank. Carrier, raised in Edmundston, the largest nearby city, loves this remote part of Madawaska County: as a young medical intern in Toronto, he heard a song about the region one night on Radio-Canada, and decided to come home. He eventually immersed himself in the history and the natural beauty of the upper Saint John, an outdoorsman's paradise of green hills and concealed lakes.

It is also a landscape shaped by an international boundary. Since 1842, the border has defined the local timber industry, the practice of religion, and the language spoken among friends. It spawned a smuggling empire in the small villages on the New Brunswick side. "Until the Second World War, the border was really a suggestion," Carrier says. "The guys from over there came to see the girls over here, and the guys from over here went to see the girls over there. There were marriages of people from both sides. But after the war, the border became stricter. Visas were harder to get." Even so, as a young man, Carrier paid it little heed. He often crossed the bridge from Edmundston, which had no public pool, to the town of Madawaska, Maine, to go swimming. His first girlfriend was from there. Today, he refuses on principle to order a passport, which the United States now requires of visitors, even those who, for decades, considered the American side of the Saint John to be part of their homeland.

In the places that matter to Carrier, on the rivers that feed his soul, he can still imagine that the border does not exist at all. At the northern end of Grew Pond, where it narrows into another channel, we come within twenty feet of another canoe. The sun is overhead and two young, beefy guys have their shirts off and their lines in the water. Maybe we stray into their country, or they drift into ours. More likely, the border is somewhere between our two boats. They are close enough to exchange greetings, in the way that men of the river do, without raising their voices.

"Is that a two-stroke?" one of them asks Carrier, nodding at his small engine.

"Yeah, a two-stroke," he answers.

"Nice day," says the American.

"You too," Carrier calls over his shoulder as we continue on.

I spot a web address on the side of their canoe, and a few days after my trip down the Saint-François, I track down the young man in the boat. His name is Benjamin Rioux, and he is a college student from Fort Kent, Maine, who spends his summers tying flies, field-testing L.L. Bean fishing gear, and guiding fishermen on the lakes and the rivers of the Great North Woods of Maine. "It's almost like you forget when you're on the water that it's two different countries," he says over the phone. "We've caught ourselves a few times when we were going to dock on the Canadian side and we say, 'We can't dock there, that's Canada.'

"People who we bring there who've never been there before think it's so cool: 'That's Canada.' They just can't get over it. They say, 'I can't believe that's Canada — that's wicked neat.'" And something else is at work on the border, something more intimate, and yet so powerful that even Rioux's guests notice it. "They sort of comment on how everybody seems so nice, and everybody's the same, and you can't really tell that there's a difference in culture, or in background."

The last incorporated municipality on the New Brunswick side of the Saint John is named for the nearby river: Saint-François de Madawaska. On the Maine side a few miles further up, directly across from the mouth of the Saint-François, is an American hamlet with an anglicized version of the name, St. Francis, though it was not always called that. "I was coming down the river once and I met a man on the American side who was fishing," Carrier says. "We started chatting. He was francophone, but I noticed his pick-up had an American license plate, so I asked where he was from. 'I'm from Saint-François,' he said. I didn't know him, and there aren't too many people I don't know in Saint-François. I said, 'You come from Saint-François?' and he said, 'Yeah. I live just up there.' I said, 'Ah, St. Francis.' 'Oui, Saint-François.' One or two generations ago, it was still Saint-François, even on the American side."

Lloyd Woods, the former head of the U.S. Immigration and Naturalization Service in nearby Madawaska, Maine, used to ask students on his school visits, "How many here have travelled to a foreign country in the last six months?"Two or three students would raise their hands. "How many of you have travelled to Canada in the last six months?" Every hand in the class would go up.

The border has been here for more than a century and a half, but it still has not completely divided what was once a single settlement. The Upper Saint John is precisely the *opposite* of Lord Durham's infamous description of British North America as "two nations warring within the bosom of a single state." Here, there is a single French culture straddling the imaginary line between two countries. "They're borders that were put here after the area was settled," Carrier says. "We have the same language, the same culture. Here it's become more francisized, and there it's more anglicized, but the DNA is the same."

On the New Brunswick side, the francophones who dominate the population of Madawaska County are known as Brayons, a mix of Acadians who came north after the Loyalists moved into southern New Brunswick and Québécois who migrated in subsequent decades. On the Maine side, there is the same heritage, though people tend to refer to their origins simply as Acadian. The towns along the American side of the Upper Saint John—Van Buren, Madawaska, Grande Isle, St. Agatha, Frenchville, Fort Kent—are all part of Aroostook County, the state's northernmost county and the one most associated with the view of Maine as a great, rustic expanse of forest. In 2000, more than twenty-four percent of Aroostook's population spoke French at home, a startling statistic to Canadians who see the United States as a cultural melting pot. In Rioux's hometown, Fort Kent, the largest town and the administrative hub of the area, only fourteen hundred of four thousand residents reported speaking English at home; the remainder spoke French, and of them, more than six hundred said they did not speak English well.

Even those numbers are historically low, however, and they continue to drop: one teacher reported in 1993 that in the Fort Kent area, only ten to fifteen percent of middle-school students understood and could speak French, even though almost half of their parents could do so. In nearby Frenchville, almost all students in the first to third grades could repeat phrases, sing songs, and understand conversations in French, but by the fourth grade, it was "more difficult to make them speak French," a teacher said. "They become self-conscious or peer pressure steps in and they don't want to try."

Rioux, the child of a Franco-American family, is typical of his generation. "In my family most of the older people speak it. I'm getting better with it, but I don't speak it myself. My grandparents are all completely bilingual, my parents are completely bilingual, so I definitely see in my family and other families that there's a big generation gap there where it's completely faded out, which is a concern. It's actually shameful, from my personal perspective, because I'd like to speak it. I think it's sad that it's fading away. What's happening up here, especially in the last five years, is so many more people are moving away, or going to college somewhere where French isn't required. Very few people are sticking around here and are in need of that second language."

Outside the northern reaches of Maine, he adds, few people even grasp why he would lament such a loss. "The whole arrogance — Americans just sort of seem arrogant about knowing different languages. 'English first,' 'English only' is a lot of what I see and what I hear, even with my close friends."

There is one culture here, but the border has created two different approaches to it. The American way has been towards assimilation, even if the Valley's geographical isolation slowed the process for more than a century. In Canada, and in New Brunswick, the notion of two founding peoples gave rise to schools and other institutions designed to protect the French language. "The American 'melting pot' tried to get rid of the French in northern Maine, while with Trudeau, on our side, French was flourishing," Carrier says. Today, "I don't think anyone would contest that English is the official language of the United States. People over there still speak French, the way others speak Spanish or Chinese." An annual Acadian festival has been held in Fort Kent since the 1970s, but daily life is less and less French. "There's a bit of a return to the roots," he says, "but it's more folkloric than anything."

Until 2001, the border still was porous enough for the Upper Valley to think of itself as a single community. But it was not quite porous enough, even then, for the French language to flourish in Maine, even with a robust official bilingualism across the river in Canada serving as an example. Today, as surely as two countries nudge up against each other here on the Saint-François, the notion of an easily forgotten border is pressing up against the reality of post-9/11 America—which often pushes back.

Yves Carrier steers his canoe back to shore and loads it onto the trailer on the back of his truck. We drive away from the lake, up a steep hill, and back onto the main road. We quickly come upon a collection of campers and trailers lining both sides of the road, a remnant of one of his many idealistic schemes for the river. In 1996, Carrier launched an eco-campground here, on Crown-owned land, envisioning a zero-impact facility that would exist in harmony with the unspoiled surroundings. Now he nods ruefully towards scattered plastic bags and empty beer cans. "That's my environmental park," Carrier says. "It didn't go the way I wanted, but hey, that's democracy. The majority prevails."

We follow the dirt road back down to the mouth of the Saint-François, the Maine shore flickering through the trees. The dirt road bends to the left when it reaches the Saint John, following the border as it enters the larger river. Two large flat islands, one American, one Canadian, sit in the current there. The Saint John is shallow today, with dried-out slopes of exposed mud and rock visible. The road is narrow, the trees press in close again, and only a few homes break the monotony of this last road at the far edge of New Brunswick. Then the road turns to asphalt, the shoulders widen out, and there are wide fields opening up to our right, running down to the river, and larger homes dotting the landscape. I thank Carrier at his house and drive on in my own car to Clair, a village with a smattering of the usual small-town essential services—gas stations, restaurants, a bank or two, and a government-owned liquor store. Clair is defined primarily, however, by the eighty-year-old steel truss bridge across the river connecting it to Fort Kent, Maine. This is the first of

New Brunswick's official border crossings with the United States that I will encounter.

The two towns were reaching out to each other, across the Saint John and the border, long before the bridge was completed in 1930. Ferries worked the river, and a privately owned footbridge, built and maintained by the Long family of Fort Kent, allowed for quicker, more spontaneous visits. Large cables, three inches in diameter, held the four-foot-wide structure in place atop half a dozen piers. It could be a nerve-wracking crossing: locals moving horses and cows across put bags over the animals' heads to prevent them from recoiling in fear from the sight of the river below. The Longs charged a nickel per crossing, and John Allen Page, a descendant of the owners, once claimed that his grandmother collected twenty to twenty-two thousand dollars per year in tolls—though she did charge a premium after the official closing time of nine o'clock at night. "A person would holler to my grandmother to open the bridge and she'd charge them fifty cents," he recalled.

There were no customs checkpoints at the time. People arriving in Fort Kent were to report at the home of the local customs officer, though enforcement was slack. Page recalled a Fort Kent man who found two pigs he needed in Clair. Rather than deal with customs, "he took a baby carriage, he went across, he put the two pigs in it, and he walked across." Workers building the steel truss bridge at the end of the 1920s used the footbridge as a staging area; once they were finished, the Canadian government tore down the older span. Now the 1930 bridge was to be replaced as well: the New Brunswick and Maine governments announced in 2010 they would share the cost of a planning study for a new link. Because there is a tradition of alternation, and Maine had overseen the recent St. Stephen–Calais project opened by Stephen Harper, New Brunswick was taking the lead on the engineering, contracting, and construction of the new Clair-Fort Kent bridge, though the two governments would, as usual, split the final bill.

I drive across and slow down as I reach American soil, edging up to the stop line painted on the pavement. On the other side of the border checkpoint, I see traffic moving along U.S. Route 1, the epic road that begins in Fort Kent and stretches more than two thousand miles down the Atlantic coast to Key West.

My reverie about the road is broken when I see a deep rectangular hole, large enough to swallow a small car, directly in front of one of the customs booths. Some new security technology is about to be installed directly below the spot where drivers stop their vehicles to check in. The construction means only one entry lane is open, so I have to wait several minutes. Finally I am signalled to advance, and I tell the officer I have come to Fort Kent to research a book about the border. He asks me to park and go inside for questioning while my car is searched.

The interview indoors is perfunctory and polite, and every item in my bag, which I left in the car, is returned to precisely the position in which I packed it. I take various Department of Homeland Security brochures from the display cases inside, including versions in French. Though they are obviously aimed at francophone Canadians from Madawaska County and nearby Québec, they are another nod to the ethnocultural reality of the Upper Saint John. The names in the weekly newspaper on the American side, the *St. John Valley Times*, from advertisements to obituaries to local baseball boxscores, mirror those from across the river: Michaud, Cyr, Guerrette, Bergeron, Thibeault, Bonenfant, Rossignol, Paradis, Faucher, Daigle.

But at the local McDonald's, where I stop for lunch, there is more evidence of what Rioux told me. Older customers are speaking French, while the younger ones converse mostly in English, another sign of how the turning of the generations is changing this side of the border.

At a nursing home on a hill overlooking the Saint John River and the New Brunswick shore, I find Marvin Jandreau, who speaks to me about life in the Valley when it was still isolated from the rest of the United States, and when New Brunswick was more of a defining fact of life than southern Maine. With a flick of his thumb, he steers the wheelchair carrying his once-powerful frame into a common room where we are able to talk. He describes learning English only when he began attending school — French was permitted outside, but not in the classroom —

and of his life working in the woods and driving a truck. Stiffened by a stroke, he describes, with an easily detected French accent, how his children speak French and how "their kids, yeah, they're coming along pretty good." He recalls his entire family going to Caribou, a Maine town just outside the French-speaking Valley, to pick potatoes. "My mother couldn't talk a word of English, and the boss, he couldn't speak a word of French," he says, but "between the two of them they'd understand each other." Jandreau is less concerned about the cultural gap that assimilation was creating in the Valley than about new security measures on the border. "I had some friends over in Clair that I'll never see again on account of needing a passport. At my age why do I need a passport to go see some friends?"

Security is the talk of the Valley. When Benjamin Rioux's fishing guests realize they are casting lines across open water into another country, "a lot of them are surprised about the lack of security," he tells me. "It would be so easy to cross and get into the woods and you're gone. That's one thing they mention — 'how do you patrol this? Is it safe with people going back and forth illegally?' That's the one thing that surprises them the most."

And, Rioux admits, they have a point: if someone wanting to enter the United States illegally goes looking for somewhere to attempt it, the Saint-François River would be a good choice. "Realistically, I'm not going to lie to you: it would probably be extremely easy," he says. "Usually my response is that it's so remote, that the chances of someone actually taking the time to drive up there and find their way down to Fort Kent, especially if they've never done it before — it would be pretty difficult. . . . I guess I have that small-town mindset that we're safe all the time." In Washington, the Department of Homeland Security is not nearly as sanguine: there are more patrols, more rigorous and frequent searches, and more complaints from local residents that something unique has been lost.

Beatrice Craig, a scholar who has studied the region for most of her career, sees the issue through the prism of the "borderland" concept, a theoretical framework used by many historians. First, she writes, come frontiers: regions with undefined or ill-defined boundaries where inhabitants "are free to interact as they see fit." When rival powers contest those regions, they become borderlands. And then, "as the borders become clearly defined and enforced, borderlands become bordered lands. Local interactions are increasingly restricted, channelled from above, and subordinated to the policies and priorities of the distant governing powers." Owing to the tradition of valley residents "behaving as if this division did not exist," Craig considers the area to have been, from 1842 until well into the twentieth century, a land "in between," not fitting neatly into either category. Now there is an inescapable feeling the Valley has become bordered lands.

Yves Carrier plans to resist the trend. He wants to take what is special about his river — that illusion of a natural, borderless land — and push it beyond the banks, into the woods, to encompass a larger part of what was once the "land in between." In 2014, the fifth World Acadian Congress, a gathering of the descendants of the original French colonists in what are now the Maritime provinces, will be held for the first time astride an international border, in Madawaska County, New Brunswick, in northern, Franco-American Maine, and in the nearby Témiscouata region of Québec, from which flows the Saint-François.

In July 2010, the premier of New Brunswick and the governor of Maine established the Maine-New Brunswick Cultural Initiative to promote connections along the entire border, but particularly to help the planning of the Acadian Congress. And intense planning will be required: the region will be flooded with francophones and francophiles from across North America, who will need to cross the border repeatedly, in both directions, for various events — a movement of people that, when it confronts American security measures, could create a logistical nightmare. The fact that the local bid to host the Congress was successful was itself a show of faith that Washington might relax, just a little.

Carrier likes the idea of the Congress: he is a veteran of grand schemes. Besides his eco-campground, he has organized several editions of an "eco-challenge" that saw participants hike, cycle, and canoe through New Brunswick's Madawaska wilderness in a race to Glazier Lake. He has also orchestrated a guided "Grande Descente" of the Upper Saint John, with passengers in large canoes making several stops on both shores for short pieces of theatre recounting the history of the region. These were all difficult to execute, but Carrier's latest river-centred project is more ambitious still, aiming not so much to accommodate the boundary as to *overcome* it.

And he wants to do so by appealing to the sentiment, passed down through the generations and etched deep in the psyches of the local population, that *it should not be there at all*.

In Carrier's mind, if the border can be forgotten for a couple of weeks during the Congress, why not erase it altogether, at least in a relatively small, secure area? In 2007, the Clair chamber of commerce organized an open forum to brainstorm new ideas for the local economy. Carrier went to the microphone and suggested an international park: set aside an area of forest on the Canadian side, logged by J.D. Irving Limited, and then add the Maine side as well, where Irving was also a major player in the forestry industry. A few people liked the idea, so Carrier organized meetings and presented the proposal at a conference on sustainable development in Edmundston.

That generated some media coverage and considerable controversy. "It divided people. Those who worked for Irving were against it. Those who want to develop a tourism industry, like around Kouchibouguac and Fundy Park, were for it. The Irvings were insulted that we hadn't spoken to them before talking about it." He wanted to gather support before approaching the company, but once the controversy upset New Brunswick's largest employer, and Maine's biggest landowner, political enthusiasm drained away. "We wanted to do something positive," he sighs. "We didn't want to start a fight."

Carrier maintains that the idea is feasible. "Those security measures are overblown. That's to please people in the south and the centre of the United States. There is no security problem here. They create little incidents to maintain jobs. It's to create well-paying federal government jobs over on the other side of the border. There's no problem at all. Other than catching the occasional person trying to sell their homegrown on the other side, there's nothing. As for terrorism, there'll never be any terrorists coming through here. The people who are going to commit terrorism in the United States are already there. They're already in there on visas. They're already set up. No terrorist is going to come through Glazier and then walk twenty-five miles through the woods to attack somebody.

"But an international park would accomplish a couple of things. First, the park would be secure. There'd only be two or three entrances to the park, and the area is so wild that those are the only places where people could go in and out anyway. And secondly, it could bring people together. Because deep down, people in the United States and Canada aren't that different. We have the same ideas, the same way of life."

In effect Carrier would re-create the world that existed here before 1842 — before customs, before white border monuments, before armed patrols, and before the large wooden structure that stands resolutely in a quiet neighbourhood of Fort Kent, Maine: a blockhouse, a cedar fort built in 1839 when the United States and Great Britain almost went to war over the Madawaska territory. The blockhouse, conveying heft and foreshadowing imperial power, is now a museum. It is locked shut when I pull up after my visit with Marvin Jandreau, but on a display plaque outside I find a set of lyrics:

We are marching on to Madawask,
to fight the trespassers;
we'll teach the British how to walk
and come off conquerors.

We'll have our land, right good and clear,
For all the English say;
They shall not cut another log,
Nor stay another day.

They need not think to have our land,
We Yankees can fight well;
We've whipped them twice quite manfully,
As every child can tell.

And if the tyrants say one word,
A third time we will show,
How high the Yankee spirit runs,
And what our guns can do.

They better much all stay at home,
And mind their business there;
The way we treated them before,
Made all the nations stare.

Come on! Brace fellows, one and all!
The Red-coats ne'er shall say,
We Yankees, feared to meet them armed,
So gave our land away.

We'll feed them well with ball and shot,
We'll cut these red-coats down,
Before we yield to them an inch
Or title of our ground.

Ye husbands, fathers, brothers, sons,
From every quarter come!
March to the bugle and the fife!
March, to the beating drum!

Onward! My lads so brave and true
Our country's right demands
With justice, and with glory fight,
For these Aroostook lands!

Next to the plaque is a boundary marker, apparently genuine but clearly out of place, bearing — as do all those along the border — the names of James Estcourt and Albert Smith, British and American commissioners who, after the 1842 Treaty of Washington, surveyed, cleared, and marked the newly created section of the New Brunswick-Maine border, including the line that divided the French-speaking people of the Upper Saint John.

This line has endured from the signing of the treaty until the present day, even if it was the product of nothing more noble than politics, diplomatic trade-offs, and deceit.

2. OSWALD'S FOLLY

RICHARD OSWALD HAD CLEARLY ARRIVED. The son of a Presbyterian minister in Dunnet, a tiny hamlet on the northern tip of Scotland, he had moved to Glasgow to find his fortune and married well. His wife was an heiress from a family that owned estates in the West Indies and North America, which soon passed to Oswald. By the standards of the eighteenth century, the two enterprises on which he expanded his fortune — war and slavery — were nothing to be ashamed of. He profited from the Seven Years' War as a contractor supplying troops in Europe, and with London partners, established an island trading station in West Africa for slaves bound for America.

And now, in 1782, this man of modest beginnings was in Paris to help shape the fates of empires. He was sitting across a table from three men who would be revered in history as Founding Fathers of their nation: Benjamin Franklin, the author, scientist, philosopher and statesman sometimes described as the "first American"; John Adams, co-author of the Declaration of Independence and later the second President of the United States; and John Jay, later the first Chief Justice of the United States. Their task was to negotiate a peace treaty between Britain and its newly independent former colonies, an agreement that would end the Revolutionary War and define the new boundary between the United States and the remaining colonies of British North America.

Despite his relatively humble origins, Oswald was highly regarded by the powerful men who had chosen him for the job. Benjamin Vaughn, an acquaintance of Lord Shelburne, the British colonial secretary who sent Oswald to Paris, said Oswald "thought for himself. His manners were such that, though perfectly simple, he was admitted into all company; his sincerity was relied upon at first and though not given to deceive others, he was yet too experienced and observant to be long deceived himself. . . . [His] views were philanthropic and expanded, and his sense was sound; and though he had little or no scholarship, yet being retired in his habits he knew many valuable books on government and on political affairs."

His six years as a young man in colonial Virginia gave him an understanding of America, and his experience in military and merchant affairs were a rare and valuable combination: King George III himself declared Oswald "the fittest instrument for the renewal of friendly intercourse" with the rebellious colonies. Even Benjamin Franklin deemed him "a wise and honest man" of "Moderation, prudent Counsels and sound Judgment."

In 1782 the United States were on the cusp of winning their independence. The Revolutionary War was winding down. The British had surrendered at Yorktown the previous October, and in London there was little political support to continue the fighting. When Lord North's government lost power in a no-confidence vote — a first in parliamentary history — Benjamin Franklin, the American representative in Paris, acted swiftly. He wrote to Lord Shelburne, the new government's colonial secretary, to propose negotiations.

At the initial meetings in Paris, Franklin boldly suggested that Britain cede Canada (much of present-day Québec and Ontario) and Nova Scotia (which included what is now New Brunswick) to the United States, in return for agreements on liberalized trade. Surprisingly, this had its attractions in London: the British could not afford to sever commercial ties to its former colonies, and complete withdrawal from North America would make it easier to carry on its war against France and Spain. Richard Oswald was authorized to arrange formal negotiations in Paris.[1]

---

1 The Americans abandoned the idea of claiming Canada and Nova Scotia when they realized France and Spain might want the two colonies as a reward for having supported the Revolution.

In fixing the new border between America and the remaining British colonies, the Paris negotiators were not starting from scratch: a river called the St. Croix, named by Samuel de Champlain in 1604, had long been considered the boundary between the colonies of Massachusetts and Nova Scotia. When King James I of England granted all of Nova Scotia to Sir William Alexander in 1621, he defined its western boundary as "the river generally known by the name of St. Croix," from its mouth to its most westerly source, "thence by an imaginary straight line which is conceived to extend through the land, or run northward" until it reached a tributary of the St. Lawrence. A subsequent land grant by Charles II of the colony called Sagadahoc (present-day Maine east of the Kennebec River) described its eastern border as that same, already-defined western border of Nova Scotia. There were other claims and disputes — the French considered the Penobscot, further to the west, as the boundary of its colony, Acadia — but the notion of the St. Croix as a natural boundary had deep roots.

In 1763, the capture of Québec compelled George III to clear up the confusion over the boundaries of all his North American colonies. He renamed all of Canada as Québec, and issued a Royal Proclamation, which introduced a new term into this story: Québec's southern boundary with both Massachusetts and Nova Scotia, it said, "passes along the High Lands which divide the Rivers that empty themselves into the said River St. Lawrence from those which fall into the sea." A month later, a separate Royal Commission finally fixed the border between Massachusetts and Nova Scotia by reviving the description used in the land grant of 1621: "a line drawn north from the source of the St. Croix." Except now, that line running north would end at "the Southern bounds of Québec" — in other words, the "High Lands" of the earlier Proclamation.

The boundaries of all three British colonies — Massachusetts, Québec, and Nova Scotia — thus appeared to be firmly fixed, creating, at least in theory, a place where they met: the point at which the line running north from the St. Croix met the "High Lands." This would eventually be referred to as the "northwest angle" of Nova Scotia.

By the time Richard Oswald got down to work in Paris in 1782, the

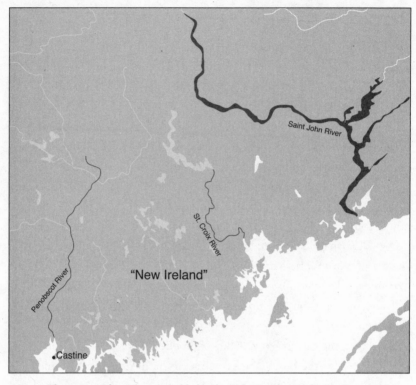

Three rivers show three possible borders: the Penobscot, the St. Croix,
and the Saint John.

British, of course, could no longer decide the boundaries themselves.
Franklin, Adams, and Jay were pushing for the Saint John River,
considerably to the east of the St. Croix, to become the new international
border between the United States and Nova Scotia. But the British wanted
a line to the west: during the Revolutionary War, they had captured the
coastal area between the Penobscot and the St. Croix rivers and revived an
old idea of establishing a new colony there. It would be called New Ireland
and would provide a home for displaced American Loyalists fleeing the
war, particularly land-owning gentry not given to revolutionary notions of
democracy. "Regulated upon correct principles, it could serve as a model
colony where institutions and men could foster loyalty to the Crown,"
writes historian W.S. MacNutt.

Loyalists were already settling in the area by the time negotiations

The negotiators sign the preliminary Treaty of Peace in Paris,
November 30, 1782.
(U.S. Diplomacy Center photo, U.S. State Department)

began in Paris. Given the American refusal to restore their property
and possessions, Oswald told the Americans that Britain would need a
more generous border than the Saint John to provide ample room for its
displaced subjects. He angled for the Penobscot, which would allow Britain
to create New Ireland. The Americans pushed back: they abandoned their
request for the Saint John, but would not agree to the Penobscot. On
November 2, John Adams wrote in his diary, the U.S. proposed "a line
from the mouth of the St. Croix to its source and from its source to
the Highlands." They had fallen back on the terms of the 1763 Royal
Proclamation.

King George III now had to decide whether to fight for the Penobscot.
Yes, the St. Croix had been fixed as the boundary as recently as 1763 — but
as a boundary between two *loyal colonies*. Massachusetts had forfeited any
advantage it had gained from the Royal Proclamation, including its title to
the territory between the Penobscot and the St. Croix, when it joined the
Revolution. The facts on the ground also favoured the British: its troops

held the area. The King might well have decided that the Americans had voided their claim and that Britain would enforce its ownership.

For two weeks, Richard Oswald would not budge. But when John Adams threatened to withdraw from the negotiations, a move that would deprive Britain of the trade agreement it needed with the United States, the King gave in. The "model colony" of New Ireland would never be. More importantly, the two nations would not have the clear, unmistakable boundary the Penobscot would have provided. Instead, Oswald settled for what one historian called the "cartographically uncertain" St. Croix and set the stage for six decades of contention that almost led to war.

The negotiators agreed to final terms on November 30. Almost immediately, Richard Oswald's crowning achievement came under attack. He was criticized in England for giving away too much, and was censured by Parliament in February 1783. Shelburne resigned, and Oswald was replaced as chief negotiator; he retired to his estate, where he died a year later. The new British government was not able, however, to improve the treaty: once the Mother Country had conceded independence, its need to maintain trade with the United States meant it had no leverage to take back what it had given away. The text of the definitive treaty was completed on September 3, 1783; the fateful Article Two described the northeastern border of the United States this way: "From the northwest angle of Nova Scotia, to wit, that angle which is formed by a line drawn due north from the source of the St. Croix river to the highlands, along the said highlands which divide those rivers that empty themselves into the St. Lawrence, and those which fall into the Atlantic ocean, to the northwestern most head of the Connecticut river."

The treaty contained other provisions. The islands in the Bay of Fundy that had belonged to Nova Scotia would remain British. Yankee fishermen would be allowed to fish the inshore waters of Nova Scotia, and to land at unoccupied harbours for shore operations. And a commission would be charged with marking the North Line from the source of the St. Croix to the highlands, a task that would not be as straightforward as expected.

But it was not nearly as contentious as Article Two. The wording had seemed clear enough to Oswald and the others, all of whom had relied on those earlier documents and proclamations referring to the highlands and the northwest angle of Nova Scotia. But none of the men in Paris had actually seen those highlands — few people had — and none could have located the northwest angle. The 1755 map by royal cartographer John Mitchell, used as a reference by the Paris negotiators, depicted a river labelled the St. Croix, but it emerged that in the settlements in the area, no one knew any of the rivers flowing into Passamaquoddy Bay by that name. And the treaty included no agreed-upon map showing the final boundary settlement.

In short, there would be opportunities for political mischief and for creative reinterpretations of the treaty, should circumstances require it. Decades of confusion lay ahead. Franklin, Adams, and Jay were destined to be secular saints of the American mythos; Richard Oswald, who had risen from nothing to become the King's "fittest instrument," would eventually be seen as out of his depth in Paris and be largely forgotten by history.

The original home of the New Brunswick Museum is a dark, solid stone building on a hill overlooking the historic harbour of Saint John, New Brunswick's oldest and largest city. It now houses the museum's archives, and it is where I have come to meet Gary Hughes, the museum's curator of history, who has agreed to show me a remarkable item in the collection — a physical relic of the border dispute.

At the back of the building in a large open area, laid out carefully on a roped-off section of the floor, beneath a clear, protective cover, is the colour, or ceremonial flag, of the 104th Regiment of Foot. On February 16, 1813, the regiment carried it as it set out on snowshoes from Fredericton to join the defense of Upper Canada in the War of 1812. Six companies marched heroically through the snow for fifty-two days, up the Saint John River to the mouth of the Madawaska river, then along the Madawaska to the great Lake Témiscouata, over the portage to Rivière-du-Loup, and on to Québec and finally Kingston, where their very presence helped deter an American attack and changed the course of the conflict.

The colour of the 104th Regiment of Foot was carried from New Brunswick
to Kingston during the War of 1812.
(Courtesy New Brunswick Museum)

It was an epic, arduous journey of seven hundred miles, unthinkable now. The historian George Stanley, a lieutenant-governor of New Brunswick in the 1980s, called it "an achievement which is surely as remarkable as any recorded in military history." Most of the men suffered from frostbite. "When we got to the end of our day's march," Lieutenant John LeCouteur recorded in early March, "the cold was so intense that the men could scarcely use their fingers to hew down the fire-wood, or to build huts, and it was dark before we could commence cooking; if sticking a bit of salt pork on the end of a twig and holding it in a fire could be so termed."

The regimental colour is more than six feet tall and five-and-a-half feet wide. The silk, jute, and metallic thread has been made brittle by the passage of two centuries, and one corner is shredded into dozens upon dozens of tiny fragments. Yet its basic shape survives, and the two concentric circles in the centre, marked "New Brunswick Reg" and "104th," are intact, along with the Union Jack. Hughes and his colleagues are making plans to restore it. They will need to move it one last time in its present, fragile state, because no conservators in New Brunswick have the skill and experience to undertake such a delicate job. Once restored, it will be placed in protective glass that will become its permanent home. The entire process is expected to cost more than fifty thousand dollars, a large sum for a small museum.

But the colour, which went to Scotland after the War of 1812 and returned to New Brunswick in 1939, represents, after all, the precise moment when the idea of a shared destiny took root among the remaining colonies of British North America. "The colour is important not only because it is a rare survivor of the era, and mute witness to important events, but also because it is somewhat of a prodigal son," Hughes says. "To me, it represents both the re-establishment of the British fact in New Brunswick after three decades of American Loyalist influence and a symbolic precursor to the eventual Confederation of the provinces. In a way, its travel overseas and return repeats that pattern."

It is also an inextricable part of the story of the border, as Lieutenant LeCouteur himself foreshadowed in his diary.

On the first of March, the regiment paused at the settlement near what is today Grand Falls, where the Saint John River takes a turn to the northwest. A map from that era shows what appears to be Richard Oswald's "line drawn due north from the source of the St. Croix River to the highlands"—the border with the United States as per the Treaty of Paris. On the map, it crosses the river just west of the falls and continues north, all the way to a range of highlands south of the St. Lawrence. The location of Grand Falls so close to the border, LeCouteur wrote, made the settlement "a very strong point of defense, the more important as it is the nearest point to the American boundary all along our line of march, and that by which the mail must pass in the winter season into Canada."

And "the only good line of march for troops," wrote LeCouteur, was to cross that north line and follow the Saint John and Madawaska rivers to Lake Témiscouata, "a level road of march on for two hundred miles, a circumstance of vast importance to the moving troops in winter, as they would otherwise have to march entirely through the brushwoods and forests, which would increase their hardships and retard their progress."

LeCouteur had unknowingly identified the strategic reality that would drive U.S.-British relations for the next three decades. For it was the wartime march by the 104th Regiment of Foot through the snow up the Saint John River that crystallized what had already been dawning on the colonial authorities: Richard Oswald had made a terrible mistake in Paris when he agreed to draw a line north from the source of the St. Croix to the highlands forming the boundary with Canada. Under those terms, the Madawaska Settlement, through which the 104th passed, was in American territory.

And if the United States realized how important that route had been to the regime, it might, in a future war, assert its claim, fill the area with settlers and soldiers, and sever "the only good line of march for troops," cutting off the Maritime colonies from Canada.

Britain had no choice but to reverse Oswald's mistake. It needed to execute what today might be called a geopolitical flip-flop. The "highlands" of the treaty were too far north. They had to be moved.

There was a complication: the territory in question, the Madawaska Settlement, was already inhabited by Acadians who had twice already been pawns in imperial rivalries. In 1784, Britain had carved out a large chunk of Nova Scotia to create a new colony called New Brunswick for Loyalists fleeing the Revolution. Fifteen hundred Acadians already lived in the colony, mostly in the lower Saint John River Valley around present-day Fredericton. They were survivors of the brutal deportation just three decades earlier. They had names that are familiar today: Cyr, Cormier, Daigle, Hébert, Fournier, and Mercure. As Loyalists moved in, demanding land, many of the Acadians petitioned the Governor of Lower Canada for permission to relocate upriver. The British were happy to agree: they wanted settlers on the upper reaches of the river to secure their claim to the area. They gave the Acadians permission to settle above the Grand

Falls, at the mouth of the Madawaska River, an area widely considered part of Canada.

Within a year of their arrival, more settlers arrived, French-speaking *Canadiens*, and the two communities merged and mingled into one, "stubborn and shrewd, honest and gay, active and intelligent, generous and full of initiative, hospitable, particularist without exclusiveness," according to Reverend Thomas Albert, author of *Histoire du Madawaska*, the first serious history of the region. By 1790 there were two hundred settlers; a decade later the population had doubled again. "For the first time since 1713," writes one scholar, "these people knew a certain sense of security and a feeling of having come home at last."

But there were already undercurrents of border trouble: in 1787, surveyors from Canada and New Brunswick met near Grand Falls to mark the precise boundary between the two colonies. The Canadian surveyor, ignoring the 1763 proclamation of "the highlands" as the dividing line, argued that the boundary was actually much farther south, at Grand Falls, putting the French-speaking Madawaskans in the predominantly French-speaking colony of Canada. New Brunswick's surveyor, George Sproule, reminded him that the highlands were the boundary, and that this gave New Brunswick more territory north of the Saint John. Sproule's argument was sound, but it carried enormous implications: if the highlands to the north were, in fact, New Brunswick's frontier with Canada, then the north line dividing Massachusetts and New Brunswick had to continue north of the Saint John River until it met them — putting the entire Madawaska settlement to the west of that line in the United States.

The matter was left unresolved for several years. The United States and Britain could not even agree on which waterway was the St. Croix of Oswald's treaty, the starting point of the north line. A commission ruled on that point in 1798, and the line was drawn north; New Brunswick's first lieutenant-governor, Thomas Carleton, noted it would cross the Saint John "little, if at all, to the westward of the Grand Falls," and continue, as Sproule had argued, to the highlands far to the north. This would cut the communications route to Canada — a consequence, Carleton wrote, that would "on strict inquiry, be justified by the letter of the Treaty."

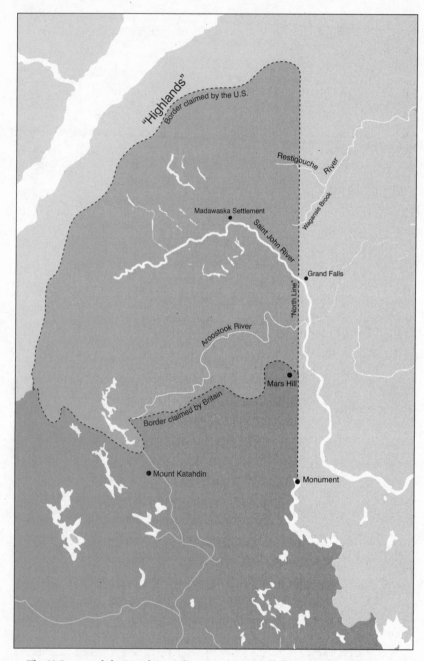

The U.S. wanted the North Line drawn to a range of hills running parallel to the St. Lawrence, which would have given them much more territory. The British claimed the "highlands" of the treaty ran west from Mars Hill.

This is a revealing admission: New Brunswick understood and accepted the consequences of its argument that the highlands were located far north of the Saint John.

The same reality was acknowledged by Edward Winslow, who had been the secretary to the commission that had settled the St. Croix debate. A different definition of the St. Croix, to the east, would have cost New Brunswick major towns such as Saint Andrews and Fredericton, he wrote in 1798, but "as it is, we lost not a single British settlement. A few miserable Frenchmen at Madawaska on the route to Canada fall within the Territory. I presume that some future negotiation will remove even this difficulty and give us a free communication with Canada."

Clearly New Brunswick felt no urgent need for that future negotiation. But by the time the War of 1812 began, the scale of Oswald's blunder was becoming apparent. A proper interpretation of the Treaty of Paris would not only allow the United States to sever the military road between Canada and the Maritimes but also place the northern boundary of Massachusetts on the highlands within striking distance of the city of Québec, allowing American troops to sweep over the hills to seize, and block, the St. Lawrence River.

The boundary had economic consequences as well: on both sides of the Saint John River, the Madawaska Settlement was teeming with virgin forests, including white pine, the tall, solid trees perfect for carving masts for ships. Napoleon's blockade of Baltic ports, Britain's main source of timber, had forced it to look elsewhere. "People really become excited over the ownership of land," remarks the scholar Charlotte Lenentine, "when it can be figured in board feet and dollars and cents." In February 1814, the New Brunswick Assembly petitioned London to do whatever it could when the war ended "to alter the boundaries between those States and this Province, so as that the important line of communication between this and the neighboring Province of Lower Canada, by the River Saint John, may not be interrupted."

And, indeed, at war's end, during the negotiations leading to the Treaty of Ghent, Britain asked the United States for a "rectification" of Oswald's 1783 boundary. The Americans, quite naturally and rightly, rejected the proposal, saying they were not authorized to cede territory. They offered instead to take part in joint commissions, structured like the one that had settled the St. Croix, to examine the question of the highlands and other outstanding border issues. The commissions would have three members: one chosen by each country, who would then agree on a third member. The British proposed instead a two-man commission who would, if they failed to agree, refer the dispute to "a friendly Sovereign or state" acting as a final arbitrator. The Americans agreed. Nothing, it seemed, could be more straightforward.

The commission's task was, in fact, enormous. The boundary it was asked to settle ran from the St. Croix up the North Line to the highlands, and then down to the northwesternmost head of the Connecticut River, then from there across the forty-fifth parallel to the St. Lawrence River. The first order of business, then, was to resolve the issue of the highlands, and in the summer of 1817, two teams, led by chief surveyors Joseph Bouchette of Montréal for the British and John Johnson of Vermont for the Americans, set out to find them on the thickly forested, sparsely populated, largely unexplored North Line.

They left from Fredericton on July 15 and ten days later reached a swampy area where a narrow brook took shape and ran south. They located some iron hoops that had been placed around a yellow birch tree in 1797, the first "monument," which later gave the little stream at the source of the St. Croix the name Monument Brook. They spent several days there, clearing brush, catching colds, and erecting a new monument, a large cedar log carved into a square beam, ten to twelve feet high, with the words "New Brunswick, July 31, 1817" marked on the east side and "United States, July 31, 1817" on the west. Bouchette's and Johnson's names were added to the north and south sides.

Moving north, the teams were plagued by weather, food shortages, and suspicion of each other. When they reached Mars Hill, a distinctive peak forty-two miles up the North Line from the monument, Bouchette speculated it was connected by a range of highlands to the majestic Mount Katahdin, visible to the west. A few miles farther north, between the Aroostook and Saint John rivers, Bouchette remarked that there was another "line of Land" that he found "extremely high."

But if Bouchette was looking for a way to move the all-important highlands south, he undermined his own effort when the teams reached the Saint John River in September. He urged the teams to continue north, and they did, reaching a small brook, the Little Wagansis, on October 8. The brook was part of the Restigouche watershed, which Bouchette wrongly considered to be the same as that of the St. Lawrence. This, then, was the end of their search: the northwest angle of Nova Scotia, where the North Line met the highlands.

This conclusion meant the territory west of the line they had just surveyed belonged to the United States, including the military road used in 1813 by the 104th Regiment. At first, the British boundary commissioner, Colonel Thomas Barclay, and his agent, Ward Chipman, accepted Bouchette's finding. Locating the highlands at the Little Wagansis was not as bad for Britain as placing them farther north, at the actual St. Lawrence watershed. The case was closed.

Then, over the winter, while the surveyors waited to resume their work in the spring, Barclay and Chipman changed their minds, and Bouchette was removed from his position.

"I cannot reflect with any degree of patience upon the manner in which our government has been humbugged from the first to the last upon the Boundary Question," an assistant British surveyor, Colin Campbell, would say years later. Bouchette, he explained, had been "gulled by and completely under the control of [the American surveyor] Johnson, who although a vulgar and uneducated man . . . was a shrewd intelligent Yankee, and an unprincipled scoundrel."

Historians have concluded that Bouchette was replaced because his conclusions did not coincide with Britain's strategic interest in securing the military road at any cost. They cite Chipman's attempt, in May 1818, to change the instructions to the surveyors: he wanted them to abandon work on the North Line and look for the highlands south of the Aroostook

River, near Mars Hill. But rivers on both sides of Mars Hill emptied into the Saint John, meaning it did not meet the treaty's definition of highlands "which divide those rivers that empty themselves into the St. Lawrence, and those which fall into the Atlantic ocean."

Still, the British became fixated on the 1,750-feet-high peak. "It was such a landmark that it is not surprising that the New Brunswickers looked to it as the topographical formation that must be the highlands of the 1783 treaty," historian Francis Carroll observes in his comprehensive account of the story. Bouchette's replacement as surveyor, William Odell, presented a novel argument: a range of small hills running east from Mars Hill divided two watersheds, that of the Penobscot and Kennebec rivers, which ran to the Atlantic, and that of the Saint John, which flowed into the Bay of Fundy. Conveniently ignoring the treaty's explicit reference to the St. Lawrence, Odell argued those hills must be the highlands Richard Oswald had intended in Paris. If so, Britain would gain not only the Madawaska Settlement but also a huge swath of lucrative forestland south of it. The Americans disagreed: Mars Hill was clearly a solitary peak, not part of a range. The two sides had reached a stalemate.

Everything now revolved around the location of the northwest angle of Nova Scotia. Oswald's intentions in Paris were now secondary to Britain's geopolitical objectives. "If this angle should be decided to be at any point in highlands northward of this river," Chipman told Barclay, "our cause will be virtually lost, and it will in such case be of little consequence where this point of highlands shall be found." The British began raising procedural concerns about the commission, such as whether witnesses had sworn proper oaths and documents had been submitted correctly. But their broader strategy was to ensure that the two competing interpretations of the 1783 wording were of seemingly equal legitimacy. They advanced new interpretations of the 1763 Royal Proclamation's reference to the highlands, and parsed references — or omissions — in the Treaty of Paris that, in their view, showed the Americans were never supposed to have access to the Upper Saint John River.

The Americans rebutted each point, and noted several cases in which the British themselves had acknowledged the clear meaning of the treaty—such as when Chipman had written, in 1798, "that this north line must of necessity cross the River Saint John." But Washington eventually recognized that the commission would never agree. Britain's position, said Secretary of State John Quincy Adams, was "one in which ingenuity maintains an endless argument against common sense." He decided to negotiate directly, government to government.

Adams, whose father, John Adams, had negotiated the 1783 treaty with Richard Oswald in Paris, was inclined to give the British their military road through the Madawaska Settlement if he could trade it for territory elsewhere. But there were political risks to this. Maine had become a state of its own in 1820, and Adams, who planned to run for president in 1824, feared that if he gave up part of the Madawaska Settlement, advocates of states' rights in Maine would mobilize against his candidacy. Even after he won the election, he told Albert Gallatin, his envoy to negotiations in London, not to give up any American territory. But Gallatin's very presence at negotiations only emboldened the British. Washington's willingness to talk was a sign, they concluded, that the Americans feared what would happen if the matter was sent to an arbitrator, the last resort in the Treaty of Ghent.

The London talks did fail, and the dispute did go to arbitration. This represented another victory for the British. In less than two decades, they had gone from conceding the U.S. claim, to concocting a rather creative interpretation of Richard Oswald's intent, to transforming that interpretation into a seemingly plausible option that would now be put before a neutral arbitrator. They had muddied the waters, including, perhaps dangerously, in their own minds. "As the years went by and as the claim was pressed in order to effect a compromise," historian J.K. Chapman observes, "there occurred a subtle transposition in the minds of New Brunswickers, and they came to regard the extreme claim not as a means to an end but as a legal right."

Years later, in 1864, the American writer Henry David Thoreau travelled on foot into what had been the disputed territory, a journey he described in *The Maine Woods*. He recounted his hike into the area that—according to the British—the Paris negotiators had considered the highlands. "I had thought to observe on this carry when we crossed the dividing line between the Penobscot and the St. John, but as my feet had hardly been out of water the whole distance, and it was all level and stagnant, I began to despair of finding it," Thoreau wrote. "Truly an interesting spot to stand on — if that were it — though you could not sit down there. I thought that if the commissioners themselves . . . had spent a few days here, with their packs upon their backs, looking for that 'highland,' they would have had an interesting time, and perhaps it would have modified their view of the question somewhat."

To Thoreau, the merits of the American case were obvious. They were to the American diplomat Albert Gallatin as well. But Gallatin, a seasoned diplomat, understood the realities of statecraft. He warned Washington that an arbitrator might not decide based on a strict reading of the treaty. He might look at earlier offers from one side or the other as an admission that their case was not solid. And he would try to avoid displeasing either party. "He has always a bias to try if possible to split the difference." It is the first recorded mention of a notion that, over the next fifteen years, became a self-fulfilling prophecy.

3. PARTITION

IN EARLY 1839, GENERAL WINFIELD SCOTT, later described as "the first soldier of his nation," was summoned to Washington. Across the city, in cabinet offices, in Congress, at the White House, there was gloom and apprehension. "Every branch of the Government felt alarmed at the imminent hazard of a formidable war — but little having been done in a twenty-four years' peace to meet such exigency," Scott would recall. Diplomacy had failed. Arbitration had failed. The United States was poised to take up arms against Britain again, this time over a remote tract of forestland known as the Madawaska Settlement. The president, Martin Van Buren, was ordering Scott to Maine to organize the troops to fight if necessary, but to avert hostilities if possible. "Mr. President," Scott told Van Buren, "if you want war, I need only look on in silence. The Maine people will make it for you fast and hot enough. I know them; but if peace be your wish, I can give no assurance of success. The difficulties in its way will be formidable."

Scott was massive at six-foot-five, seemingly as broad as he was tall. At thirteen, he had defended his Quaker schoolteacher from a drunk by knocking the attacker down with a single blow. At twenty-eight, he had become the youngest general officer in the American army, and in the War of 1812 he was a hero of the Battle of Lundy's Lane. A gentleman and an intellectual, Scott would serve fourteen presidents from Jefferson to Lincoln. "He rides well, holds his liquor, plays chess and knows how to keep a conversation going," the Canadian historian Pierre Berton wrote of him. A gourmet, a self-taught tactician, a stickler for cleanliness and discipline, Scott kept a baggage wagon stocked with biographies of great soldiers and classic texts on military strategy. He had studied Greek, Latin, French, metaphysics, mathematics, political economy, philosophy, and law, and had translated Napoleonic training manuals into English. "He is a little pompous and more than a little vain, but has reason to be both," Berton wrote.

Scott feared even his vast talents could not prevent hostilities. In Portland, Maine, "the whole population, it seemed, had turned out to greet him. All being in favor of war, or the peaceful possession of the Aroostook, the 'disputed territory,' all looked to him to conquer that possession at once, as they had become tired of diplomacy, parleys, and delays." In Augusta, the state capital, he found "a bad temper prevailing," with both parties at the legislature trying to outdo the other's fervour for what Scott called "a strip of land lying between acknowledged boundaries, without any immediate value except for the fine ship-timber in which it abounded."

Britain may have created the dispute, but Maine, a brash new state, righteously certain of its position, had become the obstacle to a compromise. In 1825 the state government and that of Massachusetts, which still owned land around the Madawaska Settlement, dispatched agents to issue deeds to some of the eighty families living there. The goal was to create what are today called "facts on the ground"— *de facto* sovereignty. Travelling up the Saint John River, the two agents, James Irish and George Coffin, encountered one of the settlers, John Baker, on his way to Fredericton. Baker, a lumberman born in Somerset County, Maine, had moved his family in 1816 to a piece of land on the north bank of the Saint John, at the mouth of a stream then called the Meriumticook. Given that he applied to the New Brunswick colonial government for payment for grain from his land, and that he was on his way to Fredericton to be naturalized as a British subject, some historians argue Baker had accepted Britain's jurisdiction. It is not known what happened when Baker met the land agents, but he decided not to continue on to Fredericton and

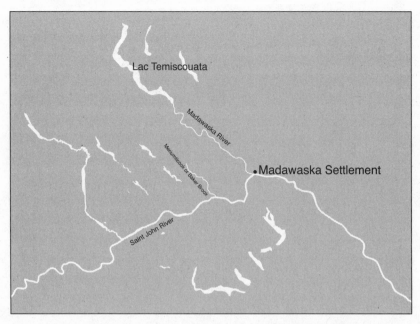

The Saint John River flows through the Madawaska Settlement,
the heart of the border dispute.

instead returned with them to Madawaska, where they issued him a State
of Maine deed for his land.

Baker became the *enfant terrible* of the border dispute. On
Independence Day, 1827, he hoisted a flag, often identified as the Star
Spangled Banner, on his land. When a New Brunswick magistrate ordered
him to remove it, Baker organized several neighbours to sign a declaration
rejecting British jurisdiction. He was arrested by the British, who were
then accused of entering Maine illegally. In Fredericton, he was convicted
of trespassing and intrusion on Crown lands and was sentenced to pay a
fine and spend six months in jail. "I am a citizen of the United States," he
declared, "and owe allegiance to that country. I live in American territory,
and hold myself only liable to the courts of that place, being the county of
Penobscot in the State of Maine. I enter no defence and call no evidence.
I do decline the jurisdiction of this court."

It was in this increasingly contentious climate that the two governments
prepared for the arbitration of the dispute by King William II of the
Netherlands. It was not uncommon in nineteenth-century diplomacy for

63

a "friendly sovereign," as the Treaty of Ghent put it, to arbitrate in this way, though the Americans later regretted agreeing to the choice of the Dutch king: they feared William's objectivity was lost after Belgium's separation from the Netherlands upset the European balance of power, and Britain came to his aid.

The governor of New Brunswick, Howard Douglas, travelled to The Hague to help the British delegation make its case in the arbitration. Douglas had earlier suggested that the Saint John River be adopted as the boundary in the Madawaska Settlement, giving Britain its military road; in return, he proposed that the United States be given Rouse's Point, on the border between New York state and Lower Canada, where a surveying error had led to the construction of an American fort on British soil. But Maine saw no reason to give up its territory in return for land benefitting another state. In The Hague, however, Douglas revived the idea of the Upper Saint John becoming the border.

Douglas also engaged in what is today called disinformation during a private meeting with the King. Albert Gallatin's 1826 warning that an arbitrator might "split the difference" had travelled via Washington to Augusta, where it was made public by the Legislature in 1828. Douglas seized on this, telling the King he should resolve the dispute any way he saw fit, "even should it be by splitting the difference, as was proposed by Mr. Gallatin." Of course, Gallatin had not proposed that at all — he had warned of it. Now his warning would contribute to the eventual undoing of the U.S. position.

King William's decision, in early 1831, did exactly as Gallatin had feared and as Douglas had suggested. The King found that, yes, the Treaty of Paris may well have intended to follow the earlier colonial boundaries described in the Royal Proclamation of 1763, but, on the other hand, there was no explicit statement to that effect. And if that had been the intent, the negotiators would not have haggled for so long over whether the Penobscot, the St. Croix, or the Saint John should become the border. The King also speculated that the change in the words used to describe the all-important watershed — from waters running to the "sea" in the

1763 Proclamation, to waters running to the "Atlantic Ocean" in the treaty — indicated the negotiators may not have intended the same border.

The King also doubted whether the British would really have agreed to a boundary that blocked their road to Québec. "One would vainly seek to discover what motive could have determined the Court of London to consent to such an interruption," he said. But the King was also skeptical that Mars Hill was part of the highlands. Therefore, he concluded, neither side's argument could be considered "as sufficiently preponderating to determine a preference in favor of either one of the two lines." There was no way to draw a border under the terms of the Treaty of Paris.

The King's decision was to split the difference. He drew a boundary north from the source of the St. Croix to the Saint John River, then along the middle of that river to the Saint-François, then up the middle of that river to the line proposed by the United States, until it met the line proposed by Britain, and then southwest until it reached the northwestern source of the Connecticut River. This boundary, almost identical to the final resolution, kept the military road in British hands, but gave two-thirds of the disputed territory, about five million acres, to Maine, and one-third to New Brunswick and Canada.

The proposal was not, strictly speaking, within the King's mandate. The agreement had been that an arbitrator would choose one boundary or the other, not something in between. This amounted to a win for Britain, which had gone from having almost no case at all to having won half of what it sought.

State leaders in Maine were incensed. The legislature denounced the decision and declared the state could not be forced to comply. In Washington, President Andrew Jackson's administration disliked the ruling, but the new secretary of state, Edward Livingston, said the reputation of the United States would suffer if it rejected the outcome of an arbitration it had agreed to. The U.S. had won most of the disputed land, and the British road between New Brunswick and Québec did no harm to American interests, he argued. If that did not satisfy Washington, the only course left was war.

Jackson submitted the decision to the Senate, where it failed to muster the two-thirds majority it needed for ratification. Administration officials then attempted to make a secret deal with Maine in which the state would support the King's arbitration in return for compensation. But when that became public, the Maine Legislature not only backed away but voted itself the power to "adopt and sanction" the ratification of any treaty — in essence, a state veto. In 1833, the Maine Legislature went even further, declaring that any future agreement on the boundary would be subject to popular approval by the voters themselves, virtually dooming any hope of a resolution. The president abandoned any hope of implementing the arbitration decision. "Maine was unsatisfied," New Brunswick historian W.S. MacNutt concluded, "and her point of view made American national policy."

Emboldened, Maine issued more land permits in the Madawaska Settlement and dispatched census-takers. Its militia began building a road from the Penobscot River north towards the territory, and it incorporated the town of Madawaska, located at the site of present-day Madawaska (Maine) and Edmundston (New Brunswick). The governor, Enoch Lincoln, admitted to the administration in Washington that his motives were economic. "The material for shipbuilding on the disputed territory may be calculated to be inexhaustible," he wrote, "and the soil so fertile that the Madawaska Settlement exports many thousands of bushels of grain."

In 1834 the Jackson administration in Washington suggested the two countries try again to make a deal. Britain eagerly agreed, proposing a border running along the Saint John River from the North Line near Grand Falls to its source. The Americans countered with a suggestion that the border be drawn along the Saint John for the entire length of the river, from its source to its mouth. Each proposal required the other side to give up more than it was willing to, and the discussions went nowhere. But the offers themselves were revealing: the two governments were no longer debating the intent of the 1783 treaty. Both had abandoned it in favour of using the Saint John River to "split the difference." Without knowing it, both were taking steps in the direction of a future agreement.

A collapse in land prices in Maine in 1837 was the catalyst for the eventual dénouement. The state relied on land sales for revenues, so it needed the border settled to resume selling tracts of forest in the Aroostook Valley. A new census-taker was dispatched to Madawaska, where he was promptly arrested by the British. The following year, Maine land agents discovered New Brunswick lumberjacks cutting timber south of the Saint John and on the Aroostook. When a civil posse was organized to stop them, the colonial governor of New Brunswick, John Harvey, mobilized the militia. The governor of Maine, John Fairfield, took that as a declaration of war and called out his own troops. "This is no ordinary crisis," Fairfield said when he reviewed northbound soldiers in Augusta in February 1839. "The time has arrived when we must make a vigorous and manly defence of our soil or ignobly permit it to be wrested from us by a foreign power. . . . I know you will not tamely submit to such indignities — to such arrogant pretensions — that you will not quail under British threats."

The Governor's motives were partly partisan: the Democrats and the Whigs were locked in perpetually close annual election battles, and standing up to foreign foes was an easy way to generate support. The New Brunswick journalist and author James Hannay, writing late in the nineteenth century, remarked wryly, "There are no people so ready to do battle and to embroil nations as those whose position would exempt them from military service, and who are not likely to feel any of the personal inconveniences of war. If those who are the strongest advocates of war were always compelled to march in front of their armies, we would hear less of warlike resolutions from congresses and legislatures."

Maine erected a fort on the Aroostook River, just east of the North Line, near where it flowed into the Saint John. British troops were sent to the disputed territory. Fairfield had warned President Martin Van Buren that "should you go against us on this occasion — or not espouse our cause with warmth and earnestness and with a true American feeling, God only knows what the result would be politically." But the very day after Fairfield's incendiary speech in Augusta, Van Buren's secretary of state and the British minister to Washington agreed to step back from the brink. The British would not eject Maine's militia from the territory; Washington, meanwhile, would persuade Maine to withdraw its troops voluntarily.

This was the mission assigned to General Scott. He had recently calmed tensions in the New York-Ontario borderlands, and "had evolved the technique of bringing a big stick, but then speaking softly," one historian observes. And in the Aroostook War, there was a happy, helpful coincidence: Scott considered himself a friend of John Harvey, New Brunswick's governor, whom he had faced in the Battle of Stoney Creek during the War of 1812. They had corresponded as commanders and had met on the battlefield under flags of truce. Scott admired Harvey for having treated captured American soldiers well, and even saved his British opponent's life during one skirmish.

Hannay describes John Harvey as "a gallant soldier, and it was owing mainly to his ability and courage that the great victory of Stony Creek was won. . . . Sir John was a man of less ability than Sir Howard Douglas, but he was quite as zealous for the good of the people whom he was called to govern." At first, Harvey had urged the seizure of the land awarded to New Brunswick by the King of the Netherlands. "I am not aware of any other course by which the spirit of my instructions can be effectually fulfilled than by taking military possession of the settled parts of the Disputed Territory," he wrote. But he was overruled by his superiors, including his rival Sir Colin Campbell, the lieutenant-governor of Nova Scotia. John Caldwell, a sawmill owner at Grand Falls, persuaded Harvey a deal might be possible in which New Brunswick would get some of the land it wanted if American interests were granted navigation rights on the Saint John River, a vital route for Maine lumbermen to get their timber to markets.

Harvey was ready to deal, and he flattered Scott—and by extension himself—as they reminisced about the earlier war and sought to avoid a new one. "If the social history of those campaigns had been given to the world," Harvey wrote, "you and I would stand crowned with the most glorious wreath which can circle the head of a soldier, viz: that of having softened the savage character of warfare and faced it with the visages of civilized nations." Scott replied, "How happy may we esteem ourselves, if a personal friendship commenced in the field and in opposition ranks can be made in any degree conducive to the preservation of peace between our countries!"

Scott told Harvey that Maine could not unilaterally withdraw from Madawaska, but if Harvey assured him that the British had stopped trying to expel the Americans, he would persuade the state to recall its troops. Harvey, in turn, agreed to limit the British presence to the Saint John River and the Madawaska Settlement, and to undertake no operations on the Aroostook. By late March, less than three weeks after Scott's arrival, the armistice took shape. Harvey would not try to seize the territory. Fairfield made the same promise and said Maine would not interrupt the road between New Brunswick and Québec. The two soldiers had bought London and Washington some time to try again for a final treaty.

Britain now made a last bid to identify the elusive highlands. London sent George William Featherstonhaugh, a geologist, and Lieutenant-Colonel Richard Zachariah Mudge, a survey astronomer, to sort out which of the competing claims was the most credible.

Featherstonhaugh had left Britain to work for the U.S. government, eventually becoming its first geologist, and founded the first successful passenger railway in the United States. He was urbane and fastidious — he carried two toothbrushes — and loathed his time in the rough backwoods of the disputed territory. In an "indifferent tavern" in Houlton, he wrote in his diary, he and Mudge encountered "the most ill-mannered ruffians imaginable." At Woodstock, they stopped at "a miserable tavern, the people just like the Yankees in their manners, as all frontier people must be like each other!" Saint John fared no better. "A vulgar fishing town," he declared. "The best emigrants always go to farms or into the U.S., whilst the low, drunker poor vagabonds unable to get any further remain in the town they disembarked at." The river, he noted in his journal, was "very beautiful," but he found the flies intolerable. "My face presents the appearance of a person just recovering from the smallpox."

Not even his partner, Mudge, escaped his withering scrutiny. "This man is of no use whatsoever," he fumed after Mudge left their documents near a fire, where they almost burned. "It would have been better if he had been left at home." Featherstonhaugh, an early riser, was also alarmed that Mudge and their support team enjoyed sleeping in. "Everyone lazy," he wrote in his diary, "can get nothing done."

But Featherstonhaugh was determined, despite the deprivations, to bolster the British claim that the highlands were well south of the Saint John River. "It will be altogether a search after ridges once connected, to be put together by geological reasoning," he wrote in early September. "I think I shall be able to demonstrate my hypothesis in a perfect manner, but it will require to be strengthened by extensive investigations conducted with diligence and prudence by all engaged in them." His bias, however, was apparent when he carved the Queen's initials, V.R., into a tree. "This is her country and we must keep it for her," he wrote in his diary.

A month later, near Lake Caucomgomoc deep in the woods, one of Featherstonhaugh's men climbed a tree and spotted what he called "a very considerable" peak. "It turned out to be what I had always believed it to be," he wrote. "The truth is that this whole country is divided by a broad range of highlands running from the Bald Mountains to Mars Hill. ... The series of views from this peak [is] most interesting, and particularly important, as they prove our case." Featherstonhaugh would argue in his report that the "axis of maximum elevation" he saw was the highlands — or had been highlands, long ago. The hills were, he argued, remnants of a continuous ridge that had existed thousands of years earlier and that had eventually been broken down by the passage of time, leaving peaks considerable distances apart.

This conclusion was greeted with derision in Maine. Governor Fairfield scorned Featherstonhaugh's reliance on ancient geology, noting that the 1783 treaty was based on conditions at the time, not "imaginary or theoretical highlands" from some prehistoric period. The editor of Featherstonhaugh's journals, published in 1988, concedes the geologist's conclusions appear "fanciful." Even the British chose not to rely on them.

Featherstonhaugh returned to England and was later rewarded for his efforts with an appointment as British consul at Le Havre, France, where a decade later, he played a minor but compelling role in another jurisdictional drama. As King Louis Philippe fled the 1848 revolution,

Featherstonhaugh provided him false travel documents in the name of William Smith. This was a geologist's in-joke: the real William Smith was the father of modern geology and a friend of Featherstonhaugh, and Smith had died in England on August 28, 1839, the very day Featherstonhaugh and Mudge had climbed Mars Hill hoping to prove it was part of the highlands.

John Harvey's reputation also suffered in the aftermath of the Aroostook War. Despite the armistice, flare-ups continued along the border as each side tried to create new facts on the ground. A Maine land agent wrote to Fairfield to suggest the state continue building its road northward "to proceed silently and quietly strengthening ourselves on the Territory, and while the two governments were negotiating we should decide the question." When a Maine civil posse moved up to the edge of the Madawaska Settlement in 1840, Harvey, anxious to preserve his carefully crafted truce with Scott, vacillated. His colonial masters lost confidence in him and gave responsibility for the dispute to Lord Sydenham, the governor of Canada. Later that year, when Americans held a census meeting at Fort Kent, Sydenham dispatched troops, and Harvey, fearful Maine would see this as a violation of the armistice, tried to stop them — then, having failed at that, warned Fairfield they were coming. "His candour exceeded the bounds of discipline," MacNutt wrote. "Now it seemed that British interests on the Upper Saint John, as well as the Aroostook, were being sacrificed to the Americans."

There is another interpretation of Harvey's actions. He may have felt more loyalty to his loose agreement with his neighbours in Maine than to his more distant fellow colonials, an early sign of a nascent, fragile New Brunswick-Maine bond. But the British could not conceive of such things. "He will bandy fine sentences with General Scott or Governor Fairfield," Sydenham wrote, "whilst the Yankees take possession and occupy the whole of the Saint John's and our road to New Brunswick to boot. They understand his character perfectly and play on it unendingly...."

It is impossible that I can go on, or take the responsibility of this business unless he is checked." In 1841 Harvey was removed as lieutenant-governor and called home to London.

General Winfield Scott fared better: a few years after averting the Aroostook War, he was the hero of the Mexican-American War, hailed by the Duke of Wellington as "the greatest living general." Nominated by the Whigs as their presidential candidate in 1852, Scott lost in a landslide, due in part to his anti-slavery views. He remained popular and was promoted to the rank of lieutenant-general by a special act of Congress, only the second American after George Washington to gain the title. At the outbreak of the Civil War, Scott advocated the "Anaconda Plan," a strategy to encircle and choke off the Confederacy. The idea was widely ridiculed, and Scott retired, to be replaced by his ambitious underling, George McClellan. Scott lived long enough to see McClellan removed for incompetence and the Union win the war by using a variation of his Anaconda plan.

The task of transforming Harvey's and Scott's armistice into a lasting peace — which required, clearly, a mutually acceptable boundary — now fell to another pair of negotiators. It is, again, the American whose name is still remembered by history: Daniel Webster, considered one of the greatest men to ever serve in the United States Senate, and a three-time presidential candidate who became Secretary of State to two presidents. The British negotiator was Alexander Baring, Baron Ashburton, the former head of the powerful Baring Brothers & Company bank, who came out of political retirement to settle all the various border disputes between the United States and the colonies of British North America.

The British government instructed Ashburton to secure a border along the supposed Mars Hill highlands if at all possible, but if not to preserve, at all costs, the north bank of the Saint John River, with its road linking the Maritime colonies to Québec. This meant gaining land from Maine, which the state refused to contemplate. Webster, thinking of the national interest, wanted a deal, and cannily invited the governments of Maine and Massachusetts to appoint commissions to join the discussions in Washington, an idea that dismayed the British. Webster calculated that bringing the recalcitrant state administrations into the process would make it more difficult for them to dissent later.

Webster played two other cards. In 1841, he had been approached by a Portland lawyer, Francis Ormond Jonathan Smith, who proposed to "prepare public sentiment in Maine for a compromise of the matter." In return for thirty-five hundred dollars plus travel expenses, paid from President Tyler's secret service fund, Smith, using a pseudonym, wrote three newspaper articles urging citizens of Maine to lobby the state government to compromise. Maine could let Britain have its military road, he suggested, in return for federal compensation and American navigation rights on the Saint John River. Smith also travelled through Maine, talking to influential political and business leaders about the attractiveness of such a deal. This nineteenth-century version of a public relations campaign bore fruit: Smith reported to Webster that public opinion was shifting "toward the necessary preliminaries of a satisfactory compromise of the dispute."

Webster's second card was a map. Early in 1841, Jared Sparks, a Harvard historian researching in London, had purchased a copy of a 1783 map used by members of Parliament during the debate on Richard Oswald's treaty. The boundary marked on it, Sparks pointed out, was "precisely as claimed by the United States," and the record indicated no one, including Oswald himself, had objected that the map was inaccurate. The following year, however, Sparks made a more troubling discovery: in the Archives Nationales in Paris, he found a December 1782 letter from Benjamin Franklin to the French foreign minister, referring to the return of a map. "I have marked with a Strong Red Line, according to your desire, the Limits of the thirteen United States, as settled in the Preliminaries between the British and American plenipotentiarys."

Sparks hurried to the map collection, where he located a map that appeared to be the one cited in Franklin's letter. "Imagine my surprise," he wrote later, "on discovering that this line runs wholly south of the Saint John, and between the head waters of that river and the Penobscot and the Kennebec. In short, it is exactly the line contended for by Great Britain, except that it concedes more than is claimed."

Sparks copied the line onto a contemporary map and sent it home to America. It appeared Richard Oswald had done quite well at Paris after all, a potentially disastrous discovery for the United States. But Webster craftily turned it to his advantage. He sent Sparks to Maine and Massachusetts to show the red-line map to state leaders, warning them to accept a compromise line before the Paris discovery completely undermined the American position. The map "produced the intended apprehension in Augusta," writes one historian.

The negotiations began in Washington in June. Ashburton, whose precise instructions from London had been delayed because of a split within the British government, nearly derailed the talks by boldly proposing that the border run west from the North Line, but along the *Aroostook* River. This boundary, south of the Saint John, went far beyond what the King of the Netherlands had proposed and would give Britain all of the Madawaska territory. Even more insultingly, Ashburton offered few concessions in return, other than navigation rights on the Saint John and some territory on Canada's border with New York and New Hampshire.

The Maine and Massachusetts commissioners were so incensed that they made noises about leaving Washington, and the entire process seemed poised to collapse before it had begun. Had Britain been willing to offer the strip of New Brunswick between the North Line and the Saint John, giving up a large piece of territory, Webster might have agreed. "But in the present posture of things," he told Ashburton, "I cannot hold out the expectation to your Lordship that anything south of the river can be yielded."

Just as the outrage was building against his opening gambit, Ashburton received his precise instructions, which allowed him more flexibility. "I shall probably give up after a little fight my cherished Madawaska Settlements," he wrote, referring to the south bank of the river. This was the turning point. Negotiations resumed, with the Saint John River again the basis for the new boundary. Ashburton told Webster he could accept such an arrangement if the United States would let the border turn southwest from the Saint-François at Lake Pohénégamook, which would move the boundary fifteen to thirty miles from the hills overlooking Québec and the St. Lawrence. This was an important modification to the King's arbitration decision of 1831 that would lessen the chance of a quick American attack on the capital. Webster agreed. "I am well pleased," Ashburton would tell London later, "that we end by driving the enemy off that Crest of Highlands so much coveted by the War Office."

Maine and Massachussetts chafed at not winning more concessions, but after a private meeting with Webster, they grudgingly assented. Six decades of contention had finally came to an end. The United States won more of the disputed territory, though less than what they would have received under the King's 1831 award. Webster and Ashburton quickly worked through some remaining issues from other sections of the border in late July and two weeks later signed the treaty at the White House with President Tyler looking on. Today, in fields and forests along the border between New Brunswick and Maine, many of the cast-iron border markers are inscribed with the date and location: "Treaty of Washington," it says on one side, and on the other, "Boundary August 9, 1842."

Britain had triumphed. Maine and Massachusetts split three million dollars in federal compensation, a significant sum in 1842, and American lumbermen gained navigation rights to the Saint John River, no small thing. Yet Governor John Fairfield pronounced himself disappointed. "The course of the British government . . . was marked by an unyielding and grasping spirit. Its liberality, if any was evinced, was in unmeaning diplomatic compliments, while its exactions were in acres and substantial privileges." But, Fairfield added, it was important that Maine support the Union. "And if she could be satisfied that the sacrifice was necessary for the good of the country, she could in that find ample consolation."

New Brunswick could now take care of some other unfinished business. It had been exercising jurisdiction in the Madawaska territory awarded to Britain, but the province of Canada claimed it as well. If, as New

Brunswick had argued during the dispute with the United States, the highlands were much farther south than what Maine had asserted, then Canada's border with New Brunswick was also much farther south. Put another way, New Brunswick's claim to Madawaska and Lake Témiscouata was based on the highlands being precisely where it had denied they were in the dispute with Maine. In 1851, London settled the disagreement by drawing a boundary that gave the Madawaska Settlement to New Brunswick and the lake to Canada. This line established a three-border corner, the equivalent of the long-sought-after northwest angle of Nova Scotia — the spot on Beau Lac where Yves Carrier took me in his canoe.

The Webster-Ashburton Treaty left John Baker, the man whose hoisting of the American flag in 1827 had reignited the border dispute, owning land in British territory. The Maine and Massachusetts commissioners in Washington had persuaded Ashburton and Webster to sign "an understanding" that if Baker did not want to live under the Union Jack, Britain would pay him a fair price to leave his land. In November, Baker petitioned the Lieutenant-Governor of New Brunswick to proceed. He said he did not "feel disposed after all that has transpired in this section of the Province to remain under the British government." In the end, however, he chose to stay at the mouth of the Meriumticook, and died there a year after Confederation. Today the stream, and the village at its mouth, are both called Baker Brook.

The people of the Madawaska Settlement did not receive the same consideration as Baker when the boundary was drawn down the middle of their community. Daniel Webster denied "that there was any cruelty in splitting Madawaska. Inconvenience, yes, but the international line need not interrupt social and family relations." The British, however, had cultivated the loyalty of the Acadians during the dispute, and their local economy and their sense of citizenship were tied to Fredericton via the Saint John River. Now, as a contemporary observer noted, "the principle that a British subject could never be alienated from his allegiance to his native country has been violated, and the people of Madawaska have been bartered as if they were common articles of traffic."

This fact has shaped the ongoing historical debate about the Webster-

Ashburton Treaty. Hannay argues that Ashburton could not have secured a better deal, given that, in Paris, Richard Oswald "had agreed to an impossible boundary on a range of highlands that did not exist or, if it existed at all, was far to the north of the river Saint John." Chip Gagnon, a Franco-American political scientist from the Valley who specializes in ethnic conflict and what he calls "political demobilization," rejects Hannay's view that Britain was hemmed in by Oswald's mistake. "It seems hard to imagine that the British negotiators in 1783 intended to cede to the United States the entire valley of the upper Saint John, given its vital military significance; or to allow the border to be drawn within 15 miles of the St. Lawrence River, as the U.S. claim to those highlands would indicate."

Worse, Gagnon concludes, the 1842 treaty paid no heed to the interests of the local population, which today remains split by an imaginary line that is ever harder to overcome. "The international border divided what was an integral community that did not see the river as a boundary or border. The result has been that while the population in New Brunswick — the only officially bilingual province of Canada — has maintained its French culture and language, the population on the U.S. side has assimilated into the Anglo-dominant culture of the U.S. The border thus not only divided the community but created the conditions which would split that community asunder."

4. GODFATHERS OF THE VALLEY

THE PLAQUE OUTSIDE THE FORT KENT BLOCKHOUSE is a model of balance and circumspection compared to most commemorations of war. It notes that Maine acted provocatively during the border dispute, granting land to settlers and "disregarding British claims" to the Madawaska Settlement. It points out that the United States rejected the arbitration decision by the King of the Netherlands. The careful phrasing adds to the sense that this spot near the river, so close to the Webster-Ashburton line, is somehow not completely, *unambivalently* American.

In some parts of the world, particularly in conflict zones, there is a heightened sense of national identification. Gates and fences bring differences into sharper focus. But on the Upper Saint John, more than a century and a half after the relatively peaceful Aroostook "War" divided the settlers here, patriotism is blunted and skewed. There is an understanding that something else exists beyond one's own sense of nationhood. Perhaps this, or a wicked sense of humour, explains why one of the streets near the blockhouse is named Highland Avenue.

I drive back across the Saint John, passing through Canada Customs without incident, to the municipal office of the village of Clair, the self-styled "frontier town" of New Brunswick. There I find another symbol of blurred nationhood: the village's coat of arms pays homage not simply to its own identity, but to its once-disputed status on the periphery of the United States. It includes the image of a bridge, representing the village's

A sign in Clair, N.B., points to the international bridge to Fort Kent, Maine.

link to Fort Kent, as well as a pine cone, a visual reference to Maine, the Pine Tree State, of which Clair might well have been a part.

The small village office, tucked inside a larger building housing a pharmacy and dentists' offices, looks more like an accountant's workplace than the seat of local government. Ludger Lang, the mayor, is seventy-three years old, and like many of the eight-hundred-odd residents of the village, the border has shaped his life. It gave him a career: he spent three decades working as a Canadian customs officer at this end of the international bridge. "You get to meet a lot of people," he tells me. "They're not all smugglers. There's a lot of legitimate business. Customs is there mainly to protect commerce. You learn quickly that there's too much emphasis on the little things. The little seizures of a bottle of booze, you have to stop that too, but the fines for those are pretty light compared to the commercial fines."

Lang's connection with the border predates him, stretching back six generations to his ancestor Philip Long, the British courier who, from a farm on Lake Témiscouata, helped move the mail along the military road between the Maritimes and Québec. Long also sheltered the 104th Regiment of Foot when it marched up the Madawaska River on its way to Kingston in 1813. All the Longs and the Langs in the Upper Saint John are descended from this single courier, who in his seventieth year moved his family from Témiscouata to Clair. He died there in 1832 and was buried in the cemetery of the closest church, at Sainte-Luce, on the other side of the river. A decade later, the burial plot of this British patriot became American soil, another irony of life on the Upper Saint John. Today Sainte-Luce is called Frenchville, Maine.

Mayor Ludger Lang has distant memories of a time in his childhood when the border seemed no more real than in his ancestor's time. People freely crossed the river here. There was Clair, and there was Fort Kent, but there were not two countries, not quite. "There was no one and nothing to say you were in the United States or Canada," he says. In those days, customs officers were based in their homes, and you knocked on the door when you had something to report, but there was little consequence if you forgot. After the Second World War, both countries began enforcing the line more closely. A new customs office — at the time, a remarkable sign of modernity and progress in such a tiny backwater — was built at the Clair end of the bridge in 1954.

Lang was hired as a customs officer in 1964. His career was fittingly unremarkable for a region with such a casual attitude towards the border. Over the years he seized cuts of meat, chickens, apples, a gun or two, but nothing more glamorous than that. In 1980, he had to ask the RCMP to arrest a man who refused to pay duty on a heating system he was hauling in his truck. Another time, two men coming down the river in a boat were spotted by New Brunswick forest rangers and began tossing boxes overboard. Lang and his fellow officers later recovered thirty-six half-gallon bottles of booze from the riverbed.

These are the anecdotes that punctuate a customs officer's career on the Upper Saint John: hardly the stuff of legend. "There's always drugs," Lang offers, somewhat apologetically, "but in small quantities."

Lang has been crossing to the country next door all his life — now retired, he still does, to visit his sisters who married Americans or to attend community events in Fort Kent — but he did not order a passport until after 9/11, when the Americans began demanding them. "More and more, the border, the law, it exists in practice, so you have to respect it," he shrugs. But he does not like it. "You get there, they check your passport. They send your car over there and they take your passport inside. They check their computer. They ask you to unlock your car. Sometimes you've only got a few minutes and you can spend a half-hour or an hour waiting."

Lang is thinking ahead to the World Acadian Congress in 2014, and whether the American security measures will impede the people attending events in Maine, New Brunswick, and Québec. For the first time in the seven decades he has lived alongside it, the border represents an obstacle.

Not everyone in Clair has treated the border as an afterthought. For one small group of men it represented a way of life, and a source of considerable wealth.

On the night of November 8, 1922, seven United States Customs and Prohibition officers raided two homes in Estcourt, a tiny settlement along the Saint-François River, fifty kilometres from Clair. Estcourt is unique: part of the community is in Québec, but the other part is at the northernmost tip of Maine, though cut off from the rest of the state by vast forests. There are no public American roads leading to Estcourt, which means U.S. residents rely on Québec for access to electricity, telephone service, and road links to the outside world.[2] This isolation is why, that night in 1922, the U.S. customs officers who seized 263 quarts of liquor from a house that was half in Canada, half in the United States, had a problem. They could not take the confiscated bottles directly to the closest U.S. customs house in Fort Kent. They had to drive down into the New Brunswick panhandle to Clair and cross the international bridge.

They made it, but only after considerable difficulty. A prankster—"un farceur," as the local newspaper *Le Madawaska* reported it—contacted Canadian customs to report that two men were on their way from Estcourt to the border with a car full of booze. The Canadian officers intercepted the American officers and arrested them. Once the Americans proved who they were to a judge in Edmundston, they were released. The

---

2   Fittingly, Estcourt is named for James Estcourt, the British military officer and surveyor who cleared and marked the border under the terms of the Webster-Ashburton Treaty. He died in 1855 at Sevastopol, in the Crimea, another area where national sovereignty has been ambiguous.

law allowed foreign officers to transport liquor through New Brunswick if it was in the line of duty, the newspapers reported. But there was another twist: "One of the men, whose name cannot be learned, was under the influence of liquor and was reprimanded by the magistrate," the Fredericton *Daily Gleaner* reported. And another: "Whilst the case was going on in the police court, some of the liquor was stolen from the cars by men gathered around the court house."

It was one of the more prosaic episodes that played out during the thirteen years that Prohibition was part of the United States Constitution, a time in which the existence of the border transformed the lives of a small circle of local men on the New Brunswick side of the Upper Saint John. They had access to a product, liquor, and there was a market ravenous for it, quite literally at their doorsteps. "Unlike the illicit booze dealers in most other parts of the province, the 'big fish' of Madawaska County did not confine themselves to any one aspect of the trade," B.J. Grant writes in *When Rum Was King*. "Their enterprises were developed horizontally."

Smuggling already had a long history along the New Brunswick-Maine boundary, but the 1919 passage of the Volstead Act, an amendment to the U.S. Constitution prohibiting "intoxicating liquors," turned the entire length of the border into an irresistible invitation to make money. At first, illegal booze was brought into the United States from large ships docked offshore. But when President Coolidge brought a fleet of First World War destroyers out of retirement in 1924 to push the rum-running ships out to sea, American importers looked to Canada for potential transit routes. One involved shipping liquor from the French islands of Saint-Pierre and Miquelon, in the Gulf of St. Lawrence, to Québec's Gaspé peninsula, or to Caraquet in northeast New Brunswick, then hauling it to isolated stretches of the Maine border.

At first, hundreds of amateur smugglers got in on the action, but the industry was soon shaken down to a small number of powerful operators. The remote stretches of the Upper Saint John, where policing was sparse, were a natural focal point. In 1921, there were just thirty men patrolling three hundred miles of border between New Brunswick and Maine. People were easily caught at crossings, but in Madawaska, local men who worked in the woods knew the back roads and the shallow points in the river, where one could wade across. They lived hardscrabble lives and were easy to recruit. A smuggler "could deliver his load without challenge and in almost perfect safety from authority," Grant writes.

"There'll always be people who'll try to get around the law because there's money to be made, so people here got into that business," says Georges Cyr, a member of the local historical society in St. Hilaire, a village between Clair and Edmundston. Cyr is sitting in the sunroom of his house overlooking the Saint John River. "You could say that in St. Hilaire, Baker Brook, Clair — well, everyone was involved," he says, his eyes alight with enthusiasm for the story. "In every house, there was someone working for the organizers. Everyone here knows who they were. There was one in every area. In this area, there was Maxime Albert. There was Alfred Lévesque, known as Fred Lévesque, who lived next door here. In Clair, it was Maxime Albert's brother, Isidore Albert, who owned a hotel. So everyone had their territory. In Saint-Léonard it was Albérie Violette. In Edmundston it was Joseph Cyr, the owner of the Hotel Royal, who was called Bébé Cyr. They became very rich."

They are gone now, all of them, and their children, too. Few firsthand accounts survive, but there are still connections and bloodlines. In Clair, Mayor Ludger Lang walks me from the village office to a nearby house that faces the international bridge the home of Ronald "Ti-Bou" Albert, one of Lang's former colleagues from the customs office. Albert's finished basement is covered with framed photographs of fishing trips, grandchildren, sports teams, weddings — the typical memorabilia of a full life. But Ti-Bou Albert has another narrative: this stocky, athletic-looking man who made a good living looking for smuggled goods is the grandson of Isidore Albert, the head of the local bootlegging operation during Prohibition.

Isidore Albert was the owner of the Clair Hotel, where much of the smuggling was planned, and it stood next door to where Ti-Bou's house is now, overlooking the bridge, the river, and the American shore. "See the road out here?" Albert asks, pointing towards the front of the house.

"There's always a crack in the road. And every time they repair it, it cracks again. I think the tunnel collapsed and that's why."

The tunnel. Legends abound on the Upper Saint John about tunnels, secret passages, smugglers crossing the river disguised as priests, booze hidden in bricks or in coffins. Contrary to one story, there were apparently no tunnels passing under the river itself. But there *were* tunnels. "My mother worked for my uncle, Albérie, before she married my father," Ti-Bou Albert tells me. "My mother worked at the hotel. What they told me, my mother, my father, my friends, was that there was the rail line that came here, and there was a train station. There was a person who sold coffins. The coffins came in here full of booze from Saint-Pierre and Miquelon. And it was stored in a tunnel below the hotel.

"The tunnel came from the hotel, under the garage that was right here, and went under the road to another garage down there, by the river. When I was a kid, we'd go down to the basement of the hotel, and there were these closets, all kinds of closets. We went in them to look for secret doors, and we could see the entrance to the tunnel, but it was blocked off. The cement was broken and caved in. The same thing at the garage down there. There was a shed and the tunnel came out there. That was where they hid the booze."

There were other hiding places: the countless barns dotting the properties on the New Brunswick side of the river, Cyr says. "Everyone had barns, and there was booze hidden in a lot of them. These big barns were where it was stored." Not everyone wanted their barns to become part of the operation, but few dared refuse when the men working for Isidore Albert or Maxime Albert or Fred Lévesque arrived at their front doors.

The next step was getting it across the border. In summer, the smugglers would use the dozens of privately owned barges that crossed the river. In winter, they went on foot. "Fred Lévesque was more daring than Maxime Albert, I've been told," Cyr says. One legend, unconfirmed, is that bottles were shipped into the area inside bricks that were used to build the church in St. Hilaire, a project made possible by the philanthropy of

Maxime Albert. "So is it true Fred Lévesque disguised himself as a bishop to bring booze over in coffins?" Cyr shrugs. "I find that funny. It's a nice legend. Did it really happen? I don't know. Could you fool the customs officers at that point? I don't know. Maybe they were persuaded to close their eyes. We do know Maxime Albert contributed to the construction of the church and the presbytery. The church is on the land that belonged to his brother, Isidore. And the presbytery is on the land that belonged to Maxime.

"Now, these guys were Mafia. They were violent. They had their muscle with them. And guns. But in the Catholic faith of that time — Maxime Albert was very religious, and he didn't want to go to Hell — the belief was, and it went back to the Middle Ages, that if you donated land for the construction of a church, or a monastery, or a religious building, your soul would be saved. And these people were real believers. This man with this money wanted to *save his soul*. He didn't want to go to Hell. So he gave a lot to the Church, to soothe his conscience."

Rain is threatening. Cyr takes me outside, around the back of the house next door. The river, just a hundred yards away, looks as cold as black metal. Cyr opens a large back door and leads me into a huge potato shed with a trap door leading to another room. This was the home of Fred Lévesque, another of the bootlegging kingpins, and the shed was where he stored some of his stock. We move on, driving a half-mile down to the centre of St. Hilaire, where the road bends sharply to follow the river. By now there are large raindrops slapping the windshield of my car. On a small hill overlooking the river sits the Complexe Maxime Albert, a large house owned by the village and used by its historical society. During Prohibition, Cyr tells me, there was a tunnel running from the rear of the house to a huge barn, "much larger than those of other farmers." As well, "there were three hotels here at one time. Maxime owned one of them. And there were tunnels beneath them."

Maxime Albert, Isidore Albert, Fred Lévesque, and Bébé Cyr had been the most important men on the New Brunswick side of the Upper Saint John, Cyr tells me. "They amassed, in just a few short years, a million dollars. In the 1920s, that was an astronomical figure. Then they each decided to go their own ways. We don't know why. They'd been a team. Maybe they quarrelled. We don't know."

Cyr has collected memories of the men for most of the previous decade, especially since his retirement as a political science professor at the Edmundston campus of the Université de Moncton. His hobby is the history of bootlegging, and for several summers, he scraped together government grants to hire local students to interview elderly residents about the Prohibition era. Their most important interview was with Rino Albert, a Roman Catholic priest and the grandson of

Maxime Albert (right) is seen with an associate during a trip to the U.S. South. (Courtesy Centre de documentation et d'études madawaskayennes (CDEM) de l'Université de Moncton, campus d'Edmundston)

Maxime. "He talked a lot," Cyr says, still marvelling at his good fortune. "He was happy to talk. There had been so many things said about his grandfather, and he had heard it all, and he had read about it in articles, and he had *fumed* — 'That's not how it happened.' He was anxious to talk. So when we called, he said, 'Yes, I have things to say.'"

Rino Albert told Cyr in 2000 that smuggling provided a better living than growing potatoes, one of the few industries in the Upper Saint John. "It was big business," Albert said. "Maxime did not approve of Prohibition. He said he was careful to whom he sold liquor and did not let anyone abuse it. His reasoning was that if the smugglers could sell, he could sell it too. So he did not feel guilty, and he considered the law to be immoral. . . . Maxime's conscience was not troubled because he drank alcohol very rarely, and he did not sell liquor just to get rich, because he had a rather modest life. He once told me he did not sell the drink to do harm, but because alcohol had its place in society. He believed the government should not take away the right to consume alcohol from people who didn't abuse it."

"But that was *his* version," Cyr comments. "He didn't want us to say that his grandfather *was* a Mafioso. Well," he shrugs, "he was a Mafioso. They were people who gave a lot of work to a lot of people, but they were violent. They were Mafioso."

Rino Albert was eighty years old when he spoke to Cyr and his students; he died a few years later. "He told us what his mother and his grandfather told him. So he's a primary source, and a reliable one, I believe. You meet people who worked in the organization, but like with everything, they have a tendency to exaggerate, amplify. It becomes a myth, to the point that today we can't distinguish what's true and what's false. It's all myth. But I consider Father Albert a reliable source."

Albert told Cyr about some remarkable connections. "My grandfather was even a close friend of the Bronfmans, the smugglers from Montréal who called him 'Le Père Maxime.' Still, I don't believe he worked with them."

Cyr smiles at this: "What does that tell us? They were close." And Samuel Bronfman's bootlegging to cities in the northern United States is well documented. "The border was right here," Cyr says, pointing at the river. Albert "could take it across, and then it was the New York market, the Boston market, the Chicago market. Maxime Albert also had connections to Al Capone. They knew each other. They visited each other. When Maxime Albert goes to Chicago and he visits Al Capone — what does that tell us?"

It appears Maxime Albert never killed anyone. But there were threats, Cyr said; they'd say to farmers, " 'Open your barn. We need to hide the booze.' If they hesitated, one of the men would take out a knife and drive it into the table. That's why some of the people who are still alive, people who remember those times, don't want to talk. There was one case — I won't name the person — where the man was eighty-two or eighty-three years old. We wanted to talk about those times. He said yes on the phone. We went the next day. We started the interview. His wife was there, sitting next to him. We asked questions. He answered: Yes, no, yes, no. And then she said, 'Don't say too much, you. You'll be hanged. Don't say too much. You've said enough.' After ten minutes, we wrapped it up. The interview was done. There were things he didn't want to talk about."

The law eventually caught up with Maxime Albert. He was charged with non-payment of taxes. Naturally, he slipped across the border to Maine, where he owned good potato-growing land in Ste-Agathe. There was no extradition treaty at the time, but Albert eventually paid the fifty thousand dollars he owed so he could return to St. Hilaire, where he died. He ended his days poor, according to Cyr, because he had done what many Canadians in the Valley did: keep most of his money in an American bank. When the markets crashed in 1929, his savings at Fort Kent were wiped out. Prohibition ended in 1933, and the other bootlegging kingpins of Madawaska were soon out of business as well.

I ask Ti-Bou Albert if his grandfather's line of work had made it difficult for him to land his first job with Customs. No, he tells me, no one looked askance at it. Nor did he seek the job to redeem Isidore Albert, or Isidore's nephew, Albérie. "At that time, the way I see it, you did what you had to do to live," he says. "You worked in the woods, you gathered wood to heat your home, and you sold booze."

Rum-running was a response to one of the fundamental facts of life on the Canada-U.S. border. "There are two markets," Albert says, "and the products are always better on one side or the other. When it's better in one place, people come across." Governments can establish borders, but people with a strong-enough motivation will always seek to surmount them. And money, in large amounts or small, is one of the greatest motivators. This is Ti-Bou's philosophy, and — albeit from the other side of the law — it was probably Isidore's as well. But I don't have to take Ti-Bou's word for it: before I leave Clair, he agrees to introduce me to an old acquaintance.

I follow Albert's small SUV on the road leading out of Clair, heading back upriver in the direction of the Saint-François. After only a few minutes, we pull into the driveway of a small, neat bungalow, where a woman at the door points us down a grassy track next to the driveway. In Albert's SUV, we follow it slowly towards the river, finally emerging into a large, flat expanse of field. In the distance, a man is driving a ride-on lawn mower. He stops and comes over. He has white hair, a white moustache, and eyes that twinkle a greeting for Albert, who makes the introductions: this is Carmel Boulay, convicted smuggler.

"When I started I was just this tall," Boulay says. "Everyone smuggled. Everyone, not just me, but everybody. It was the only way to survive. There was no work."

"Bootlegging was the same thing," Albert interjects.

"Yes, bootlegging was the same thing. You smuggled whatever you could. Same thing with the Alberts," he winks. "They were big smugglers. When I started, I was married, and there was no work. I was just trying to find a way to make a living. If you've got a job paying three or four dollars per day, my friend, there's no way to live on that. You can't pay rent with that. Smuggling was a job, just like anything else."

And the product Boulay smuggled fit the bill. It was available and cheap on one side of the border but was restricted, and thus in demand, on the other.

"I'd buy a case of margarine over on the American side and I'd pay three dollars for thirty pounds," Boulay tells me. "I'd buy it in stores, and I'd row across the river with it, and I'd resell it in Québec for six dollars per case. That was a good profit. I could live on that."

In the 1960s, Ludger Lang explained to me earlier, it was illegal to bring margarine into Canada from the United States. Customs officers seized small containers. For larger amounts, they levied fines. Provincial legislation in both New Brunswick and Québec banned or restricted what were called "imitation dairy products," a measure designed to protect farmers. But margarine was also much cheaper than butter, and that made it appealing to anyone on a budget, including public institutions.

This proved to be Boulay's undoing. "There was a police officer in the hospital in Québec," Albert recounted earlier, "and this hospital was in business with Boulay. So one morning the cop takes a bite of his toast and says, 'That's not butter, that's margarine.' There was no margarine in Québec in those days, so he says, 'Where's that margarine from?'"

The hospital identified its supplier, and soon police in New Brunswick pulled over Carmel Boulay when they saw him driving his truck along the river. It was full of American margarine, and he spent a night in jail and had to pay a two-hundred-dollar fine. "At the time, that was a lot of money, two hundred dollars. I was partly retired by then. I had some other jobs after that that allowed me to make a living. So I paid the fine and moved on to other things. But I don't regret a minute of it. I'd do the same thing over again. It was a way to survive, and it wasn't only me doing it. Don't forget that."

Smuggling may be human nature, but Boulay and Albert both agree it was never as difficult as it has been since 9/11. "It doesn't bother me," Boulay says of the increased security. "I have the right to cross. They can't stop me. I can go over and get some stuff that I want. I bring my passport, even though I don't need it." Boulay is Maliseet, one of New Brunswick's aboriginal nations, and under a 1794 treaty, he can, in theory, cross the border unhindered, as long he carries identification that proves his Maliseet heritage and as long as he is not transporting something to resell.

Ti-Bou Albert, on the other hand, shakes his head at the longer searches on the U.S. side. He doesn't go over anymore, he says, without a very compelling reason. "I went over to get my friend in Fort Kent, who lives down in the States. He comes home once a year. I cross two or three times a year. It's not that I dislike the U.S., it's just that I don't have any reason to go." Albert was shocked during one visit to Fort Kent when his car was searched not only on the way in, but also again on the way out. It strikes him as absurd that the Americans would care what he was taking out of the country. "Crossing is different," he sighs. "You need a passport. But other than that, things haven't changed here. Relatives, friends, that hasn't changed. It's just the security at the border that has changed."

Some crimes, such as smuggling, are the result of borders. They capture the imagination because of the natural human instinct to defy arbitrary, administrative boundaries. Clair and Fort Kent have seen other crimes that resisted being romanticized, crimes that, though not created by the border, were complicated by its presence. It is impossible for me to cross the bridge between the two communities and not think back to a young man named Dean Michaud.

In 1996, I came to the home where he grew up in Clair. "I believe one hundred percent that he is innocent of that," his father, Lucien Michaud, told me back then while sitting at the kitchen table, fidgeting with a coffee mug. "It's very, very difficult for us to believe that our oldest boy could be arrested for something like that. Everybody around here, the school principal and everyone, everyone comes by and says they don't believe that Dean could do that."

Dean Michaud was nineteen years old at the time and had been a successful student, baseball coach, student-council president, and air cadet. A few days before my interview with his father, Dean crossed the international bridge to Fort Kent for a volleyball game and was arrested for murder.

A chasm opened that day between Clair and Fort Kent. On the New Brunswick side, village residents rallied to the Michauds, convinced that Dean could never have killed anyone, and that the unforgiving American justice system was out for vengeance. To people on the opposite riverbank, and to the mostly American student body at the University of Maine at Fort Kent, the prosecution's case looked solid: Dean Michaud was jealous that his ex-girlfriend, Barbie Ouellette of Frenchville, Maine, had started dating another student, Tommy Maki of Massachusetts. Michaud invited Maki to take a walk along the Saint John River and had smashed his head with a rock. "Everybody was thrilled," a student senate member, Jennifer Sirois, told me after Michaud was arrested.

Michaud had dated Ouellette, a tall, striking, blonde, blue-eyed biology student, for eighteen months. He had attended the Université de Moncton but transferred to the Fort Kent campus to be with her. After all, though the campus was in another country, it was a five-minute drive from his home, and in the Valley, people had been crossing the border for love for as long they'd been crossing it for money. Michaud had broken up with her in the spring of 1996, and Ouellette tried to win him back, but she eventually gave up and started seeing Maki.

I have long wondered why Michaud crossed the bridge for that volleyball game. He knew by then he was under investigation. Had he remained on the Canadian side of the river, he would not have been arrested and could have at least played for time during the extradition process.

The police spoke to him the day of Maki's death, when he ran from the river, soaked, to Barbie Ouellette's house in Frenchville. He told the police he had taken Maki to the river to see Ouellette's "special place," a small island, and as they waded back to shore, Maki had fallen in the river by accident. "I'll tell you guys right now that I didn't fight," he told them. "I didn't fight at all." [3]

The next day, his story changed. He said he and Maki had never reached the island but had stopped in the current to talk. The day after that, his account evolved again. He told investigators he and Maki had indeed fought — Maki threw the first punch, Michaud insisted — and, after a struggle, the next thing he knew, Maki was lying unconscious in the river. "I was scared because I knew our confrontation went way too far," Michaud explained later in court, "so I did what I felt was the best thing to do, but what it ended up being was the mistake of my life. I lied about what happened. I didn't want to tell anyone that we had fought beside the river. But after realizing what had happened, I decided to tell the truth." The lie would haunt him: the judge, in convicting him of manslaughter, said it undermined his credibility.

So Michaud had known when he crossed the bridge to play volleyball that he was in trouble. Perhaps, like others in the Valley, he simply could not think of Fort Kent as being in another country. If so, that soon changed: during his trial and subsequent appeal of his conviction,

---

3 The Saint John River is so narrow at the place where Maki died that when the judge in Michaud's trial went to Frenchville to see it during the trial, she crossed the international bridge so she could look at it from another angle, from St. Hilaire, New Brunswick.

Michaud's defence lawyer argued that the police interview tapes were not admissible. Michaud's francophone background, the lawyer argued, made it difficult for him to understand the investigators. A New Brunswick reporter who viewed the tapes in court agreed Michaud "appeared to be confused several times" and spoke "in awkward English." The Maine Supreme Judicial Court brushed that aside, another sign, Michaud's father said, of unfairness. "We knew from the beginning that he didn't have a chance because he was Canadian," Lucien Michaud said. "We know he's innocent of what happened there."

Sentenced to sixteen years in prison, Michaud eventually lobbied to serve out his sentence in Canada. To build support in New Brunswick, he granted media interviews from the maximum-security state prison in Warren, Maine. Had the incident taken place in Canada, Michaud told a reporter from Fredericton, the verdict might have been different. He would have had the right to a trial in French and would have been comfortable enough to testify in his own defence. "During the trial I had a hard time understanding everything they said because of the language barrier," Michaud said. "It was a bit tough for me to even work with my lawyer. We had to translate and sometimes it's tough to translate the words because they don't have the same meaning."

In early 2006, Michaud was transferred to a federal prison in Springhill, Nova Scotia, under the terms of a 1978 treaty. That November, he was granted parole. The day he stepped off a bus in Edmundston to greet family members and friends waiting in the rain, it had been ten years and a week since the fateful trip across the international bridge, where he had found the sheriff waiting for him. Now he was home and would live with his family, though his parole conditions required that he report daily to the provincial jail at St. Hilaire, directly across from, and within sight of, where Tommy Maki had died.

The chasm remained: a family friend from Clair, Louis Labrie, told a Maine reporter at the bus station that Michaud never should have been put on trial. "I am still convinced after all these years that he did not throw the first punch in whatever happened at the river. He was never a violent person." Tommy Maki's mother, in an e-mail, said Michaud got off easy.

"He served a mere ten years for callously and maliciously taking my son's life with his bare hands."

During my journey through Clair, I decide not to inflict myself, or this retelling of the story, on Dean Michaud's parents. They were innocent victims of whatever had happened on the river.[4] That moment will, of course, remain with Dean Michaud forever. For one thing, this young man who grew up on the border will probably never cross it again. His manslaughter conviction all but certainly means he is barred from entering the United States. This would be a potential inconvenience to any Canadian, but a serious handicap to someone from a community where a trip across the line is a staple of life.

The day Tommy Maki died was the day the border changed for Dean Michaud forever: September 11, 1996 — five years to the day before it changed for everyone else.

---

4   I sent Dean Michaud a message by Facebook to request an interview. He did not respond.

5. "A FEW MISERABLE FRENCHMEN"

BELOW CLAIR, THE MAIN ROAD ALONG THE RIVER changes designation and becomes New Brunswick Route 120, but it continues to twist and wind its way in a roughly eastern direction along the Saint John. Near the village of Baker Brook, where John Baker planted his flag in 1827, the road swings low to within a hundred feet of the water. On the opposite shore, the hills of Maine are deep and green, covered with pine. Next is St. Hilaire, where Maxime Albert hatched his schemes. At a place local residents call "la pointe," the road bends sharply left and veers north. Here the Valley is so narrow, and the surrounding hills press in so closely, that it is hard to tell from a car which way the road will turn next, and whether the wooded hills folded in on each other up ahead are in Canada or the United States.

Another visual trick presents itself as I follow the border. In the distance, a plume of effluent bleeds into the sky; below it is the manmade structure from which it comes, a mill belonging to Twin Rivers, the rebranded, restructured forestry company once known as Fraser Papers. But I cannot discern which of the company's two mills I am looking at: the pulp facility in Edmundston, New Brunswick, or the paper plant in Madawaska, Maine. Then I crest a rise, and the river, visible again, stretches out ahead, and both mills come into view. Between them I see the second of the Saint John River's international bridges.

I slow down as I enter Edmundston's city limit. The outskirts of the town of Madawaska take shape across the river. I pass the bridge, then drive through the heart of the small city. Just past City Hall is the mouth of the Madawaska River, where it empties into the Saint John. Several generations of government grants have beautified the riverfront with boardwalks, parks, and a cycling trail, but its most striking feature remains a pair of long, green pipelines snaking along the western riverbank. I park and walk down a gravel path to look at them.

The larger tube, marked "Steam," has an arrow pointing towards the Saint John and a label saying "From Edmundston to Madawaska Mill." The narrower tube below has a sign that said "Condensate Water" and an arrow pointing in the other direction; its label says "From Madawaska to Edmundston Mill." These are actual physical links — chemical, organic, but above all economic — between the two communities straddling the Saint John River, at the very site where the Madawaska Settlement began in 1785. The Webster-Ashburton Treaty may have politically severed the settlement in 1842, but money, in the form of constantly flowing timber and pulp, has kept its people literally connected.

The Edmundston complex is huge and sprawling, its giant buildings dwarfing the cityscape, its dank smell of pulp invading the nose and mouth. Catherine Delafield, the mill's process manager, leads me through large, cavernous towers, along metal walkways, past massive valves, and through flickering control rooms. She runs her fingers along a ten-tonne tank holding groundwood pulp, then guides me to a large red pump that sends the pulp through a tube under the Saint John River and into the mill in Madawaska, Maine. "I can look at this and it will tell me what's being pumped over to Madawaska," she says during a stop in a control room filled with monitors and computer screens. "I can see the concentration of the pulp and we can also see the pressure in the line and the amount that's going over. This says they're running and they need the flow. This tells us whether to slow down or speed up."

In another building, bark is stripped from wood and fed into boilers where it is burned to create steam. "It's wood residual that no one's going to do anything else with," Delafield tells me. Once bark was waste, but in an era of high energy prices, it has become a cheap source of cogeneration power for both mills. Some of the steam makes electricity for the plant in

Edmundston, and the rest is fed into yet another large tube that Delafield shows me outside, the start of the green snake down by the riverbank. "That's coming out of the steam recovery plant and going down by the river and all the way over to Madawaska," she says. This is cross-border traffic of a different sort: people from Edmundston or Madawaska using the bridge to visit relatives or to shop may be facing longer delays after 9/11, but the raw product of international commerce can still shoot across the line at high speed.

Ron Beaulieu shows a schematic of the connections between the Maine and New Brunswick mills.

Donald Fraser built his first mill in 1877 at River de Chute, east of the so-called North Line and almost a hundred kilometres from the confluence of the Saint John and Madawaska rivers. More followed up and down the Saint John. Fraser died in 1911, but his company, Fraser Papers, continued, opening the Edmundston pulp mill in 1918 and the Madawaska paper mill seven years later. At the time, the United States imposed tariffs on finished paper but not on raw pulp. The company's solution was to make the pulp in Canada, then push it across to Maine in a tube, where it could be turned into paper and sold in the American market tariff-free.

Over the decades, the physical connections grew. In his office in the Edmundston mill's administration building, Ron Beaulieu, a project manager, shows me a schematic of the facilities. "That's all the pipes," he says, sliding it across his desk. The drawing resembles some kind of dystopic, H.R. Giger-spawned organism: two giant heads, everything else tendrils. No fewer than seven black lines span the river. On the drawing, the border is not marked; Canada and the United States are not labelled.

"When you make pulp, it's one-point-five percent wood fibre, ninety-eight-point-five percent water," Beaulieu tells me. "That's what's pumped over there. They take the fibre out to make their paper, and they send the water back here to make more pulp." That tube, too, runs under the riverbed. Reusing the water saves money, but it also helps Twin Rivers avoid the thorny problem of disposing of it, because it cannot be dumped into the Saint John. "Environmentally we wouldn't be able to operate," Delafield says. Adds Beaulieu, "A hundred years ago you could have, but not today."

Then there is the steam, sent across in the big green tube that is encased in its own narrow bridge over the river. The mills were powered by oil until the 1980s, when the Edmundston mill saw its fuel costs drop, thanks to the Trudeau government's National Energy Program. "Because oil was cheaper on the Canadian side," Beaulieu explains, "we shut down those boilers on the U.S. side and put in more steam capacity on the Canadian side, and we built that pipeline that sent steam over to the U.S side. It's still cheaper now, but not because of oil prices. Today, we generate not just the pulp on the Canadian side; we generate all the steam on the Canadian side in the co-gen boiler." The steam comes from the bark, which is cheaper than oil. And the cross-border loop continues with condensate from the steam, water, sent back across to Edmundston to be reused.

Lastly there is electricity. Steam cannot power the mills on its own, so Twin Rivers buys electricity from New Brunswick Power, the province's publicly owned energy utility, and sends some of it across the river to the paper mill. The northern edge of Maine remains sparsely populated, and it has been prohibitively expensive for Maine electrical utilities to build large-capacity transmission lines to the area. There is enough power coming from downstate for homes, Beaulieu says, "but for the mill, there's no ability to provide that power in Madawaska at this time. There's not enough capacity. They're not interconnected with the rest of the U.S. grid. So there's a whole block in northern Maine where the power is really from New Brunswick, and the Madawaska mill is the biggest one of all that."

"They are Canadian electrons," Delafield adds simply. "That's it."

Delafield leads me through more buildings, down more stairways clanging with the echo of our footsteps, along more dimly lit walkways. In another monitoring station, several sinewy men dressed in coveralls lean back in their chairs, glancing from their screens over to Catherine and to me. They are monitoring the last step in the process of creating pulp, where the last impurities, small flecks of fiber, are removed before the material is pumped across the border. The men are in constant contact with the Madawaska mill, Delafield says, but have never met their American counterparts who check the arriving pulp. "If they ran into them on the street, they wouldn't know them," she says. "These guys here would never have any reason to go across to the other mill."

One of the men seems eager to point out that it is the Edmundston mill that is central to the entire Twin Rivers operation. "We supply their water, we supply their electricity, we supply their pulp. We supply them everything. They make the finished product, for *Time* magazine, everything like that. But it all starts here." The border does not matter to the company, but it matters to its employees: during the restructuring in early 2010, employees in the Edmundston mill were forced to accept a thirty-percent reduction in their pension plan, while just across the river, the pensions of their American counterparts were protected by law. The perceived inequity and unfairness has created resentment and envy among the Canadians, and feelings are still raw.

But, Beaulieu tells me, there is no way that the men will ever stop dealing with their counterparts in Maine. The two mills are locked together. "This system is so enmeshed, it would be very difficult to separate it," he says. In theory, Twin Rivers has to periodically allow American companies to bid to supply electricity to the Maine mill; in practice, no one will ever beat the cross-border price from New Brunswick, which in 2010 is almost half that of Maine. And during the restructuring, all of Fraser's American assets were sold except the Madawaska mill, because it would have been impossible. "The pulp and water and steam, you can't separate it," Beaulieu tells me flatly. "It's one complex."

Fraser Papers did not pioneer this international approach to forestry: the border has long made it a necessity. "Even during the height of the international incident," historian Richard W. Judd wrote, referring to the border dispute, "lumbermen from Maine and New Brunswick were forging economic links that would provide a basis for rapid expansion of the industry once political issues were resolved." The river was vital to moving timber to market, so there was no choice but to cooperate once it became an international waterway.

Even before the Aroostook War — to the frustration of Maine land agents who were under orders to not cooperate with the British — there were partnerships between New Brunswick merchants and American settlers. The conflict itself fuelled growth as both sides encouraged settlers to move into the area and built roads to help them get there, and at its height, revenue from seized timber was placed in a "disputed territory fund," to be divided up based on the eventual boundary settlement. The timber industry's growth attracted more people: between 1870 and 1920, Fort Kent's population quadrupled; Edmundston's grew from eighteen hundred to nearly five thousand. Saint John, New Brunswick's main port, boomed as American lumbermen established sawmills to process wood coming down the river from northern Maine, another manifestation of the symbiosis between the state and the province.

But if the Upper Saint John Valley remained economically and culturally homogenous, its administrative and political fate was dramatically different. Partition began immediately. The first U.S. post office was established at Fort Kent the year after the Webster-Ashburton Treaty. Eight years later a British telegraph line was run through Edmundston, connecting Halifax and Québec City. Land surveyors returned to confirm ownership on both sides of the border. Schools were brought under local control. Cross-river Catholic parishes under the diocese of Fredericton, and later of Saint John, survived for three decades, until American congregations were brought under the Bishop of Portland. This was the start of two distinct realities: the survival and eventual flourishing of French in New Brunswick, and the gradual but unstoppable assimilation of the language in Maine.

American nativism compounded the challenge. The French of northern Maine were seen as different. "They are light-hearted, improvident, unenterprising people, more fond of the fiddle than the hoe, and content to remain stationary while all around is progressing," a journalist from southern Maine wrote in 1858. The sentiment grew harsher in the 1870s, when a wave of French-Canadian immigrants, mostly from Québec, poured into Maine and other New England states to work in textile mills and shoe factories. In a referendum in 1892, Maine voters amended the state constitution to state no one "who shall not be able to read the Constitution in the English language" had a right to vote.

Three years later, a bill was introduced in the state legislature to eliminate funding for schools teaching in a language other than English. Major William Dickey, the state representative from Fort Kent, opposed the bill, calling it "an impossible task" to teach in English in the Upper Saint John Valley. "Would it be equitable that for this reason thousands of children might lose the benefit of the schools? Would it be equitable to confiscate their rights to education, because being born of French parents and having learned in their prime infancy but the French tongue, one of the most beautiful languages in the world, they labor, as a matter of course, under the want that French may be, more or less, spoken to them for school discipline and instruction?" The law failed to pass, but the sentiment behind it persisted.

The backlash coincided with an Acadian renaissance in New Brunswick. Beginning in 1881, the tiny Acadian élite — mostly church leaders and a few political representatives — launched an effort to reestablish a sense of national identity, adopting a flag, a feast day, and a hymn. This would grow into a movement for greater equality within the church, the school system, and the political arena, culminating in legislative and constitutional equality a century later. These developments reflected the very different demographics in New Brunswick. Francophones grew from fifteen percent of the province's population in 1870 to twenty-four percent in 1914; sheer numbers, and their deep roots in the province, translated to growing political clout that could not be ignored. In Maine, French-speakers represented only one-tenth of the state population in 1900, and the vast majority were recent economic migrants, creating a greater rationale for their assimilation.

The anti-immigrant sentiment in New England gathered strength after the First World War, fuelled by a perception that some ethnic communities had not sufficiently supported the war effort. In 1919, supporters finally succeeded in passing a ban on French in Maine schools. At first it was enforced loosely in the Valley, but eventually teachers, even francophones, were required to punish children who spoke their mother tongue. "At the convent school I attended," wrote local historian Cleo Ouellette, "a system of cardboard tokens was established in which students were made to take a token from any classmate who spoke French. At the end of the week, those having too few tokens were punished, and those having the most tokens were rewarded. . . . Speaking French became a clandestine activity. The sense of betrayal by one's very own sparked anger and bitterness."

Even the growth of the Fraser Papers mills contributed. The Franco-Americans who aspired to senior positions found themselves held back, while English-speaking Canadians moved into executive office jobs in Edmundston. "The Franco-American of the valley was now caught in an English-speaking world on both sides of the border," Ouellette writes. Some changed their names: the Roys became the Kings, the LeBlancs became the Whites.

A revival began in the 1960s. Partly as a result of the Civil Rights Movement, the U.S. government began funding bilingual education programs in 1965. Four years later, Maine repealed its English-only law, and school districts in the Valley created one of the first bilingual programs for French-speaking children in the United States. At the same time, a pride in the area's French history became more tangible with the creation of Acadian festivals, and there was a growing academic interest in the history and culture of the valley. State representatives from the valley would eventually hold weekly meetings at the legislature in French, reciting the Pledge of Allegiance and singing "The Star-Spangled Banner" in French.

But these actions were gestures, primarily nostalgic and folkloric, more a celebration of the valley's past than an assertion of a present-day identity. The future was English. "The monumental task of reinculcating a love for a language which has caused so many people so much suffering," Cleo

Ouellette reflected, "has been all but impossible to accomplish." Those bleak words were written in 1993, just two years before a small group of local school officials made a final attempt to rescue a dying culture.

From the Twin Rivers pulp mill in Edmundston, it is a short drive back around to the Madawaska River, where the steam and condensate pipes run down to the international bridge and across to Maine. The paper mill looms over the customs checkpoint and, indeed, the entire town. Mill Street leads up the hill to U.S. Route 1.

The sky is clear over the Valley, and my pace is unhurried and meandering as I drive southeast. At St. David, just outside Madawaska, I follow a narrow lane down to the river to see the large white granite cross that commemorates the one planted on the same spot by the first Acadian settlers in 1785. At a church cemetery in Grand Isle, a few miles farther downriver, I listen to the roar of a train across the river in Canada as I stroll among headstones bearing the names Tardif, Ouellette, Fortin, Picard. The inscriptions on the oldest stones are in French; those of people who died in recent decades are in English.

"The past is never dead," Faulkner said. "It's not even past." But if French still has a chance in Maine, it is not amid the markers of history, but among future generations of Madawaskans. So I continue on along the border, each gentle bend in the road revealing a new church and a new community of a few houses and businesses, until Van Buren, the first significant town since Madawaska. Named for the U.S. President who sent Winfield Scott here to defuse the Aroostook War, Van Buren consists of U.S. Route 1 as its main street, a number of side streets, and yet another bridge to New Brunswick, connecting to the town of Saint-Léonard. The schools in Van Buren are easy to find: both elementary and secondary schools are housed in a single, modern building with a bold blue façade, visible for miles. A student escorts me to the classroom of Diane Michaud, the elementary school French teacher.

Like other Madawaskans, Michaud appears brassy and forceful, but she also seems harried as she struggles to hold the attention of a fourth-grade class. The kids are staring at the ceiling, playing with their hair, shuffling in their seats, or even talking back to her with startling rudeness. One girl starts applying makeup, which Michaud takes from her.

"You guys can tell me what the difference is between those two," Michaud says in English, pointing to some words in French. "Think about what we've been doing. Think." The response is sullen silence.

This is not an immersion class: Michaud speaks mostly in English, and her teaching method itself is built on simplified comparisons to English. Nothing is happening organically in French. "You know when I speak English, I make mistakes, like I often forget to pronounce my 's' at the end of the word," Michaud tells the kids at one point, trying to illustrate the silent last letter of plural nouns in French. Some of the students perk up. The teacher is acknowledging her own accented English — a weakness, a foible. Now *this* is something they can work with. "Like 'th,'" one girl says, leaning forward in her desk, repeating it as a hard t.

"'Th' is harder," Michaud says, promising to come back to that and returning to the silent s.

The girl persists. She is not interested in the s, which had no comic potential. "I remember, like, when we were in third grade," she says, "if you got mad, you'd say 'You guys are in *turd* grade,'"

"Third," Michaud says, not getting the joke. "Okay."

"*Turd* grade," the student says, getting some classmates to chuckle at the same scatological pun that has been a staple of French-second-language classes across Canada.

During a break, Michaud shakes her head at the behaviour. Kids will be kids, regardless of the cultural context. A majority of the students in the class have at least one parent or grandparent who speak French, she tells me. "We even have students who start to speaks French at home, but once they come to school they speak English and they lose their French. The kids spend their days here. Their friends speak English. They spend their days in English. So when they go home, they've spent their whole day in English. In their heads it's English. So we have to remind them to speak French at home. I have students that I teach for half an hour twice a week. You can't perform miracles in an hour.

"The goal is we'd like them to at least understand French, to be able communicate with their grandparents. Many of them have grandparents who don't speak English at all. They don't have any choice. It's like a barrier between generations. I'd like them to leave here being able to understand and communicate in French."

Students get some French instruction in every year from kindergarten to high school, where it is mandatory for only one year. The lessons start at a very basic level: the alphabet, simple vocabulary, colours. More vocabulary and verbal skills are added in the third grade. By fifth grade, the curriculum becomes more demanding. The level of apathy or interest depends on the student. "There are some who say they want to learn for when they visit their grandparents," says Michaud, a Canadian from Edmundston whose husband, from Van Buren, has roots on both sides of the border. "There are others where there's no one in their family who speaks it. I had one student, the first day, who was in tears. Didn't want to learn French. Two weeks later, she was one of the highest in the class. If it's important at home, they'll do well."

It helps when the children have francophone relatives across the river in New Brunswick, though Michaud says many don't even grasp where they are going when they cross the bridge. "I would say there are kids who don't realize Saint-Léonard is another country, because it's so easy to go."

Like Madawaska and Edmundston, Van Buren and Saint-Léonard began as a single community, Grande-Rivière, straddling the river. By the time of the 1842 treaty, twelve hundred people, almost all of them French-speaking, lived in equal numbers on both sides of the river. Like elsewhere in the Valley, though the population was suddenly governed by two different political jurisdictions, economically it remained integrated. Mills were the economic engines of both Van Buren and Saint-Léonard, and for decades wood products from the American side were carried across the border first by ferry then, after 1910, on a new bridge, to be sent to market on Canadian rail lines passing through Saint-Léonard.

Culturally, however, the two sides grew apart. A 1999 study by Louise Gravel Shea identified language as the biggest difference between the two towns. In Saint-Léonard, people lived in French; in Van Buren, despite the Franco-American heritage, English was dominant. "The idea of the Canadian-American border as one of the most open in the world," Shea concluded, "seems more and more like a myth and less of a reality."

In 1995, local school officials set out to end that growing divide. The U.S. government approved a grant of more than a million dollars over five years for four school districts— Van Buren, Grand Isle, Madawaska, and Frenchville— to set up a kindergarten-to-eighth-grade immersion program. It was the next logical step after the return of partial French instruction in the 1970s. Almost immediately, old attitudes emerged, even among Franco-Americans in the Valley. Rumours spread that immersion would take away resources from other programs, even though the curriculum was voluntary and funded entirely by Washington. In March 1996, the Frenchville school board voted to put its participation on hold, even before the program had started.

Daniel Béchard, a school board member, told me at the time there was little need for French in the global marketplace or even in the Upper Valley. "There's not too many grandparents left who don't converse in English," he said. Charles Collin, an employee at the Fraser mill in Madawaska, Maine, said his children did not speak French: during a trip across the bridge to the Edmundston mill, he noticed most of the commercial signs were in English. "That tells me the universal language, the language everyone can understand, is English," he said. "I don't have a problem with French. It's a plus, especially if you're living here in the Valley. But my priority is to have my kids excel in English. You can speak fifteen or twenty languages, but if you can't excel in one, you won't go far."

Other parents were incensed. "I can't believe they would take it upon themselves to deny my children's future for me," said Carol Roy, a mother of three boys whose skills in French began to vanish the moment they started attending daycare. Even Jerry White, the school superintendent answerable to the board, criticized the decision. "Sometimes the adults get in the way of good learning," he said. "Reason did not enter into this." White, who initiated the federal grant application and who was to administer the funding for all four districts in the Valley, was forced to hand over the responsibility to the adjacent Madawaska district.

I went to Madawaska, Maine, in 2001 to check up on the program. The federal grant had run out, but administrators had managed to keep it running with local funding in the three remaining districts. At Madawaska's elementary school, I met a ten-year-old boy, Shawn Parker, who crossed regularly to play hockey in Edmundston with New Brunswickers. Remarkably, this American boy was playing the role of interpreter. "Some speak French and some speak English, so I have to speak both languages to help them communicate and stuff, so it helps me out," he said. Shawn, who had roots on the New Brunswick side of the border, played the same role at family reunions, translating between his unilingual francophone grandparents and his New Hampshire cousins, who spoke only English. Shawn was the bridge.

It felt, in 2001, as if something akin to pre-1842 Madawaska, a single community, was reasserting itself. "It's like crossing from one street to another as far as I'm concerned," Rosanne Gendreau, Shawn's teacher, told me of her trips over to Edmundston. "It's second nature to us. It's not really another country because we're so interrelated." That, in turn, contributed to the local sentiment that the immersion program made sense, or at least was not a futile effort. "One of the reasons we're able to sustain it to the extent we have is because we're so close to Canada," the school superintendent, Tom Scott, told me proudly. Officials in Washington had selected the program as a "Portrait of Success," one of five bilingual programs across the United States so recognized, and the U.S. Department of Education later declared the Madawaska elementary school a Blue Ribbon school, in part because of the immersion program.

During this visit, nine years later, I am less optimistic. In Madawaska's district, a scaled-down immersion program continues; in Van Buren, it is gone, replaced with French as just another subject. I walk from Diane Michaud's Van Buren classroom to the office of Clayton Bélanger, the superintendent for the local school district, who speaks with a captivating mix of New England and French accents. Bélanger is in the middle of

Clayton Bélanger is the superintendent of the Van Buren, Maine, school district.

trying to sort out details of a school lunch program when I arrive, and his eyes twinkle with that strange mix of energy and exhaustion common in public school officials.

"It was going to be in stages," Bélanger says of the immersion program. "The first year was ten percent in French. I think the goal was — we never made it — fifty or sixty percent. We were supposed to teach math in French, which we did, and social studies, I think, in French." Now most children only get French instruction two or three times per week. "We're back to where we started from. I don't like it. We don't like it. But it's money. It's a matter of money.

"Number one, you need a full-time coordinator. We bought the materials. They cost a lot, the first couple of years. And we have all that stuff, and do we use it? Not anymore, because you have to have somebody *on it* all the time. You have to have courses, you have to have meetings, you have to have training. It can't be static. And people leave. We trained a lot of teachers. They were well-trained. But a lot of them retired. Someone else comes in and they haven't been trained, and guess what happens?"The children, saturated with American pop culture, find it difficult, he says. "The kids are bilingual, but you talk to them at school and they'll speak to you in English." Class trips to Québec City have brought this home, painfully. "The tour was in French, the literature was in French, and the kids were having difficulties."

Local opposition had not killed the immersion program; demographics had. "It was well-received in the community. We had a lot of group things, after-school things," Bélanger says. But in Washington, the funding programs for bilingual education focus increasingly on the growing Latino population. "The people running the program are Spanish and it was,

'What do you need French for?'" Bélanger says. At the same time, the once-isolated Upper Saint John Valley is welcoming more and more families with no roots here and therefore without a whisper of French at home. Just a few years ago, there were a hundred students from homes where English was the second language; now, in 2010, there are eighty. And despite the new arrivals, there is a net population decline. The district served six hundred students when the immersion program began. Now there are fewer than four hundred. "We're losing kids," Bélanger says. "It's like ten a year. Sometimes it's twelve." Smaller classes make staffing more expensive. At a certain point the numbers could no longer justify the cost.

For Bélanger, the proximity to the border, and to French-speaking Canada, is the last, tenuous argument for holding on to some kind of French-language instruction. "English is such a strong language and we're being overwhelmed. The only reason we stay this way is because we're so close, in the Saint John Valley. But the population's on the other side. It's not here. We'll always have that undercurrent, there'll always be movement, but not to the extent it was twenty years ago. I'm talking about the influence of French. It's changing. As we go on, I think we're going to have less commonality. I pick it up. When I go to Saint-Léonard, I'll hear the discussions in French, and I come here and there's a little difference in the actual vocabulary. We tend to lose it here a lot faster. Since 9/11, we have a lot of people here who don't even cross the border anymore."

As I leave Van Buren to continue my drive southeast along the Saint John River, towards the edge of what was once the Madawaska Settlement, I feel I am witnessing the death of a culture in slow motion. "If we can't be who we are," Valley educator Marcella Violette Bélanger said in 1971, "we're only half living. Psychologically, we're half a person." And each side of the Valley is now half a community, because of the political compromise of the 1842 treaty.

"In some ways it seems that, yes, it is still somewhat of a community," Chip Gagnon, the political scientist from Frenchville, says, "but in many ways I think the border and the assimilationist pressures that have increased, especially since the 1940s, as well as U.S. patriotism that does not seem to have room for multiple, cross-border identities, have created two communities. One is francophone, secure in its French heritage and political representation in Fredericton. The other is slowly bleeding away into the U.S. anglophone majority, its French roots coming closer to the kind of hyphenated ethnicity seen by other assimilated groups such as Italian and Irish Americans."

Britain and the United States compromised on the border because each got what they wanted—America's timber and Britain's road—and neither side was willing to fight for what Edward Winslow had called "a few miserable Frenchmen at Madawaska." There was, of course, no conception at the time of a future Canada as a vibrantly bilingual nation, or of New Brunswick as an equally bilingual province.

And this is why Winslow's dismissive remark seems ironic today: the new border was cruel to the newly American Madawaskans but inadvertently kind to those who became New Brunswickers. The 1842 treaty may have condemned the French-speaking people on the south bank to assimilation in the American melting pot, but it *saved* the French language on the north bank. Had Britain allowed Maine's claims, all of Madawaska would be American today, and the loss of French would almost certainly be more advanced. By refusing to give up its military road, Britain ensured that the New Brunswick Madawaskans became, along with other Acadians, part of a political constituency capable of preserving its language and culture. Today they enjoy the legal and constitutional right to deal with their government, to appear in court, and to school their children in the language of their ancestors.

The Franco-Americans of Maine can only look on with envy: in keeping part of Madawaska British, Britain unwittingly ensured it remained French.

6. REMAINS

THE TOWN OF FORT FAIRFIELD, MAINE, is on the last major bend in the Aroostook River before it heads east across the border into New Brunswick, where it empties into the Saint John River. The Aroostook was, after the Saint John, the other strategic river in the border dispute: logs harvested in the contested territory were sent down the Aroostook towards the Saint John and into British New Brunswick, until state authorities authorized the use of a boom, a large chain net suspended in the current, to stop the logs. The Americans built a fort next to the boom so that soldiers could watch over it. The fort was named for Maine's

Many road names, like this one in Hamlin, Maine, reflect the nearby border.

bullish governor, John Fairfield, and around it grew the town of the same name — a community created by the Aroostook War.

I left Van Buren heading east on Main Street along the Saint John, driving past State Street, where U.S. Route 1 turned south towards the town of Caribou. Instead I followed Route 1A along the river to stay close to the border as long as possible. The Saint John was flat, calm, and undisturbed. Occasionally I saw cars speeding along the Trans-Canada Highway on the opposite shore. Within a few minutes, Route 1A curved sharply right; a small side road, Boundaryline Road, continued on along the river for another mile to a border crossing. It was the first land crossing between Maine and New Brunswick on my journey, and it marked the end of the United States on the south bank of the river, and the end of the border's run down the Saint John. It was the point where the North Line — the land boundary agreed to in the 1783 treaty — met Webster and Ashburton's river border of 1842.

Now I am following Route 1A south, driving parallel to the North Line, past potato fields and through the small town of Limestone, where I see Albert Michaud Park, the last French name on my journey and the southernmost point of Franco-American influence. I am leaving behind the story of cultural partition, but there are other legacies to consider.

At Fort Fairfield, Route 1A crosses the Aroostook on a modern concrete bridge. The town's main street is a typical New England combination of old red-brick buildings and modern gas stations and stores. And there is the blockhouse, where Bill Findlen is waiting for me in the large wooden doorframe. He has cartoonishly large ears and an enthusiastic smile. "Come on in," he says.

The blockhouse, I am disappointed to learn, is not the original structure. That was torn down in 1862. "We don't know why," Findlen says. "It wasn't being used anymore. It was just sitting here and it was probably starting to rot. So they actually just sawed it up into lumber." During the United States Bicentennial, a local group got together and decided the town needed something to celebrate its history. They settled on a symbol of the best story Fort Fairfield had to tell: the Aroostook War.

Bill Findlen greets visitors at the Fort Fairfield blockhouse.

A forestry company donated the wood, farmers volunteered to haul in their trucks, and the blockhouse was reborn.

Findlen, whose grandfather Patrick landed in Saint John in 1839, at the height of the Aroostook War, and came north to settle here, is now the museum's caretaker. "I hated history in school," he laughs. "All it amounted to was memorizing who the presidents were, and what war happened in what year." But after serving in the military, farming, and teaching woodworking in school and in college, his dabbling in antiques led him to the Fort Fairfield Frontier Heritage Historical Society. "Of course, the more you get into it," he says, "the more you're interested."

Findlen's love of history is that of the generalist and of the community booster: the blockhouse is not a museum of the Aroostook War itself but a repository for just about any object that turns up locally and that happens to predate living memory. "We take most anything in," Findlen says, "anything that's to do with Fort Fairfield, or the county, or Canada even. So one day this boy comes in. He had been in before. He was probably six or eight years old, and he says 'I've got something for you. I'd like to donate it.' So I said okay, and he brought in a little, rusty, flat washer. And we've got it in the showcase here. We kept it."

There are actually a handful of items from the border dispute: a piece of board from the original blockhouse, an original key, and a clump of chain from the original boom. "I love the condition of it because it's all rusted, almost completely out," Findlen says, lifting it up. "It was found right out back here, along the river. This is where the boom went across." He smiles, amused at the banality of the dispute. "Where was the line?" he asks rhetorically. "'Those are our trees!' 'No, those are our trees!'"

Findlen does not get very exercised about the Aroostook War. It is, as they say, ancient history. But perspective matters. In 2008, the historical society published a new edition of the 1904 town register. Its introductory essay simplistically blamed the dispute on Maine's realization "that considerable lumber was being stripped from her public lands and shipped to England." Not long afterwards, Findlen showed the blockhouse to staff and managers of King's Landing, a tourist-oriented re-creation of a New Brunswick Loyalist community near Fredericton. The manager, Findlen laughs, "looked at the history that we have here and he said, 'That's not the same story we have on our side of the border.'"

Findlen shrugs. "I think it's like our politics, at least like we have in the U.S. today," he says of the eventual compromise. "It was a trade-off. It was about the politics, and the politicians doing the trade-off." He shrugs again. "Right or wrong, who knows?"

Monument 82 marks the border near the Aroostook River.
(Photo: International Boundary Commission)

The end of the border dispute in 1842 was not the end of the debate. At the time, everyone had an opinion about the Webster-Ashburton Treaty. Many were convinced it had been a grave mistake.

The very day the treaty was signed, August 9, 1842, Daniel Webster showed Lord Ashburton the map on which Jared Sparks had copied, in Paris, what seemed to be Franklin's red line supporting the British claim to a boundary down below Mars Hill. At least, Ashburton *claimed* this was when he first saw the map. In the very same letter in which he told Lord Aberdeen, the foreign secretary, about the map, he also referred to spending almost three thousand pounds "to compensate Sparks, to send him, on my first arrival, to the Governors of Maine and Massachusetts. My informant thinks that without this stimulant Maine would never have yielded."

This astonishing note has led historians to surmise that Ashburton secretly worked *with* Webster, to use Sparks's map to persuade the governors that a compromise boundary was the best they could hope for. This leads logically to the conclusion that Ashburton knew there was a map that supported Britain's position. If he compromised regardless of this powerful piece of evidence, it may have been because of his financial interests. His family's banking house, Barings, held guarantees on a large tract of land on the west side of the St. Croix that would gain value with a settlement.

The existence of the Sparks map, and of another map of questionable provenance that also seemed to support the British claim, was revealed late in 1842. Both maps were cited during the U.S. Senate's secret debate on ratification of the treaty, which inevitably became public. When word reached London, Ashburton was criticized for giving away too much. The government of Sir Robert Peel decided to conduct its own research, and a diplomat dispatched to the Paris archives found still more maps. Each, he wrote, "follows exactly with a crimson line, the boundary claimed by the United States!!"

Ashburton himself learned of yet another map, from the collection of King George III, which had been given to George Featherstonhaugh to help him prepare documents for the negotiations in Washington. The King George III map, as it became known, was particularly damning. Its marking included a red line showing the border claimed by the United States, with "Boundary as described by Mr. Oswald" handwritten in four different places. It was the only map that "seems to have had the annotations added and then erased as part of the negotiation process," according to Matthew H. Edney, a professor at the Osher Map Library of the University of Southern Maine. Featherstonhaugh had kept the map to himself, leading to accusations Britain had withheld a map damaging to its own case — the same charge levelled against the United States when the Sparks map was revealed.

Defending Ashburton in Parliament, Peel argued there was no proof either map had actually been used in Paris to illustrate the final terms of the 1783 treaty. "Nothing can be more fallacious than founding a claim upon contemporary maps, unless you can also prove that they were adopted by the negotiators," he said. The controversy eased, but Ashburton was haunted by the map debate. Though he wrote to Webster that the controversy in both countries meant the treaty was well-balanced and that "the map question now fortunately only interests historians," he later told an acquaintance that had he known of the King George III map, he might not even have gone to Washington.

One last map emerged in 1843. Albert Gallatin, now eighty-two, the diplomat who first made the self-fulfilling prediction that an arbitrator might "split the difference" on the Saint John River, unearthed a map that had belonged to John Jay, one of the American negotiators in Paris. This map mostly conformed to U.S. claims, but it showed the Saint John as the border between Maine and New Brunswick. Given this idea was rejected early in the Paris discussions, the map was plainly not a reflection of the final agreement.

It did prompt a special meeting of the New York Historical Society, where John Jay's grandson read Gallatin's paper, and where Daniel Webster himself was invited to comment. Webster defended the treaty, noting that Maine had won navigation rights on the Saint John for its timber industry, and suggested the controversy had run its course. "Though in party times and in contests of men, some little dust may be thrown in the air, some little excitement of the political elements may be produced occasionally, yet as far as we know, no considerable fermentation in the subject exists."

Webster was wrong. After he returned to the Senate, a congressional committee brought charges against him over the secret payments he made to Francis O.J. Smith for his pro-compromise propaganda campaign in Maine. Former president John Tyler, testifying for Webster, said he had authorized the payments because war was looming and the administration's perspective needed to be heard in the state. "Political parties in that state had not marshalled themselves against each other," Tyler reminded the committee, "but rather vied with each other in the effort to go farthest in the assertion of the territorial rights of that State." Webster was exonerated, but the affair revived the notion that trickery had helped bring about the boundary compromise.

In 1937, the controversy flared again when two scholars, Lawrence Martin and Samuel Flagg Bemis, published a paper arguing Jared Sparks had copied the wrong map in Paris. In the archives in Madrid, they discovered a map by cartographer John Mitchell, marked with a red line supporting the American claim. By examining French and Spanish correspondence, they concluded *this* map, and *not* the one discovered by Sparks, was the one Benjamin Franklin was referring to when he said he had "marked [it] with a Strong Red Line" in 1782. "We think that Jared Sparks's communication to Webster . . . ruined a perfectly good American title to five thousand square miles of territory abandoned by the compromise. It is too bad that Daniel Webster had no better cartographical advice."

This is the closest anyone has come to proving that Richard Oswald had also made a terrible mistake in Paris, and that the negotiators had intended a boundary that gave all of Madawaska, as well as Lake Témiscouata, to the United States. By then, it was decades too late. The treaty, flawed though it was, had stood for almost a century, and passions had cooled. It had been difficult enough to establish that the treaty was flawed; rectifying its flaws was, of course, impossible.

History is littered with mistakes and attempts to correct them. After a quick look at the second floor of the blockhouse, I ask Bill Findlen if he will take a quick drive with me across the Aroostook. I tell him what I am looking for, and he thinks he can help me find it. We drive back over the bridge and down into Riverside Cemetery, moving slowly between the headstones. Findlen directs me to the very centre of the graveyard, where its two main car pathways form an axis. Suddenly I see the marker and stop the car.

It is not all that different from all the other tombstones: it is large, but relatively nondescript—certainly not ornate in a way that draws attention to itself. If Bill Findlen were not with me, it would take a thorough search of the entire cemetery to find it.

John Baker is in the ground at my feet.

What is remarkable about the grave is that it is here at all. John Baker, after all, chose to live out his days in New Brunswick, whose jurisdiction over his land he had denied in 1827 but implicitly accepted after 1842. He died near the mouth of the Meriumticook, now called Baker Brook, and was buried—accounts vary—either in the family plot near the brook, or at a Baptist church in nearby St-François.

So Baker apparently reconciled himself to the location of the border, and what it meant for him. Others plainly did not. In 1895 his body was exhumed and reburied in Fort Fairfield, with a new gravestone. The front says he was born in 1796 and died in 1868. The back bears an inscription:

Erected by authority of a Resolve
of the legislature of Maine A.D. 1895,
to commemorate the Patriotism of
JOHN BAKER A Loyal son of Maine
in maintaining the Honor of his Flag
during the contentions on the disputed Territory 1834-42

It was a remarkable ceremony, with bands playing music and chevaliers of the International Order of Odd Fellows marching in formation. State Representative William Dickey of Fort Kent was there, as was Maine's Secretary of State, Nicholas Fessenden, a native of Fort Fairfield. After an elaborate laying of three foundation stones, Captain E.E. Scates of the local I.O.O.F. chapter placed various items—a set of scales representing justice, a dagger and olive branch representing war and peace, and a copy of the state resolution authorizing the burial—in a receptacle in the grave, along with Baker's remains. Scates was the son-in-law of an elderly woman seated in the front row: Adaline Baker Slocomb, John Baker's daughter.

It is hard to fathom why a daughter would want to see her own father exhumed and reburied. John Baker never hesitated to assert his will, and if he had wanted to be buried somewhere other than in the Upper Valley, he surely would have said so. The Maine Legislature clearly did not ponder that possibility when it voted overwhelmingly for the move.

Historian George L. Findlen, a native of the Fort Fairfield area and a nephew of Bill Findlen, scoured primary sources for evidence of mass pressure or patriotic sentiment. He found none. In fact, Findlen discovered there was but a single name on the petition that moved the Legislature to action: that of Adaline Baker Slocomb.

Slocomb, Findlen discovered, was what we would call today a good networker. She used her local connections to get her way. Her husband and son were members of the Masonic Lodge with E.L. Houghton, the state senator from Fort Fairfield, who agreed to introduce the resolution in the Legislature. The timing was also good: Findlen notes that Civil War memorials were a fad at the very moment Slocomb began lobbying for her father's repatriation — though, he points out, officials in Washington and Augusta had been embarrassed by Baker and worried his actions would inflame the border dispute.

But Slocomb's effort to correct what she obviously considered a historical mistake was itself based on a series of errors that Findlen points out in his article on the repatriation. Her petition to the state said that John Baker worked his land with "unremitting toil," but his brother Nathan, who arrived in the area first, cleared the land and erected houses. It said he raised "an American flag" on his land on July 4, 1827, when in fact it was a white banner with an American eagle and a semicircle of red stars sewn by his wife Sophia. The petition said he was jailed because of the "vengeance" of New Brunswick authorities, but it was because he refused to pay the fine in Fredericton. It said he was charged with treason, but he could not betray a country other than his own. It said his property was "destroyed and confiscated," despite the side agreement by Webster and Ashburton to compensate him if he chose to move across the river.

"John Baker is not a patriot," Findlen writes. "He is, instead, naive, a bully, a poor follower, and an embarrassment both to his state and to his country." The 1895 reburial was the result of a solitary effort by one woman, his daughter, "to get the State of Maine to say that her father was a Special Somebody, not a Misguided Nobody, and the State agreed with her." But, he adds, cities and towns across America are dotted with memorials that seemed like good ideas at the time but are now largely forgotten.·

There are no patriotic pilgrimages to John Baker's grave in Fort Fairfield. Bill Findlen tells me he is rarely asked for directions to the cemetery. The grave is not mentioned in the publications of the Frontier Heritage Historical Society. Nor was George Findlen denounced for his article. "No one gave me any flak about my article," he tells me by e-mail. "No one cares. All too far back. Today, all those who cared about where the U.S. border should be have died, and the superiority complex [manifested by both Baker and his daughter] has found other issues to attach itself to."

John Baker's grave reveals little except modern indifference towards his actions, his cause, and any thought of refighting the Aroostook War. If Adaline Baker Slocomb was trying, with her petition, to register her anger at a larger historical error — the outcome of the dispute — she was alone in that anger.

Or so I think as I stand there with Bill Findlen. I have yet to meet a woman named Bertie Williams.

The 1837 Foundation of Northern Maine, according to its Web site, seeks to honour "the men and women who, by their character, integrity and actions created, built, protected and defended both the ideals and territory of the Aroostook, St. John and St. Croix Rivers and their tributaries in Northern Maine in the Post-Treaty of Paris years." The foundation's headquarters is located in the living room of Bertie Williams's apartment in Mattawamkeag, Maine.

Williams, listed on the foundation's Web site as its director of research and development, is, I quickly realize, its driving force and perhaps its only active member. Her apartment is in what appears to be a converted roadside motel near where the Mattawamkeag River empties into the Penobscot. The place is decorated with Desert Storm paraphernalia and crammed full of stacked milk crates holding files and books. Two old computers sit precariously on boxes. Williams herself has wispy grey hair and remarkably lively eyes, which light up mischievously whenever she is about to reveal the point of a story or an observation.

"I'm not mad at anybody except the Orwellian textbook people who can't get it right," she tells me when I ask her if she is angry about the Webster-Ashburton Treaty. "Of course it's legitimate, because both sides agreed to it. But was it coerced? You betcha. What matters to me is they perpetuate the lie that it was a bloodless war and the only fighting was in a barroom brawl in Houlton, and there were no casualties. Wrong."

Williams and the foundation have two goals: to create the Aroostook Expeditionary War Historical Trail, commemorating the route the militia used during the border dispute, and to have the graves of those men officially recognized and marked as military graves. That this has never happened is, to Williams, further proof that the boundary compromise was orchestrated by a duplicitous government in Washington that trampled on states' rights when it refused to stand up for Maine. "I'm a Jeffersonian Democrat," she tells me. "I believe in a constrained federal government."

Williams is hardly an uneducated yahoo. Her knowledge of the border story is breathtaking. "I am a non-traditional thinker," she says, an observation I cannot dispute after our ninety-minute interview. "At fifteen, I was told I was too stupid to go to college. They refused to let me take the SAT." She eventually earned degrees in history and education and taught in juvenile detention centres. She also has ADHD, she tells me, and will not let me take her photograph because she fled an abusive relationship and cannot risk being found. She consents only after she conceals her face behind a denim jacket on which she has cross-stitched the words "The 1837 Foundation of Northern Maine: The Protectors of the Disputed Aroostook Territory."

"This is where it gets sticky," she warns me as she launches into her version of the story, "because if you go in all the research, you'll never find this." In 1825, she explains, New Brunswick acknowledged Maine's claim to the territory north of the Saint John. When the state land agents Irish and Coffin journeyed up the river that year, they encountered two members of the New Brunswick Assembly and two lumbermen from the province. As Williams recounts it, the New Brunswickers told the Americans about a proposal to give Maine land between the North Line and the river, in exchange for the north bank of the Madawaska Settlement. "That's the acknowledgement by the New Brunswick provincial assemblymen that we controlled the property north of the

Saint John,"Williams says. "They were asking us to swap it. You can't swap it if you don't own it."

The whole point of the Americans' trip, she adds, was to collect settler information from New Brunswick authorities, whom, she insists, were registering Madawaska landowners *on behalf of Maine*. This was why Baker had applied to the province for payment for grain from his land. "Apparently from what I can figure out, there was a quasi-agreement that rather than us having to send someone up there, if the provincial authorities in Fredericton would act on our behalf, keep a record, write the permits, collect the money, every couple of years we would send somebody up there to get it. That again is recognition that it's ours."

Never mind that New Brunswick's acknowledgment of the American claim is widely cited by historians, or that there is evidence that Britain executed its political flip-flop on the territory in 1817, eight years before that river trip, or that Williams might be confused over Irish and Coffin's river encounter, during the same trip, with John Baker himself: she was adamant that she had discovered the truth. "There wasn't a dispute until October 7, 1825. That's what I'm trying to tell you. That's the night of the fire." The great Miramichi forest fire destroyed sixty thousand acres of timber in New Brunswick, and, according to Williams, led Lieutenant-Governor Howard Douglas to look to Maine. "Douglas issues a proclamation saying that if New Brunswick as a colony is going to survive, we're taking the Aroostook wood, regardless of if Maine likes it or not," she says. "That's when the problem started."

There is much more to Williams's account, which at times mixes pedantry and what seems like Tea Party paranoia. She describes President Andrew Jackson's "hijacking" of the Constitution, treaties with Spain, the discovery of gold in the Appalachians, wars with Indians, and the Missouri compromise, which, she says, was not really a compromise. All of it was somehow part of Washington's effort to deprive Maine of its rights.

What matters most to her, though, is winning recognition for the twelve thousand men who mobilized for the Aroostook War: the original posse dispatched to deal with trespassers, the thousand men called up to augment them, the rifle companies, and the militia itself. "We want headstones and markers for these soldiers," she tells me. "None of those guys have ever gotten credit for it, for the job." She shakes her head when I point out the Aroostook War was not actually a *war* because there was no fighting. "World War Two guys got markers for showing up at Fort Dix. Right? You get called to war, you get called to war. You leave your home, you leave your job, you run the risk of, you know, getting hit by a train."

She pulls out a roster listing the names of the twelve hundred men who were members of the original posse. "These are the various divisions. These guys were all draft eligible. You're not old enough to remember what it was like to be nineteen years old in 1969. You get your draft notice, that's really scary. Your whole life goes on hold. That's all these guys. Every one of these guys. And these guys would be eligible." She flips through the pages of names. "Sick. Died, September 11. Died, April first. Sick. Sick." They may not have died in combat, but they suffered for their state and their country.

Williams feels the injustice in her bones. She is a descendant of John and Mary Knowlen, two settlers who moved to the disputed territory in 1834 at the behest of the state government. John's agreement with the state was that his payment for clearing the land would be half in cash, half in sawed lumber, but the lumber was caught in the boom downstream and seized by the state to build Fort Fairfield. He lost his homestead as a result. "Twenty years later, John had no problem sending three of his sons to the Civil War for a nation that cost him his home and his land," Williams tells me, her tone hushed and dramatic. "Two of his sons didn't come home. The third one came home disabled. His fourth son drowned in the Aroostook in '74. The fifth son was my great-great-great-grandfather."

Williams's brother fought in Desert Storm in 1991, and afterwards she began wearing "I Vote in Honor of A Veteran" buttons, issued by the state, whenever she cast her ballot. There were different buttons referring to individual wars, but in 2002, Williams realized, "they don't have one for the Aroostook War. I grew up on the stories and I thought everybody knew the Aroostook War was a major war."

She tells me she sees a parallel with the treatment of modern American soldiers. "We're barely recognizing that the guys coming back from Iraq and Afghanistan are suffering from some serious PTSD. These guys, for four years, got up in the morning — Captain Thomas Bartlett and ten guys would go out on patrol up to the de Chute river and pray that they didn't run into twenty-five armed New Brunswick trespassers every single day. Our federal government said, 'We're not involved. We're not going to help you.' And these guys are entitled [to be recognized as veterans]."

Williams has managed to get the Maine State Legislature to recognize her efforts, not a particularly difficult achievement if Adaline Baker Slocomb's petition is any measure. But as of mid-2010 the graves are still not officially recognized as military graves. Her challenge may be that history is written by the victors, and there was no clear victor in the Aroostook War, only a muddled compromise — Gallatin's "splitting of the difference." The dispute has not been etched in the collective memory of America as a triumph or as a defeat. Though the historian Francis Carroll views it as setting a precedent for the peaceful resolution of all subsequent disagreements, it is not widely studied as a turning point in U.S.-Canada relations.

It has been left to those with roots in the disputed territory to debate the meaning of the Aroostook War. Even in Fort Fairfield, Bill Findlen tells me, it arouses no passion and no anger. "No, not really. We see it in the history books, that it was a trade-off, but there's not really much sentiment about it, no."

And there are more immediate border issues. The question of how the boundary was drawn is not as pressing as how it is being enforced.

PART TWO
HOLDING THE LINE

Every place in the country that has this problem has a larger source.
In eastern Maine, ours is Canada.

— Lieutenant Michael Riggs, Washington County sheriff's office, 2003

Muhammad Atta had a passport, and he slipped right through
St. Stephen, they say.

— Anonymous comment, bangordailynews.com, 2010

7. GOOD NEIGHBOURS

I AM GETTING READY TO LEAVE FORT FAIRFIELD when Bill Findlen asks me if I have seen the brand-new Department of Homeland Security building just outside town. At Bill's suggestion, I drive back up Route 1A to take a look. It is huge: twenty-six thousand square feet, complete with helicopter landing pad, electric fencing, detention cells, and office space for fifty employees. From its location atop a hill, it offers a good view of the border. But it cost more than six million dollars and is widely scorned by many of the locals. For one thing, it is much larger than the DHS building it replaced, a modest structure right across the road built only a few years ago. The old office is already sporting a real estate agent's name and phone number on a sign out front. In a statement read at the new building's official opening, Maine Senator Olympia Snowe called the facility "undeniably essential," a sentiment that prompted only more eye-rolling in Fort Fairfield.

The hills beyond the building are in New Brunswick, and I am curious how close I can get to the border here. I drive a little farther and spot a side road called McNamee Road, which heads east. I follow it, but it bends and turns several times, and within minutes, I have lost my bearings. I spot a disheveled old man at the end of his driveway, and I ask him if the border is nearby. He says it is, and I should follow the road. He tells me he is a Second World War veteran from New Denmark, a community in

New Brunswick. "I wish I was in hell," he says. "I fought for this world and I hate it." I drive on.

It is unlikely I will accidentally cross the border, but I know it is not impossible. The North Line, running from the head of the St. Croix to the Saint John, cuts through forests, hills, and potato fields, and there are still remote areas with old roads leading right up to it. I am not worried about being arrested by Canadian border guards as much as I am about mistakenly crossing into Canada and then back, which would probably give me a firsthand look at those new detention cells in the DHS building back on the hill.

I reach a stop sign. A road marker tells me I am at Russell Road. I know the road — I have driven it several times — but I cannot tell where exactly I am, nor which country I am in. I back up, turn around, and return to Fort Fairfield to take the safer, conventional, *legal* route to Russell Road: along the river, past the cemetery, and up a long hill to where two countries meet in a most unusual circumstance.

A river border like the Saint John has its advantages: roads cannot run through it. But many roads have run perpendicular to the North Line. Major ones tended to become ports of entry, to use the official term, with customs checkpoints and security searches. Over the years, minor ones were barricaded. But Russell Road is different: it does not run *to* the border. In effect, it *is* the border, and this is what has perplexed residents and security officials in the years following 9/11.

For a mile and a half, the road follows the North Line almost perfectly. Almost, because they are not quite aligned. The boundary runs ever so slightly diagonally down that mile-and-a-half section, so as you drive from the southern to the northern end of the contentious stretch, the road becomes more and more Canadian.[5] The effect, though, is the same: the eastern shoulder of the road is in Canada and the western shoulder is in the United States.

---

5 Adding to the challenge of describing the configuration of Russell Road is the fact that the "North Line," surveyed after 1842, is a geodetic line, not a true north line. Geodetic surveying takes into account the curvature of the Earth, which can make the line on a two-dimensional map appear to curve. The North Line thus subtly curves slightly to the northwest on maps, even though this is difficult to detect.

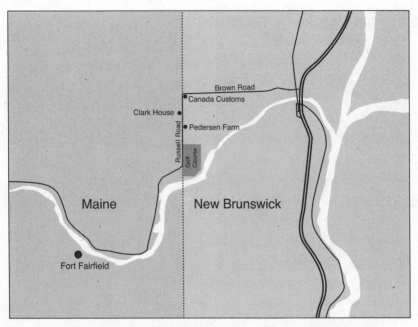

Russell Road runs almost perfectly along the border for a mile and a half.

This did not pose particular challenges to the residents of the road until January of 2003, the same month the Bush administration created the Department of Homeland Security. Marion Pedersen was driving to the large white farmhouse she had shared with her husband Nickolaj for fifty-three years, the only home on the Canadian side of the road, when she was stopped by the U.S. Border Patrol right in front of her driveway. "He said, 'I'm going to take you in,'" Marion told me when I interviewed her two months after the incident. "'In where?' I said. And boy, he meant it. He wasn't fooling. And I said, 'Well what's wrong?' He said, 'You jumped the border.' And I said, 'Well, maybe yes, maybe no.' I said. 'If I have, I've done it for fifty-three years.'"

Marion had come to the house from the north, using the shortest and most convenient route from the nearby New Brunswick village of Perth-Andover, where she'd been running errands. She had come west on the Brown Road, which ran straight to the border, where it ended as it met the northern tip of Russell Road. The appearance is of a road that suddenly turns sharply left. At that corner, a large sign warns *No entry: United States*

Nickolaj Pedersen's family had no
border problems until 2003.
(2008 photo courtesy Joyce Pedersen)

Border. No Vehicles. No Pedestrians, but
there is no U.S. checkpoint.

That day, Marion did what she
had been doing since the 1960s,
when Washington closed its border
post. She made the left turn onto
Russell Road, into the United States,
and drove south along the border,
assuming that when she reached
her home, she would turn left again
into her driveway, back into Canada,
just as she always had.

Except this time, the U.S. Border
Patrol stopped her right in front of
her house.

No one had ever taken the border
very seriously on Russell Road, but when the border officer accused
Marion of jumping the line, she knew what to do. She defiantly shifted
her car back into drive and pulled into her driveway, safely back across the
border in Canada and out of the patrolman's reach. Only then did she get
out and, remaining on her property, tell the officer to call his supervisor
and get the situation sorted out. After he had spent a few minutes on
the phone, he turned back to Marion. "He said, 'Mrs. Pedersen, you're
alright, but you're not allowed to have anybody else here. No family.' I said,
'What — no family?, 'No, and no friends.' I said, 'What happens tonight
if, say, the water stops? And I have to call a plumber?' 'Nope, not unless
they come around by Fort Fairfield and report.' I said, 'Well, how can
they get back in here? This is Canada.' Well, that was going to be the way."

Marion had pointed out the conundrum that she and her husband
Nickolaj were suddenly facing. With the U.S. Border Patrol enforcing
the boundary to the letter, the Pedersens were in a Catch-22. If their
visitors did as the officer suggested and took the long way around, crossing
legally at the U.S. checkpoint at Fort Fairfield, they could drive from the
town out to the Russell Road perfectly legally, as I have. But the moment

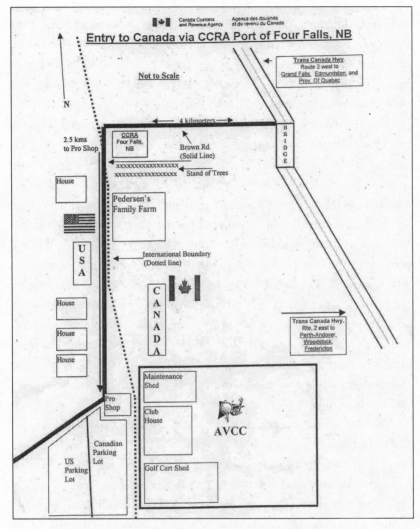

A map, not to scale, created by Canada Customs, illustrates
the unique problem the Pedersens faced.

they turned into the Pedersen's driveway, they would be entering Canada
illegally. And, of course, they would be crossing into the United States
illegally when they left the driveway.

By the time I visited the Pedersens in March 2003, their newspaper
delivery man had been stopped by the Americans. He started leaving the
paper with their friends on the Brown Road, forcing Marion to drive a

mile every morning to pick it up. A tenant who rented an apartment the Pedersens owned in Perth-Andover had been detained and searched on her way to drop off a rent cheque, and she swore she would never come back. The mail was still getting through, though Marion figured it was only a matter of time before Canada Post gave up too.

John Dolimount, the regional director for Canada Customs, told me in 2003 that he would try to show some flexibility towards people visiting the Pedersens. "Technically they are re-entering Canada illegally if you want to take a broad view of the law," he said. "But the fact that we're aware of it and the RCMP are aware of it, we recognize it is a unique situation and we'll be flexible and creative with our arrangements with those people. We haven't prohibited anyone from going to the Pedersens's farm." He also promised to look at getting special ministerial exemptions for Canadians who had to visit the property regularly. That, of course, would only solve the problem of entering the driveway. "A ministerial exemption won't do anything from a United States Customs point of view," he said. "It's wholly a Canadian exemption." The moment someone left the Pedersen driveway, they were subject to arrest. "You know, what U.S. Customs or U.S. Border Patrol, what they do or don't do is something I can't comment on," Dolimount said.[6]

Marion told me she could think of only one other possible solution. "I would like to see them buy us out. I want out. It's ruined my life here. . . . Before that I didn't want to leave. It was my home. It'll be difficult. Yeah. But you have to do what you have to do."

There was another Canadian victim of the Russell Road's unique configuration. The Aroostook Valley Country Club sits half a mile south of the Pedersen farm, on the curve where the road bends towards Fort Fairfield. It too is a relic of a more relaxed era, its pro shop and parking lot on the United States side of the border, the clubhouse and course on the

---

6 I repeatedly requested an interview with a spokesperson for the U.S. Department of Homeland Security during my research for this book. I was promised written answers to questions I submitted by e-mail about Russell Road and other border issues. I never received them. The office of U.S. Senator Susan Collins also promised to provide her written responses to four questions I sent by e-mail. I did not receive them either. In February 2011, Senator Collins called for increased security on the border to stop drug smuggling, a topic discussed in Chapter 9.

A border marker illustrates the problem for the Aroostook Valley Country Club.

Canadian side. At first, both countries seemed to make special allowances for it: Canada Customs operates a seasonal checkpoint at the north end of the Russell Road for golfers returning to Canada that way (a checkpoint that also helped people returning to Canada after visiting the Pedersens during golf season). The U.S. Border Patrol allowed people to continue entering and leaving the course via Russell Road as long as they had entered the United States legally to get there. But staff at the golf course lived in fear that the next crackdown could end that special arrangement.

At the opposite end of Russell Road's mile-and-a-half run along the border, on the American shoulder not far from the corner with Brown Road, is the home of Clarence Clark and his wife. For decades, Clark walked across the road each spring, into a patch of Canadian forest, to tap maple trees for syrup. The Clarks were also lifelong friends of the Pedersens. "When we came out here we had three daughters. It was 1966, I think. And they were six, eight, and ten." The Clark girls became friends with the Pedersen children, all girls, and Clarence Clark recalls cutting a trail through the woods so they could ride their horses through the potato fields and down to the Tinker Dam on the Aroostook River. "We loved Nick and Marion, and loved the family," Clark tells me, sitting in his sun porch. "They were good friends and close friends — the closest friends we ever had. We enjoyed their company."

It was not as if the Russell Road was incident-free over the years. Clark remembers a van carrying five Filipinos that was been stopped on the road. Police started tracking it on the I-95 in Maine and watched it as it crossed into Canada. RCMP picked up the surveillance as the van drove to Fredericton, then headed up the Saint John River to Perth-Andover and out the Brown Road to the Russell Road. It was likely a case of human smuggling. But Clark says the occasional bust like that did not justify an overzealous Department of Homeland Security cracking down to the point where neighbours, even international neighbours, found their lives turned upside down.

"When they first landed here," he says of the build-up after 9/11, "there was no concept of what they were here for, except to nail everyone. This is not the Mexican border. They're dealing with people, both sides of the border, whose parents probably lived here. They're old farming families who've been here for a hundred years or more. I haven't met anybody who's been happy over the situation. I'm eighty-eight years old, and I'm sick and tired of talking about it, you know what I mean? It's a *fait accompli* as they say. It's here. It's done. I can't envision anything about it ever changing."

Marion Pedersen died in January 2004, less than a year after I visited her on the farm. Her children and her neighbours, including Clarence Clark, were convinced the stress of the security crackdown contributed to her death at the age of seventy-three. And there was one final indignity, Clark told me. Despite his visit to the local Homeland Security supervisor to convince him to keep his officers out of the way, Border Patrol vehicles followed every car heading to the Pedersen house for the wake. "They intercepted everyone who came to the border and they followed them down [to the house]," he says. "And how effective is that? Just sticking their goddamned nose in, upsetting the family even more, to accomplish what?"

"Up until 9/11 it was great," Bill Findlen tells me. "My mother was from Canada. Half of the people here are from Canada or married across the border. I thought it was just super. I used to go over to my uncle Mike's not far from the border. It was in the country near Andover. We used to go out there all the time. But I just don't go over anymore."

Bill's nephew George, the historian, adds, "My grandfather's sister lived directly opposite him in Saint-Léonard civil parish, having been courted by a young man who grew up on a farm directly opposite the one on which she grew up. As a child, I easily crossed the border to shop or go to the dentist. Then, most of the crossing guards knew my face. Today, I must present a passport and explain where I was born."

Finding Aroostook County nightlife a little dull, the American servicemen at the now-mothballed Loring Air Force Base, north of town, used to cross the border to visit bars in Edmundston and Grand Falls. Some went further: in the 1950s and 1960s, African-American soldiers would drive all the way to Saint John, the closest city with a black community, to date women of the same race. This all unfolded without much trouble.

Even border "tensions" were rarely tense. "Canada was bringing over, quote, 'cheap potatoes,' and all of a sudden the farmers over here got really disturbed about it," Bill Findlen recalls. "My son was farming at the time, and my other son was working for Delta down in Boston. And he looks at the paper down there, the Boston paper, and there's a picture of his brother dumping potatoes on the border. The farmers, including my son, went over here to the border — they went to all the borders — and they stopped the Canadian potatoes from coming over by dumping potatoes in the road. They literally blocked the road with potatoes. I have a picture of my son standing with the mound of potatoes, and the unique thing about the picture is one of the women who lived right at the border — she was Canadian — she was there. And one of the Americans who had dumped the potatoes there, my son-in-law, was picking out some good potatoes and giving them to her."

Bill knows the Russell Road well: one night, his son was on potato blockade duty near the golf course, and Bill and his wife drove out to bring him something to eat. "The Border Patrol—American—shows up. We happened to know the guy. He's in our church—great singer. So he pulls up and we think, 'Oh boy, we're in big trouble,' and he says, 'Could you guys move that pick-up truck you're sitting in about fifty feet down the road? You're sitting right on our buzzer and it's driving us crazy.'" Bill laughs heartily at the memory of accidentally tripping a sensor. But he shakes his head when I ask him about the Pedersens. "It's just junk," he says. "Junk." It does not surprise him, however.

In the hours after the terrorist attacks of September 11, 2001, the U.S. government briefly closed the border altogether. When it reopened, it was under a Code Red Alert, with thorough searches leading to long lines at major crossings. There were media reports based on speculation that some of the 9/11 hijackers had entered the U.S. by crossing from Canada into Maine. That was soon debunked, but the myth lived on and would be repeated, erroneously, for years, including by members of Congress and by Barack Obama's Homeland Security Secretary. "It took on a life of its own, like a viral infection," the Canadian ambassador to Washington, former New Brunswick premier Frank McKenna, said in 2005.

As recently as 2010, an anonymous online comment on a *Bangor Daily News* story about the decline in cross-border traffic said, "Muhammad Atta had a passport, and he slipped right through St. Stephen, they say." Even American news organizations that managed to avoid the mistake in 2001 characterized Canada as "an entry point and staging ground" for Islamic terrorists. "The U.S.-Canada line is little more barrier than ink on a map," wrote the *Seattle Times*.

In 2003, border security was placed under the new Department of Homeland Security, which began planning the creation of "smart borders": systems that would allow the U.S. to monitor everyone entering or leaving the United States. And there are many: five hundred million people, two-thirds of them non-citizens, enter the U.S. annually, the vast majority at a land border. There is also more than a trillion dollars in commerce in each direction, so delays could also create economic harm. Some business leaders began pushing the idea of a North American security perimeter, a tighter system of customs and immigration controls around the continent that would allow for looser restrictions along the border itself. Meanwhile, the RCMP, U.S. Border Patrol and other agencies expanded their Integrated Border Enforcement Teams, which share resources, data, and facilities across the border.

The impetus to keep traffic flowing came from Canada, and it was largely commercial. "We are seeing the cost of cross-border trade rising and our exports to the U.S. declining," Allan Gotlieb, a former Canadian ambassador to Washington, lamented. Individual persons, such as those who used the Russell Road to visit the Pedersens, or others who frequently crossed between Maine and New Brunswick, were less of a priority. Programs such as Autopass and Nexus — allowing pre-screened, low-risk travellers with special cards to breeze through security — were cancelled by the United States. By 2009, anyone entering the U.S., including Americans returning from a quick trip to Canada, was required to show a passport as part of the Western Hemisphere Travel Initiative.

Many residents of border communities refused to purchase them on principle or because they were too expensive.[7] The number of cross-border trips continued to drop: by the spring of 2010, they were down twenty-one percent compared to 2005 in both directions at Calais and St. Stephen. There were similar numbers at all Maine-New Brunswick crossings. "You've turned America into a fortress," one St. Stephen resident told *The Bangor Daily News*, "and your own people find it a hassle to get back in."

Nickolaj Pedersen continued to live on the farm alone after Marion's death. The Americans relaxed enough to let his daughters visit him without being harassed. But in 2008 there was a new crackdown. Joyce Pedersen, who lived in Fredericton, was stopped when she tried to reach the farmhouse. The road was completely blockaded. No Canadian traffic

---

7 During my stop in the Fort Fairfield area, it was front-page news in the local weekly paper that the passport fee for adult U.S. citizens was increasing from a hundred to a hundred and thirty-five dollars.

was permitted. "He hasn't been able to sleep," Joyce said of her father, who continued to shy away from interviews. "It upsets his pattern. And it means he's isolated. People do not want to come and visit because they do not know what's going to happen. And we're concerned about his safety, being at the farm by himself." A spokesman for the Department of Homeland Security said, "This is just one location among many other locations where we are enhancing our border security."

Mike Allen, Nickolaj Pedersen's Member of Parliament, was prevented from reaching the farmhouse, perhaps the first time the American government has prevented a Canadian MP from meeting a constituent. Allen, a Conservative and therefore a supporter of Stephen Harper's pro-security agenda, sounded sympathetic to the American and Canadian border patrols. "Both parties are concerned that it's really seen as a bit of a weak spot because there's not much patrol on it, and there's only a seasonal border station, and that's only Canada Customs. You can certainly see how some areas like that could be a real problem." Allen said his understanding was that the blockade "was very much of an information campaign to the people who were going along that road, that they were doing that against regulations and that there is a potential that they could be stopped and they could be fined."

After speaking to officials from the office of U.S. Senator Olympia Snowe, Allen said he hoped security officials from both countries could show more flexibility. "My heart goes out to Mr. Pedersen. He's eighty-five years old, he's a veteran, and certainly is deserving of his services, and we have to find a way in the short term to accommodate this, and in the long term to accommodate the golf course." Allen recognized, though, that there was no way to get around the double illegal entries required to reach and leave the Pedersen farm. "If you look strictly at the regulations, it doesn't work."

Later that year, U.S. Border Patrol officers extended the crackdown to golfers heading to the Aroostook Valley Country Club from Canada via the Brown Road. "They caught a guy passing some dope out on No. 6 fairway," Clarence Clark tells me, gesturing towards the course. "And that's the number one thing they throw at you, if they're asked what the threat is. Well, there's no backbone in that statement. It probably has happened since then all along the border, except there weren't two dummies who was passing it. This is a long border. They've got some surveillance up now, but if two sharp guys wanted to smuggle something, I don't care if it's a washing machine or some cigarettes, they could do it."

A U.S. Border Patrol official confirmed the crackdown was prompted by a drug sale on the course and that all golfers would have to take the long way around and enter the United States via Fort Fairfield. "It may not be a drug transaction next time," he said. "It could be something a lot worse." U.S. Senator Susan Collins of Maine urged Homeland Security to set up a small seasonal border post, similar to Canada's, at the corner of Brown Road and Russell Road, but to no avail.

There is more at work here than the unique configuration of the road, Clarence Clark tells me. The Border Patrol officers themselves are changing, he says. "A couple of those guys I was really friendly with. They'd stop here and we'd have things to talk about. One of them was a trapper. He'd trap down back of my farm." Now, fewer are from the local area, and the new arrivals keep to themselves. "They do what they're told to do. I don't know of any of them who are close to anyone but family." Their model is the Mexican border, Clark says, and there is no allowance for friendships across the line. "These guys weren't told any more than, 'Here's your card; get out; do your work on the border.'"

Clark remembers one border officer from the area who, before 9/11, would offer to bring rookie patrolmen out to Russell Road to introduce them to the residents. "What he would say was, 'Listen, I'll go out with you. I know all the people out there. They're good people. They want to help you get along.' But they never took advantage of something like that [after 9/11]."

Nickolaj Pedersen died in 2009 at the age of eighty-six. "Nick died when Marion died," Clarence Clark says, in a tone that suggests he wants to set me straight. "We took him out once or twice to eat. The four of us used to eat a lot of Chinese. We'd go out over to the Jade Palace over in Caribou. I bet we went there every five or six weeks." But after Marion's death, Nickolaj lost interest. "He didn't want to go there. He didn't want anything to do with the country club so we couldn't go down there and eat. I'd say, 'Nick, how about this?' 'No, I'm not really up to it.' I could see what was coming down, so I didn't press him."

In his final months, Pedersen was not even allowed to drop in to visit his dear friends the Clarks in their home. "He used to stop right here at the end of the driveway — he wasn't supposed to come in here — and my wife and I would come out and we'd have a nice big schnapps right there. He might have got out of the car a couple of times, but he was parked there at the end of the driveway and he was in Canada. He'd park right about there.

"It's a funny thing. Nick and Marion never asked us to smuggle anything. They never said, 'Would you bring us this or bring us that?' I'll tell you, I gave him a bottle of booze now and then. He liked gin. But I didn't stand out in the middle of the road and brag about it. But they never asked me [to bring them anything], and the rest of the people on the road would tell you the same thing."

There has been one slight alteration to the intersection of Brown and Russell roads in the two years since my last visit. In the westbound lane coming from Canada, there are now orange pylons to make it slightly more obvious that no one should drive on. But the road continues to perplex. A family of six from New Brunswick was detained by the Americans for four hours in March 2010 after assuming that the border was on the western shoulder of Russell Road, and that they would still be in Canada if they stayed on the road. "I saw the marker that says 'Canada' and saw the sign that's in the farmer's field," Derek McDaniel said. "When I looked at that I assumed I couldn't go past where the sign was and go into the farmer's field, which I wouldn't."

Clarence Clark can't tell me how it will end. He is angry that his own country's Border Patrol sometimes harasses him for driving on his own road, simply because they don't notice him pull out of his driveway; they assume he has entered illegally from Canada. "As long as the border stays there, I don't care if they close it right down and put a cement wall up right there. I'm going right straight this way," he says defiantly.

At other times he sounds defeated. "I'm giving this house to my two grandsons. One's a senior in college, one's a senior in high school. It's too bad, because if I was buying the place and I looked out and saw the Canadian border right there, and looked at the situation, if it was worth a hundred thousand dollars, I wouldn't give you ten for it. You're just buying trouble."

Clark's change of mood is a reflection of his country. The United States has spawned a security-industrial complex of vast scope and power, forceful and uncompromising, but ultimately it is a blunt instrument that reveals a fundamental American weakness: the inability to recognize and respect the dignity of an individual citizen. In this case, it is a harmless old man, unable to welcome into his home the best friend he had ever had, all because of an invisible line running down the middle of their road.

8. INVASIONS

THE NORTH LINE IS A VERY DIFFERENT BORDER from what exists in Madawaska. The Saint John and Saint-François rivers may not be much of a barrier to movement, and the line drawn there may have been a socio-cultural mistake, but there is an inherent physical logic to using rivers to separate two political jurisdictions. There is no such natural boundary on the North Line, as Nickolaj and Marion Pedersen found out.

Nor was the North Line ever considered a single, functioning community, as the Madawaska Settlement was before 1842. Many of the towns and villages along the line did not exist, or were barely settled, when the line was established in 1797. Some, such as Fort Fairfield and Houlton, were creations of the border dispute farther north. So there are no remnants of organic communities cut in two by the line. There is no geopolitical wound still festering. Rivers connected people in the nineteenth century, but the people of the North Line never shared a river. While there have always been exchanges and relationships across the border, the North Line is not a single place with a common story.

And yet, sooner or later, all aspects of the border dynamic play themselves out there, albeit in smaller, more isolated episodes.

If Madawaska is where the line's tumultuous history can be most vividly observed, the North Line is where its troubled present springs to life.

The large white farmhouse stands out as I drive south from Fort Fairfield on Route 1A. Straight ahead, the distinctive hump of Mars Hill rises above the potato fields of Maine and New Brunswick. I am watching the right side of the road, looking for my destination, but the house on the left catches my eye, and I glimpse a small election sign on its front lawn. "Don't Tread on Me," it says. "Tea Party Patriots."

I pull into the parking lot of the Celebration Center, a Pentecostal church across the road, and walk over to the house and knock on the front door. In early 2010, the Tea Party, a grassroots right-wing movement, stacked the policy convention of the Maine State Republican Party and passed a platform full of populist and occasionally paranoid language. It promoted, among other things, the elimination of the federal Department of Education, a "return to the principles of Austrian Economics," and the prohibition of "any participation in efforts to create a one world government." And it urged the United States government to "seal the border and protect U.S. citizens along the border and everywhere, as is the prime directive of the Federal Government."

Even in a year when the Tea Party seemed to be driving the national political agenda, the adoption of such a platform in Maine, known for its independent politics and its embrace of moderate Republicans, drew attention from afar. "Do our friends Down East fear an invasion from the Canadian Maritime provinces?" a *Washington Post* columnist asked mockingly, calling the platform a "manifesto for insanity." Even one of the candidates seeking the state party's nomination for governor admitted he had no idea what was meant by the reference to "Austrian economics." An editorial in *The Bangor Daily News* noted that sealing the border would shut down more than a billion dollars in annual trade between Maine and New Brunswick. "Not a good way to improve the state's economy," it said. One of the Republicans who helped write the document hastened to clarify to the New Brunswick *Telegraph-Journal* that he did not want to close the border with New Brunswick, only beef up security.

Maine's independent streak has bred a surprising array of movements with names such as the Maine Patriots and the Maine Highlands Defense Force. The bestselling novelist Carolyn Chute, who has been compared to Faulkner and Steinbeck for her portrayals of poverty in rural Maine, has been a key player behind the Second Maine Militia: a collection of libertarians, secessionists, home-schoolers, Second-Amendment advocates, Marxists, and vegans. Something about Maine's remoteness and its large expanse of forest seems to attract, or breed, a free-thinking spirit that combines with skepticism of big government, big business, big anything. "Voters who don't identify with any party — independents outnumber both Republicans and Democrats," Mike Tipping, a political blogger, tells me by e-mail.

So the Tea Party and its anti-government rhetoric is only the latest manifestation of this strain of thought. But I still find it odd that someone living within five miles of the Canadian border, someone who can see a foreign country from their house, as it were, is given to isolationist thinking.

A Star-Spangled Banner lies on the front porch, rolled around a pole. I knock several times, then walk around to a side door. No one answers. "I suspect if you had found that person at home near Fort Fairfield," the former governor of Maine, Angus King, will later tell me, "he'd say 'I'm against this, that, or the other thing, but I don't want to seal the border with Canada.'" The Tea Party, he says, is part of a cyclical, periodic backlash common in American politics during times of economic uncertainty. "Fear and distrust of foreigners rises, and there's a fear of newcomers, of immigrants taking American jobs. That happened in the 1880s. It happened in the 1920s," says King, who was elected twice as an independent.

Indeed, George Findlen points out that much of the anti-Hispanic rhetoric common in 2010 echoes the nineteenth-century nativist backlash against French-Canadian migrants to Maine. "It's not an unprecedented reaction," King says, "and I don't think it has anything to do with Canada or Canadians. I can tell you when I was in office Bill Clinton tried to put some kind of border-crossing tax in place. Everybody in Aroostook County went nuts. They hated it, because they wanted to go back and forth. I don't think too many people up there would want to seal the border. They want people to come shop at the mall in Presque Isle. In Washington County, they want people to come shop in Calais."

Mike Tipping says elected officials in Maine seldom feel bound by their party platforms, and he doesn't expect the Tea Party-backed winner of the governor's race, Paul LePage, to be much different. The platform, he says, was spawned by national trends. "When Tea Party activists took control of the Republican convention they adopted that agenda wholesale, without thinking of the consequences such a policy would have for the northern border." That, of course, is precisely the problem: the loud American debate over border security tends to drown out the quiet voices, and the quiet places, that speak to a different, more nuanced approach.

A few miles south of the Tea Party farmhouse is the small, modest Friends Church, a Quaker meeting house that tells another part of the border story. There is no parking, so I stop my car on the lawn and step out. Across the road, past a potato field with a large pivot sprinkler sitting idle, is New Brunswick. The weight of history is as present on the front lawn of the church as it has been anywhere else on my journey: once, desperate people set out from this very spot, and across those very fields, seeking an invisible line and the promise of freedom on the other side. For them, a porous border was not just a convenience but a life-altering blessing. For this humble little church was one of the northernmost stops on the Underground Railroad, a secret network of safe houses that allowed escaped slaves from the south to make their way north and cross into the colonies of British North America, where slavery had been outlawed in 1834.

Arthur Mraz — like Bill Findlen, another aging citizen of Aroostook County with an outsized interest in local history — arrives in a car driven by his daughter. He practically bounds out of the vehicle despite his eighty-six years. Wearing a baseball cap, enormous glasses, and suspenders that hold up his pants, he cuts a comic figure. Mraz is from Wisconsin, but his wife Ruth, whom he met in Boston, was a local girl. "When I saw her I just couldn't let her go," he says. It was Ruth who was fascinated with the history of the Friends Church. As a child she heard whispers about the Underground Railroad. "My wife's grandmother grew up out here in the

The Friends Church in Maple Grove was a station on the Underground Railroad.

woods, and there were stories back in those days," Mraz tells me. "And Joseph Wingate Haines, who built the church, he'd come home some nights from being at the church, and the children would be up in the balcony listening in, and he'd say 'Well, they're safe tonight.' They didn't talk about it much, but the kids [heard] these stories."

The church is another product of the Aroostook War. Members of the Society of Friends, the Quakers, settled in Maple Grove, south of Fort Fairfield, in 1844, two years after the Webster-Ashburton Treaty established the border. Maine, anxious to shore up its jurisdiction at the time, was generous with land grants. Haines was granted a thousand acres on the condition he build a sawmill for other settlers. "I think the Quakers were good people at taking advantage of situations like that," Mraz says, delicately. "But as far as what they did as abolitionists, they kept quiet about that." More Quakers came in 1858, and two years later the church was built.

It is estimated that thirty thousand blacks fled to Canada via the Underground Railroad. Little is known about how many of them hid in the church in Maple Grove because no records were kept. "Nothing was ever written down that would imply their illegal activity," Ruth Mraz wrote. "It was too dangerous." Slavery had been abolished in the north, but an 1850 compromise, meant to preserve the Union, required that authorities return fugitive slaves from the south to their masters. It also created the position of federal commissioner — one in each county of the United States — to hear cases of recaptured slaves. Anyone who interfered with their capture and return could be jailed for six months and fined a thousand dollars, a small fortune at the time.

Ruth Mraz also tried without success to get church records from Quaker headquarters and sought to track down descendants of escaped slaves for interviews, but as Arthur tells me, "Oral history sometimes gets lost. They'll say 'Oh yes, we heard something,' but there's never any documentation. It would not be a big number. It's fairly far north. It's a long trek. There were the Hoopers. There was a family down in Easton. I think there are at least four families that you can identify."

Arthur Mraz opens the combination lock on the door. The church is small, and at the front of the room is a small platform. Beneath that platform, decades ago, there was a hollowed-out hiding place. In 1906, it was boarded over with wood from packing crates used to ship the glass used for a stained-glass window installed in the church that year. "We covered up, supposedly, the trap door," Mraz says. "It's interesting they took the packing boards and changed something that was here. I have no idea why they would do that, with all the lumber we had."

The space would have been barely two feet deep, and not much wider than six feet across, enough to hold two or three people at best, and not comfortably. But it would have sufficed. From that hiding place the slaves would emerge at night to be spirited by the Quakers southeast across fields and through woods to Monson Pond, just a half-mile this side of the North Line. They would then sneak across the border, to be met by New Brunswick Quakers at Tomlinson Lake. What became of them after that is not known, as least not in Fort Fairfield. But they were free, and that, Arthur Mraz marvels, is worth remembering. "To help the slaves in those times, in the 1830s and the 1840s, before the Civil War — they were very dangerous times."

Arthur Mraz inherited the role of unofficial historian of the Friends Church after his wife died. He is now the one who tells visiting schoolchildren about the flight through darkness to Canada. It was another example of how important the border has been, and how it has affected so many lives. "There was a very close relationship," Mraz says, "and from a slave area to a free area, there was a lot [of interaction]. And of course people up here who were Quakers, who were abolitionists, they felt really close [to sympathizers in New Brunswick], because they knew anybody that came to them, they could take over to freedom.

"I think between the individual people who lived on both sides of the border, there was a lot of mutual understanding and a lot of mutual friendship. I think that our governments are making it more difficult because we have to have passports and such. The free flow that we had ten years ago, or five years ago, isn't as free. But that does not affect the relationships between individuals." Still, he says, the line is not completely secure. "I live right near the border, and there's the helicopters going and this and that, and we have border patrol cars going by all the time, but it isn't a foolproof border."

Mraz's enthusiasm for the Underground Railroad makes him sound like a conventional American liberal. But his sympathy for the escaped slaves, who, after all, were slipping across the line illegally in search of a better life, does not carry over to those trying to cross the southern border from Mexico. "The view in the U.S. today is we welcome *legal* immigrants," he explains matter-of-factly. "We do not welcome illegal immigrants." The slaves, he says, occupied a different moral plane. "We forcefully brought the blacks and the Africans into slavery and whatnot. Remember, the majority of people back in those days were people who owned slaves. And I think today it's totally different.

"We don't have the strong feelings here that are prevalent down in Texas, down in Arizona, that area, because there is so much damage [down there]. We haven't had the robberies and the drugs and so on. But I think we feel that it might be easier to get into Canada and then smuggle someone into the United States, especially right here on the East Coast."[8]

Arthur Mraz's face brightens. He has an idea, one borne of his own good will, and his faith in international brotherhood, but one sure to send shivers down the spines of Canadian nationalists. "I think everybody would love to see the United States and Canada secure our perimeter," he says happily, "and then we wouldn't need to protect the border between us."

The former governor of Maine, Angus King, has advocated a similar idea for years. "It's ridiculous to me that you can drive from Italy to Norway, between countries that fifty years ago were trying to kill each other, without slowing down, and yet you can't cross the largest undefended border in the world, between the two best neighbours, without going through a lot of rigmarole," King told me. "The problem is the two countries have very different rules and views on things like firearms. But I always argued we should work to harmonize our immigration policies and our legal policies so we could move towards opening up the border between Canada and the U.S. I made that statement in the weeks after 9/11 and everybody told me I was crazy, but that's what I think."

It seems crazy. Or it would, if I were not seeing firsthand how strongly New Brunswick and Maine are tied together. The more time I spend on the border, and the more deeply I feel the state and the province reaching out to each other, the less crazy it seems.

---

8   In fact, the *Winnipeg Free Press* reported in September 2010 that in 2008, for the second year in a row, more people tried to sneak into Canada from the United States than the other way around.

The North Line was once dotted with official border crossings: at least six closed from the 1950s to the 1990s, often as newer, more centralized stations were built on busier roads nearby. Many others closed long before that. In some cases, the customs houses were torn down. In others, they were sold and became private homes.

The most recent closure was in 1994, on the Aroostook River near Fort Fairfield. A road ran from the Saint John River along the south bank of the Aroostook, past a small hydroelectric dam to the border, and then continued into the town. In April that year, an ice jam upstream burst, and the river flooded the banks in Fort Fairfield, bringing large chunks of ice with it. The flood also drowned two Canada Customs officers trapped in their car at the crossing. The checkpoint was closed not long afterwards and the road was barricaded. Today, similar barricades with "No Entry" signs mark many of the former crossings, and sometimes a few feet of asphalt have been torn up as well, just to reinforce the idea that it is the end of the road.

I begin to expect such a barrier as I travel east down Ladner Road. I turned onto it from Route 1A, south of Easton. A white U.S. Border Patrol SUV was parked at an abandoned gas station on the corner, and a large barn had a sign above the door that read "McCain Champion Grower." My map shows that Ladner Road leads to a still-functioning crossing, and the road seems pleasant and lively with white farmhouses and barns set back in the open fields. But as I near the frontier, the road slopes down, hills and trees close in, Mars Hill looms ever closer, and the setting feels suddenly remote. When the asphalt ends and the dirt road begins, I am convinced I will soon be backtracking to Route 1A.

Then I round a final bend and, to my relief, see two customs checkpoints ahead: the United States Border Patrol office, a small prefabricated hut with its now-familiar yellow radiation-detecting poles for incoming traffic, and beyond it, Canada Customs.

The Canadian officer barely looks at my passport before waving me through. I park at the Customs office and walk back towards the line. About halfway between the two customs buildings, I find the telltale clearing, running through the woods to the north and south. This

Monument 61 sits near the Easton River de Chute border crossing.

twenty-foot buffer, known as a vista, is cut and trimmed regularly by the International Boundary Commission. The IBC also maintains the white numbered markers, known as monuments, which dot the entire land border between Canada and the United States. There are almost three hundred of them along the North Line. I can see one of them about a hundred and fifty feet up the hill, in the middle of the buffer clearing.

The Commission, created by a treaty in 1908, may be the only institution in the world to use the word "monument" as a verb. Its 2007 annual report described a stream on the Québec-New Hampshire border that shifted position over the decades, making it "necessary to monument the many turning points." The practice of clearing a vista along the border, ten feet on each side, was codified in a subsequent 1925 treaty, although the concept dates back to 1817, if not before. The two countries divide up the work on various sections of the border, with the Americans maintaining the North Line. "The IBC represents a true sharing of resources, intellect and goodwill between the two sovereign nations," the commission said in the same 2007 report, "with little fanfare, less hoopla, and no jingoism."

Still, the commission, like other public agencies, often faces funding cuts. The same document noted "a significant lag" in maintenance because the U.S. Congress had not approved enough money. And its authors knew what card to play: the war on terror. Increased border security, the commission's 2009 report said, made its work more important than ever. "Quite simply, the need for enhanced demarcation is clear. People must be able to easily recognize the boundary and avoid inadvertent crossings." To reduce costs, the IBC was seeking partnerships with other agencies to pay for mapping. The North Line itself had been mapped as a pilot project with help from the RCMP and the U.S. Geological Survey.

An American officer comes out of his office as I approach the line, and I brace myself, but he waves. "I'm a reporter and I'm working on a book," I call to him. "I'm not going to cross. I just want to see the marker." He nods, and I walk up the hill, careful to stay on the Canadian side. He walks up the vista on the American side, and we meet at Monument 61, a small, squat, white concrete obelisk on a wide base marked "Treaty 1842." We stand there chatting, five feet apart but in our respective countries. "I can't quite see the next marker," I tell him, squinting up the line. Each of the white monuments is supposed to have a clear sight line to the next one in either direction.

"Look high," he says, pointing, and at the very top of a long hill, I can just make out Monument 60A, almost a kilometre away.

"You're very relaxed compared to some of the crossings I've been through," I tell the officer.

He puts his arms up, gesturing to the surrounding, as if to say, "There's nothing here. What do you expect?" And he is right. This is probably the most remote crossing I have encountered. The next time the budget axe falls in Ottawa or Washington, this port of entry could cease to exist.

I photograph the obelisk and walk back down the hill. Monument 61A is just across the road. It is a newer version, with a thinner, taller, stainless steel obelisk protruding from the same traditional cement base. Across the small, winding River de Chute, I see the next one, Monument 62. Beyond it, the twenty-foot-wide clearing continues north to the horizon.

Soon I am back in my car, continuing my drive into New Brunswick. I come to a junction with Route 560, where I finally see the name of the road leading into the province from the border: Smuggler's Road. Yes, I think, the American officer was right. This road has seen busier days.

From Route 560, I follow the Saint John River south until I meet the Trans-Canada Highway, which takes me to Woodstock, the largest town in Carleton County. There, I exit onto New Brunswick Route 95, the only highway in the province with a two-digit designation not in the teens. This is because Route 95 leads to the border, and to U.S. Interstate 95, the twin ribbons of asphalt that decades ago replaced U.S. Route 1 as the primary coastal road running from Maine to Florida.

The I-95 begins at the Woodstock–Houlton border crossing. A young, fresh-faced officer opens the window and asks me why I am entering the United States. To my surprise, when I tell him I am researching a book on the history of the border, his face brightens and he asks if I am researching the Aroostook War. "You must be a local guy," I laugh.

"Yeah, a local guy," he nods.

Aaron Bell could not be more local. The border station itself was built on land the American government bought from his mother's family, and he is the third generation of his father's family to work on the border. His grandmother is the curator of the Aroostook County Historical and Art Museum in Houlton. I absolutely have to go speak to her, he tells me.

The museum is in a stately house painted yellow, a block from Houlton's quaint, old-fashioned downtown. Many of the storefronts on Main Street are empty, and have been since well before the market crash of 2008. The rationale for putting a town here was not clear when the first settlers arrived in 1807 to farm; Houlton grew into a town only after federal troops were dispatched to the area in 1828 because of the border dispute. "A lot of the boys up here were West Point graduates, and they sent them up here to give them a little taste of the frontier, and to build roads," Kay Bell tells me. The most important of the roads they built ran from Mattawamkeag to Houlton — now part of Route 2. The stretch within the town limits of Houlton is still called Military Road.

Upstairs, Kay shows me an old map from the time of the Aroostook War, depicting the Saint John, its tributaries, and the various forts and encampments along their banks. The museum is filled with items from those days: coins, cannonballs, buckets. Anything from Hancock barracks, which the troops built and where they were stationed, is an important part of the collection. The United States had only four thousand federal troops at the time, but two hundred of them were sent here. "It really made Houlton grow," Kay tells me as she leads me through the exhibits. "It probably made it possible that the settlement stayed. Because who knows? They might have thrown their hands up and said 'We can't hàck this.' It was a factor in Houlton's stability and permanence."

Kay Bell's father was from the Miramichi in New Brunswick. When he came to Houlton in 1909, customs officers climbed onto the train at the border and collected a head tax. "When I was a kid a long time ago, I don't even

Kay Bell, curator of the Aroostook County Historical and Art Museum, shows a century-old survey map of the border.

recall there being a customs office at the line coming in. It was down near the county church." Kay landed her first job with U.S. Customs in 1957. "I started in as a secretary because they needed somebody who could take shorthand to take investigations and things like that. It was fun. I liked the job a lot. I really did. The guys were great." She eventually became a supervisor in the radio room. "Stations were a lot smaller then," Kay says. "Houlton had one supervisor and four officers. The border was not nearly as active as it is now." The district headquarters and the ports of entry, she said, are "splitting at the seams."

Fewer staff were needed in Kay's day because crossing was second nature, and an honour system was at work. You could use an unguarded road provided you drove straight to customs to report, without stopping. "They were back and forth all the time," she says. "People from here went over there to teach. People from over there came over here to work. Almost every family in Houlton seems to have some roots in Canada." The traffic is still flowing in 2010. "On the weekend here at Houlton Regional

Hospital, a big percentage of the nurses are Canadian; Houlton likes it because they're available and they're good nurses." But other crossings are down, she says. "It used to be you went over there to shop, but not so much now. A lot of Canadians still come here for cheaper gas."

Kay retired from the border in 1990. One of her sons, Aaron's father, works at Bridgewater, across from Centreville, New Brunswick, while the other retired to Tuscon, Arizona, after flying helicopter patrols on the border with Mexico. Aaron's brother is working on the southern border as well. She speaks about their work in only the most general terms, and is discreet, even decades later, about her own career, gently dodging requests for anecdotes about specific incidents. She has heard all about the Pedersens's case — "petty," she calls it — but is ambivalent about the heightened security in general.

"It's a different world. And sometimes it seems like it's over-protection, and then other times, you know, things . . . happen and you think maybe it isn't enough. If you're an outsider, you just don't know. I don't know how active the northern border is compared to the southern border. I know the southern border is almost an invasion. But if the Mexicans and the South Americans didn't come, the crops wouldn't get picked. Or employers would have to pay more money and food would cost more. They are *workers*. I've been down on the southern border a lot, and I visited Tuscon and El Paso and all those places, and it's not the Americans you see out picking the crops or working on the roads in hundred-degree weather. It's Mexicans.

"It's a fact of life. A lot of people gripe about the fact that they have to have a passport. Unless today's world changes, it's probably going to stay the way it is. It's so different from when I worked for the Border Patrol, or when I was growing up. So many things have happened. Even in Houlton, which is such a quiet town, you have people who come in from somewhere else. And of course there's a lot more subsidized housing and things like that. And there's a lot more drugs. Drugs is probably the big problem."

Kay goes out back to find something she thinks I will want to see: a set of maps that someone found in their basement. They planned to throw them away. Then they decided they had better show them to Kay.

She unrolls a couple of them on a table. "They're not in good shape and neither am I," she says. The paper is yellowed and brittle. There are long cracks along the edges. But they are remarkable and exciting to see. They are a series, all early drafts of the survey maps — "advance copy subject to correction," says a handwritten note — of the North Line drawn under the terms of the treaty of 1908, which established the International Boundary Commission. Each of the border monuments is marked, and it is possible to identify all the roads that once crossed the line, most of them now closed. If arranged end to end, the maps would form a portrait of a more innocent border, from a more innocent time.

Kay is ninety-one years old. Her life accounts for more than half of the years that have passed since the treaty of 1842 and the final, definitive marking of the North Line. She is conscious of history and understands in her bones what a century means. "My father used to say that he lived from the time there was nothing but axes in the woods, no saws, until when they put a man on the moon," she laughs. "That was his lifetime. And I got thinking the other day: what am I going to say? I thought, well, I lived from the time women got the vote until the time when two women can get married. So you wonder what'll happen in, say, Aaron's time, and will it be better or worse?"

9. THE PERSISTENCE OF ATLANTICA

HOULTON'S DOWNTOWN IS ITSELF LIKE A MUSEUM, a scale-model diorama of a prosperous past, when the town's Market Square was still worthy of its name. This was where citizens and visitors congregated for parades and speeches and other civic events, and for the all-important activity of shopping, which fuelled the buzz of activity up and down the few short blocks of Main Street. Now all that remains are indicators of retail decline: a Salvation Army, a martial arts school, a pet grooming salon — the last desperate twitches of economic activity.

In Houlton, as elsewhere, people vote with their feet and their dollars. All the traffic and the energy are out on the sprawling stretch of Route 1 near the I-95 off-ramps. That is where Wal-Mart, a small mall, and a handful of other box stores and discounters have touched down, sucking the oxygen from the downtown core. Shoppers come to the strip from north, south, and west, zooming in on the interstate or meandering down the old highway from Mars Hill, or up from Danforth or Hodgdon. And they came from the east, from New Brunswick. Canadians are helping to fill the box-store parking lots on Route 1, tightening the chokehold on Main Street.

Cross-border shopping is as old as the border itself, but in the late 1980s, the presence of so many Canadian licence plates in towns like Houlton took on the feel of a national crisis. The dollar was rising in value and would peak at eighty-nine cents U.S. in November 1991.

Its buying power was soaring at the very moment cranky Canadians wanted to protest the Mulroney government's new goods-and-services tax. The rush for the border, and its bargains, was on. With the recently adopted free-trade agreement in the mix, Canadian economic nationalists were wringing their hands, as if the country itself was being sucked whole into the United States market.

American entrepreneurs near the border moved quickly to exploit the opportunity, building malls and stores conveniently close to the line. The Aroostook Center Mall opened in 1993 in Presque Isle, near Fort Fairfield, perfectly situated to draw New Brunswick shoppers from Edmundston to Fredericton. But the loonie proved fickle: it was already down to seventy-six cents by the time the doors opened, and as it continued to drop, the cost of a shopping trip went up for New Brunswickers. By 2001, the dollar was worth only sixty-three American cents, and Canadian shoppers, once fifteen percent of the Aroostook Centre's traffic, represented only one percent. The mall, appraised at twenty-three million dollars, sold in a bankruptcy auction for ten million. "We do local TV which is in Presque Isle, which broadcasts to Canada," the manager, Dennis Hussie, told me at the time. "We have advertised on radio in Canada. We do direct marketing in Canada. But all of these things will not replace the exchange rate falling."[9]

The flood of shoppers across the border didn't just stop; it reversed course. Canadian goods became temptingly cheap to Americans, and Maine licence plates were suddenly easy to find in the mall parking lots of Carleton County. "We buy a lot of things over here, all types of groceries, construction stuff, and stuff like that," Jerry Thomas, a Smyrna Mills resident, told me in 2001. His car, parked at a Woodstock grocery store, proudly sported a George W. Bush bumper sticker. The U.S. dollar was so strong that a real-estate company in Woodstock selling pre-fabricated houses reported that ninety-five percent of its sales were in Maine. "The saving they're finding, depending on the size of the home of course, is anywhere between twenty and thirty-five thousand dollars," the company's

---

9   The drop in Canadian shoppers was not the only blow to the mall. In 1994, the nearby Loring Air Force Base was closed, costing the area hundreds of jobs.

co-owner told me. The increased traffic in Woodstock forced the town to install its first traffic light, then its second, on Connell Road, its own box-store strip near the Trans-Canada Highway.

Another decade has passed, and as I travel the border in the spring and summer of 2010, the loonie is flying high again, reaching parity. Oddly, there is no national agonizing this time, no talk of a border-shopping crisis. The flight of shoppers to the U.S. is not repeating itself. "Cross-border shopping volumes . . . pale by comparison with the phenomenon observed two decades ago," Statistics Canada reported in 2007. There was once a relationship between the exchange rate and the number of same-day car trips by Canadians into the United States, the agency said, but after 9/11, the two trendlines decoupled. Day trips edged up only slightly, from 1.7 million in 2002 to 1.9 million in 2007, despite the Canadian dollar gaining forty-four percent in value in the same period. Border security was almost certainly the main cause, though another was likely the recent retail expansion on the New Brunswick side: when the loonie was low, Wal-Mart and other large chains came to Edmundston, Grand Falls, and Woodstock, providing more selection and better prices. This created new shopping habits less vulnerable to a rebounding loonie.

The 2007 Statistics Canada report also said online shopping was not making much impact on cross-border shopping trips. It pointed out that courier shipments from the United States to Canada, "the dominant route to receive a product ordered online," had increased steadily, but not strongly. But the border itself offers an alternative for mail-order shoppers, and in Houlton, that alternative is directly across the street from the Aroostook County Historical and Art Museum. When I finish my interview with Kay Bell, I walk over.

PAC Electronics, a former Radio Shack franchise, is a packrat's delight, jammed full of boxes, radio supplies, wires, electronic components, signs, baseball caps, fishing gear, and other assorted detritus. People are constantly coming and going. The owner, Neil Cowperthwaite, a large man with white thinning hair and glasses, never quite stands still, though he shuffles more than he moves, constantly pawing at his inventory, looking up each time the bell over the door rings to signal the arrival of another customer.

"I had a package delivered here," a man says as he approaches the counter. He is about forty and has come from Fredericton. He gives his name.

Cowperthwaite pokes through a wheelbarrow full of cardboard shipping boxes: nothing. "Do you have a box here?" he asks.

"No," the man answers, but he gives the name of a friend who does.

"That doesn't help you," Cowperthwaite replies.

"Oh, that doesn't help me. Okay." Now the man has the nervous look of someone who is doing something vaguely illicit, though the transaction he is trying to complete is perfectly legal.

"Unless your name is on his box," Cowperthwaite adds, correcting himself. "What's his box number?"

The man calls his friend and gets the box number. Cowperthwaite disappears into a labyrinth of back rooms lined with shelves. He emerges with the parcel and informs the Fredericton man it will cost four dollars to claim it. Then Cowperthwaite's demeanour begins to shift. His studied impatience with the uninitiated gives way to something approaching forgiveness. Then he begins his sales pitch.

"Now he only has one person on his box," he explains as he hands over the man's parcel. "You are allowed to share your box. If he so desires, and you're going to do this a lot, he can call me and put your name in there, at which time you would pay one dollar."

"Sounds good to me."

"Now I'm going to give you an instant rebate here because I feel guilty charging you all that."

"Perfect."

"You talk to him and if he wants to put you in the box, he just calls me. Not you. Him. He owns the box."

Another New Brunswicker arrives, a non-subscriber picking up several packages. "That's four dollars, four dollars, four dollars, four dollars, and four dollars," Cowperthwaite counts, tallying up the pick-up fee for effect. "Five times four is twenty dollars. A box rental is thirty dollars Canadian." Then he spots a sixth package. "That's yours also? Okay, you've got

Parcels shipped to Houlton wait to be picked up by New Brunswick shoppers.

six times four, so you're at twenty-four dollars. A box runs you thirty dollars a year, at which time you pay a dollar a package. You rent a box today and I'm going to give you the packages."

Cowperthwaite lost the Radio Shack franchise when the chain pulled out of downtown Houlton and moved to the mall. He decided to stay put: he was developing a sideline in the store, a post-office-box service, an address of convenience, for Canadians doing mail-order from the United States. For a fee of thirty dollars a year, two families share a box and pick up parcels for a dollar each. Picking up without renting a box costs four dollars per package.

Cowperthwaite understands a fundamental trait of human nature: people love to save time and money. And people living near an international border are almost genetically programmed to try to save even more time and money on the other side of the line. One customer tells me it once cost him seventy-six dollars in shipping, taxes, and customs brokerage fees to have a twelve-dollar radio tube shipped from California to Moncton. He rented a box after that. Another man, from Woodstock, explains that a thirty-dollar set of blueprints would cost him thirty-six dollars in brokerage fees alone if they were shipped to his home. Instead, he drove to Houlton and saved the money. "And it's faster, too. It takes three or four days longer to get there," he explains, nodding his head east towards Canada. "This way, if you want it that week, you can get it."

"Hey, it saves big money to come over here and get your own stuff," Cowperthwaite says. In recent weeks, he has handed over, in addition to the usual mail-order items, tires, an excavator, even an aircraft engine. "You name it, it's been through here." The system works in the opposite direction as well: two members of a church group in Woodstock are in the store shipping earthquake-relief supplies to Haiti through Cowperthwaite's store. They will reach the stricken island more quickly, and the lower shipping cost means more of the money they raised is going towards helping people.

"I started out with about twenty mailboxes and now I'm at about eighteen thousand," Cowperthwaite says as he returns to the back of the store and sifts through long shelves crammed with shipping boxes. "Ninety-eight percent of them are Canadian. They come through on a vacation, on a forty-eighter, and don't have to pay taxes." (A forty-eighter is border slang for a trip to the United States lasting at least two full days, after which a Canadian can bring home four hundred dollars worth of purchases duty-free.) "It's word of mouth. I've got 'em from Québec to Nova Scotia to Newfoundland, as well as New Brunswick. Some people drive here from Prince Edward Island. ...They come over to Bangor or Portland to fly, and they pick their stuff up. I don't have any storage fees. I don't charge if they don't pick it up. If they don't pick it up after a while, I inherit it."

And it is all perfectly legal. Only once has Cowperthwaite run into problems. Before 9/11, a Woodstock man used the store to ship illegal satellite TV chip cards to the United States. The cards, which bypassed the encryption on DirecTV digital satellite signals, were shipped C.O.D. "The money came back to me and he would pick it up," Cowperthwaite says. "So when the F.B.I. did the money trail, it came to me, because I was the shipper. My name was on the C.O.D. tag." Federal agents showed up at the store one day. "I said, 'Yeah, sure, he comes here all the time, rents a box, ships stuff C.O.D.' They said, 'Where is he?' I said, 'Well, he's in Woodstock.'" The cops couldn't get him, but they had Cowperthwaite.

They charged him. Fortunately, Cowperthwaite had paid the Woodstock man his C.O.D. money by cheque. "He wanted me to pay in cash. I do not pay cash to anybody. I want a paper trail." Because he could prove he made no money on the chip sales, he was found not guilty in Bangor. The chip man in Woodstock "has not been across," Cowperthwaite says. "There is a federal warrant for his arrest for one-point-five million dollars, and he will get caught eventually. Someday he's going to forget about this. But when he comes through with that licence plate and that ID, bingo!"

There have been no problems since then. What Cowperthwaite provides to his New Brunswick customers is what many Canadians secretly covet: a piece, however tiny, of United States real estate and the free-market privileges that come with it. "I have more customers than I can handle," Cowperthwaite tells me. "If I advertised, I'd be here seven days a week."

Even the dip in traffic due to the new security regime is balanced by the online shopping boom. For every New Brunswicker afraid to cross the border, there are even more signing up to receive parcels from Amazon, eBay, and a range of other sites. "It did affect me for about a year," Cowperthwaite says of the crackdown, "because you've got to have a passport. But it didn't take a year before that was solved. Everybody got a passport. If you want to go to America and get free gas and free milk, you've got to get a passport." Cowperthwaite is proof of a fundamental economic law: money does not recognize borders. "I am," he tells me, "in the right place at the right time."

Neil Cowperthwaite is embracing a reality that is hardly new but that was recently given a fancy new name for the twenty-first century: Atlantica.

The term was coined to describe the concept of a single economic unit covering the New England states and the Maritime Provinces of Canada, and, occasionally, Newfoundland and Labrador and parts of eastern Québec. "We have more in common with Atlantic Canada than we do Iowa or other states," Tanya Pereira, an economic development official with the town of Brewer, Maine, told a 2010 Bangor conference devoted to Atlantica. A third of Maine's exports were to Canada in 2008, and more than thirty thousand jobs depended on cross-border trade.

"Atlantica has long been a *de facto* historical concept," says a 2007 study, "Historical Atlantica," by the Atlantic Institute of Market Studies, a right-wing Halifax think-tank that advocates free trade, deregulation, and economic integration. AIMS pursues its own self-interest—a corporate-sponsored, ideological agenda vigorously opposed by the Canadian left—but the report's grasp of history is undeniable. Cross-border commerce in the region, it notes, dates back to the seventeenth century, when borders were not even firmly established.

Despite their respective loyalties to competing empires, John Winthrop, the British governor of the Massachusetts Bay Colony, was intrigued when, in 1641, he was approached by Charles de Saint-Étienne de La Tour, the governor of Acadia, to sign a trade agreement. Winthrop turned down a formal accord, but the geographic proximity of the two colonies made commerce between them inevitable. La Tour hoped to use his new links to Massachusetts to undermine his rival for the governorship of Acadia, Charles de Menou d'Aulnay, but in the end, their violent internal feud undermined their own colony. The French considered the Penobscot River the western boundary of Acadia, but Massachusetts took advantage of the instability to expand its fur trade east of the river, towards their new settlement at Machias, not far from the St. Croix. This commercial impetus would lead to confusion about colonial frontiers, and more than a century later, caused the St. Croix, not the Penobscot, to be seen as the natural boundary.

Trade continued to grow in the eighteenth century, and after the fall of Québec in 1763, Atlantica was briefly united under the British flag. Following American independence, coastal merchants treated the new border as little more than a nuisance, turning Passamaquoddy Bay into a busy smuggler's market. The profit motive helped resolve the diplomatic impasse in Madawaska, when Maine accepted the Webster-Ashburton Treaty in part because it gave Americans the right to float their logs the length of the Saint John River. Maine entrepreneurs were soon buying or building mills in Saint John, at the mouth of the river. "The Ashburton treaty broadened Aroostook Valley horizons immeasurably as Yankee loggers fell heir to the worldwide markets of the British empire," wrote historian Richard W. Judd. "The provincial port city welcomed Aroostook's forest resources and offered in exchange goods from all over the world."

Logs from northern Maine could float down the river because, under the treaty, they were treated as a product of New Brunswick. This had disadvantages as well: the wood was thus subject to both an export duty by New Brunswick and an import tariff by the United States. A Reciprocity Treaty in 1854 ended the tariffs and duties, but in 1866 that treaty was allowed to lapse, a victim of domestic American politics. Maine Congressman Frederick A. Pike of Calais quickly introduced a bill to let timber that was cut on the American side of the Saint John and St. Croix rivers, and milled in New Brunswick, re-enter the United States duty-free. Lumbermen elsewhere in Maine opposed the legislation, but loggers on the Saint John, the Aroostook, and the St. Croix understood their prosperity hinged not on their fellow Americans but on the British colony with whom they shared a border. They lobbied hard and the bill passed, "legitimizing the unique international economy that had developed" along the border, according to Judd.[10]

Some forms of border commerce are not governed by laws or treaties. In a spartan meeting room at the RCMP's J Division headquarters in Fredericton, Inspector Daniel Goodwin nods knowingly as I describe the remote places I am visiting during my journey. "You go up to Glazier Lake or Spednic Lake, and it's beautiful, but you're also thinking, 'Man, what a

10 The Pike Act lapsed in 1911, but by then Aroostook County had been linked to Bangor by rail for almost two decades.

place to smuggle. Where would you go? What's on the other side?' When you drive a boat down the St. Croix River, you realize how close the two countries are. It's a stone's throw. It would be seconds, not minutes, trying to cross there with contraband. The Saint-François River is very shallow this time of year. It's not a hindrance at all."

Smuggling is as old as borders themselves. The North Line was not even finalized and surveyed when, at the beginning of the eighteenth century, the mouth of the St. Croix River and Passamaquoddy Bay were the scene of a contraband free-for-all. In 1858, Thomas E. Perley of Woodstock wrote to Samuel Leonard Tilley, the provincial secretary, to complain that liquor from the town's taverns was being transported to Houlton duty-free. Perley confessed he did not "practice the principles of total abstinence, yet these disqualifications . . . do not blind my eyes to the stupendous fraud upon the Revenue which I daily see going on around me. If people want to use liquors they should pay duty upon them."

Even *The New York Times* discovered, in 1892, what it called "four hundred miles of boundary for smugglers" between Maine and New Brunswick, including "convenient ferries and bridges where no questions are asked—an army would be required to enforce the law." Men from Eastport and Lubec, Maine, travelled to New Brunswick's Campobello Island to buy "dutiable goods" and bring them back without scrutiny. Saint Andrews was a base from which clothes, silks, and other products from the port of Halifax were shipped illegally to the U.S. At Vanceboro, Maine, smugglers used the international rail bridge spanning the St. Croix, "right under the noses of the officers," the newspaper reported, "who are only supposed to look after freight trains." Most egregiously, the *Times* correspondent discovered "a collection of liquor shops" catering to Americans at the Canadian end of the Calais-St. Stephen bridge. Further, the *Times* man reported, he himself had crossed the bridge several times "and has yet to be checked or asked a question by any Custom House man."

Today border officers, their numbers bolstered by large anti-terrorism budgets, catch more smugglers, but modern-day contraband, mostly drugs, still gets across. Washington County, bounded by the St. Croix River and New Brunswick, had 2.5 percent of Maine's population in

2010, but seven percent of its illegal drug seizures. "Every place in the country that has this problem has a larger source," Lieutenant Michael Riggs of the county sheriff's office told hearings in Washington in 2003. "In eastern Maine, ours is Canada." Nicholas Ames, serving time in jail for a robbery to fund his addiction, told the *Bangor Daily News*, "There are a lot of people standing in line, ready to sell, coming across the border, hiding drugs in their bodies."

"Our addicts often go to Canada for pills," Lieutenant Riggs testified in Washington. "They go for two reasons: U.S. money is worth more than Canadian, and prescription drugs are cheaper there.... They can be delivered by boat, Jet Ski, ferry, or just by walking across the St. Croix River in some places. One dealer takes his fishing boat near the Canadian shore and runs a remote-controlled toy boat to shore. His connection puts the pills in the boat. The fishing boat has never landed in Canada and the remote-control boat is too small to see from surveillance distance.... My Canadian law-enforcement counterparts are aware of the problem and are willing to assist any way they can, and I appreciate their help. I believe their primary focus at the moment is cocaine. Security at the border works both ways. Its intent is to keep unwanted things out of each country, but in doing so it also makes my ability to conduct surveillance on an American going to a Canadian drug dealer's house and back impossible."

In 2006, the Criminal Intelligence Service in New Brunswick linked some drug-smuggling operations on the border to Québec-based organized crime groups, who, it said, were attracted to "wooded areas and small rivers ... with limited detection." This made the border attractive as a two-way transit point: "Marijuana grown in New Brunswick is traded for cocaine." That was borne out two years later, when police, border patrol agents and federal drug agency officers in New Brunswick, Maine, and Québec busted a group of men planning to bring three hundred kilograms of cocaine from Colombia into New Brunswick. The plan was to bring it across the Saint John River between Edmundston and Saint-Léonard, then return to Maine with methamphetamines and Canadian-grown marijuana to be sold in the United States.

Few New Brunswickers, even few police officers, understand this

An unidentified border monument sits south of the Woodstock-Houlton crossing.
(Photo: International Boundary Commission)

dynamic as well as Inspector Goodwin, an amiable cop with thinning red hair. His first exposure to the border was in the mid-1990s, when he worked on the RCMP team fighting tobacco smuggling. The cooperation with counterparts in the United States Drug Enforcement Agency led him to work for the Mounties' drug section, and for customs and excise. He was later seconded to national security operations and became the senior Canadian officer for the Integrated Border Enforcement Team on the New Brunswick-Maine border. "We got to see a lot of things, especially dealing with IBET," he tells me.

IBET is designed to allow for more seamless joint operations by the U.S. Border Patrol, the U.S. Immigration and Customs Enforcement, the U.S. Coast Guard, the RCMP, and the Canada Border Services Agency. It makes it easier to share information and conduct joint patrols. The RCMP has desk space at the U.S. Border Patrol office in Houlton, while the Americans get a desk at RCMP headquarters in Woodstock. "I never really appreciated the border until IBET," Goodwin says. "You were just made more aware. Your ability to go out on the border, see the vulnerable areas, and then mix in the terrorism aspect — the whole reason you're there is because of 9/11 — it makes you look around, and open up a little more and say, 'Wow, you could smuggle anything through here.' You started caring about everything. Not that I didn't when I was with one of those other sections, but I guess 9/11 woke everyone up: 'This is our country.' And we got out and did our job."

IBET's stepped-up efforts against terrorism are catching more than drug smugglers. In 2005, the team got a tip from a hotel employee in Woodstock that three guests of Asian origin were acting strangely. Two other men, also Asian, had come to the hotel several times to see them. "We had reached out to partners and said, 'Look, if you see anything suspicious, give us a call,'" Goodwin says. "And this is where that worked." The RCMP put the men under surveillance and determined that the two men visiting the hotel guests were human smugglers, and the guests were their Korean customers. One night, "they loaded the three Korean nationals into a vehicle and took them out to a location close to the border, close to the Houlton port of entry. We had U.S. Border Patrol on one side, prepared to follow them."

Human trafficking and human smuggling are often confused, Goodwin explains. Human trafficking, rare on the New Brunswick–Maine border, preys on people who can't afford to pay. They often find themselves working in prostitution or in menial, under-the-table jobs to pay their debts to the traffickers. Human smuggling is more straightforward, a simple fee-for-service with no ongoing relationship between smuggler and customer. "It is a single transaction," Goodwin says. "The payment is a one-shot deal. No strings attached. Here's the border, you're across, see you later."

And it is happening with increasing frequency along Goodwin's border—still only once, twice, or three times a year, but he sees it as a portent. "It's the balloon theory. You squeeze one part and it goes to the other end. We're seeing that, there's no doubt. There's increased enforcement the whole length of the border, and they'll try out new areas. We've had people tell us that when we caught them. Why Woodstock? Proximity. You've got the I-95 corridor there right to Florida. You can hop off the Trans-Canada anywhere in New Brunswick and sometimes be yards from the U.S. border."

That night in Woodstock in 2005, the RCMP were unable to arrest anyone until the Koreans stepped across the border, because until that moment, there had been no crime. "It's a fine line," Goodwin says. "If we had had the grounds to believe these people were going to be smuggled into the U.S., we would have arrested them. Unless you have sources within a particular operation, it's difficult. When the grounds don't exist, the only proof you have that they want to cross the border illegally is when they cross. And then our jurisdiction ends."

So the RCMP watched and waited, albeit with a pretty good idea of where the smugglers would be taking their clients. It was a spot Goodwin won't identify, for obvious reasons. "The fact of the matter is, people are going to go to the easiest spot. We were conducting surveillance. We'd seen how they were dressed. We knew they weren't going to hike through anywhere. So we thought, 'Where would they go?' And sure enough, the surveillance indicated where they were going, and we followed them to this location, and we knew there was one way in and one way out. It's a familiar location to us, because we've apprehended people there before." The U.S. Border Patrol arrested the Koreans after they crossed, and the RCMP nabbed the smugglers, Min Kyeong Hwan and Yang Cheoul Bae, as they drove back to Fredericton. They pleaded guilty and were sentenced to seven and five years in prison, respectively.

Goodwin says Min and Yang told investigators the Koreans had paid five thousand dollars to be taken to the border. "They would be part of a network. It's word of mouth. It's word back home. . . . In the Asian community, for instance, 'Here's who you call' if you want family and friends to come over and join you. Mostly, that's what it is: people entering Canada, using it as a transit point to enter the United States to be with family, nothing more. When you look at some of these isolated areas and you understand what people would go through to get to the U.S., nothing surprises you any more. The most isolated terrain New Brunswick has to offer? Seen it. It's amazing what people will go through to get where they want to go."

"History embodies both permanence and change," the AIMS paper on Atlantica concluded, "and both have long-term effects. Specific policies, good and bad, come and go, while natural forces producing the circumstances from which these policies arise persist." Geography makes the movement of goods and people between the Maritimes and New England inevitable, the logic goes, so why not remove the constraints altogether? The small but dedicated community of left-wing activists in New Brunswick loudly protested that philosophy during a 2006 Atlantica symposium in Saint John. They argued that large American corporations would use open borders to colonize the Maritime economy and undermine labour and environmental standards.

These, of course, were the same activists who often lament that a single New Brunswick group of companies, the Irvings, have poor labour and environmental records, *because* few other companies are able to compete with them. There is another irony to their rhetoric: if there was any economic colonization going on across the New Brunswick–Maine border, it was happening in the other direction.

On my drive south from Fort Fairfield to Ladner Road, I glimpsed a massive industrial complex in the distance, near the town of Easton. The property was once a modest potato processing plant owned by Fred Vahlsing, who in 1965 provoked what was later called "the nicest international incident imaginable." The potato facility and Vahlsing's adjacent sugar beet-processing plant were dumping foul-smelling waste into the Prestile River, which flowed down to Mars Hill and over the border into Centreville, New Brunswick. Residents there, angry about the smell and the fact that fish in the river were dying, protested by using tractors to dam the river at the border. The publicity from their protest prompted a U.S. boycott of Vahlsing's products, contributing to his company's eventual bankruptcy. Not long after that, two ambitious brothers from New Brunswick swooped in.

Harrison and Wallace McCain founded their frozen-french-fry company, McCain Foods, in 1956. They expanded first by selling frozen fries overseas, and then by buying up processing plants, and eventually competing companies, around the world. McCain is New Brunswick's only truly global brand, with twenty thousand employees in more than fifty plants on six continents, producing one-third of all the frozen French fries on the planet. In the United States, McCain has plants in Illinois, Washington, Wisconsin, Idaho, New Jersey, Nebraska, and in Easton, the heart of Maine's so-called "potato triangle" of Caribou, Presque Isle, and Fort Fairfield. In 2000, Harrison McCain cut the ribbon on an eighty-million-dollar expansion and upgrade to the Easton plant, which doubled its production capacity.

As Bill Findlen pointed out, the import and export of potatoes across the border has often been political: in the 1980s, Maine farmers blamed price slumps on Canadian dumping, prompting a rash of protectionist duties, tariffs, increased inspections, and permit requirements. Such measures "are very political," one industry insider told me on the condition he not be identified. "Politicians have taken advantage of that by saying 'We're going to do something about the other country.' But it's their country, and they have a right to [impose tariffs and other measures]. Things happen on the border and our gut reaction is 'It's political.' Usually there's a reason for it. But this isn't water flowing downhill. It works both ways. If Canada stopped monitoring my food that comes in from other countries, I'd be upset." In recent years, technical agreements and harmonized inspection standards have overcome many of the irritants. "That border is just a line," the industry veteran told me. "You've got the same farming techniques and the same production techniques [on both sides]."

In the early 1990s, McCain Foods used fears in Maine about New Brunswick dumping in an unprecedented battle with the province's other outsized corporate player, the Irvings. The two sides will argue about which first violated a long-standing, unspoken agreement not to compete on the other's turf. Regardless, when Irving entered the frozen food industry by buying a small Prince Edward Island producer and renaming it Cavendish Farms, McCain saw a threat. And when Cavendish announced it would build a large frozen-French-fry plant at Grand Falls, right on the border with Maine, with $29 million in federal and provincial subsidies,

McCain fought back. Knowing potato politics, the company raised the spectre of Irving flooding Maine with artificially cheap fries. Soon the state's political leadership was calling on Washington to impose tariffs if the Cavendish Farms plant went ahead. Irving cancelled its plans.

Despite that fight, or perhaps because of it, the Irvings and the McCains are often thought of in tandem. Both families built their fortunes by processing natural resources, both grew to a scale far larger than anyone would expect in a small province, and both inevitably expanded into Maine.

Irving's gas stations are its most visible presence in the state, and New Brunswickers travelling there have the comfort of knowing those blue, white, and red service stations will provide them the same remarkable variety of convenience store products, the same clean washrooms, and, more recently, even the same decent coffee. K.C. Irving began supplying New England service stations from his Saint John refinery in 1969 and was soon buying up the ones that other companies decided were not viable because they were too far from their refineries. For Irving, of course, they were only a short and inexpensive trip across the border.

"The Maritimes are closer to New York and Boston than to Toronto," Arthur Irving, who ran the oil company after his father K.C., once said. "The richest market in the world is in the northeastern seaboard of the United States. That is the natural way for us to go." Author John DeMont speculates in his 1991 biography that the Irvings were typical Maritimers with a strong affinity for the "hard-headed Yankees" of New England. "Maine, a mirror image of New Brunswick with its untapped forests, rural unsophisticated economy and clannish citizens, is the natural place to begin an assault on New England," he writes.

J.D. Irving Limited, the family's forestry operation, moved into Maine even earlier, when K.C. Irving acquired a Van Buren, Maine, sawmill in 1946 as part of the purchase of the Reversing Falls pulp mill in Saint John. Two hundred thousand acres of forest in the northwestern part of the state were part of the sale. The company increased its holdings in Aroostook County in 1985, when it faced a shortage of wood in New Brunswick.

By June 2010, Irving Woodlands LLC was managing 1.2 million acres of forest in northern Maine, and the company was routinely referred to as the largest landowner in the state.

The Irvings have encountered vociferous resistance in Maine. Local communities fought the location of some gas stations, and the state Legislature passed regulations to deter Irving Oil from strong-arming local competitors. In Aroostook County, some residents complained about the environmental impact of JDI's clear-cutting practices. "I hate to see Canadians control my country," a storeowner in Aroostook County complained to DeMont. In 1996, thanks to Maine's referendum law, Irving faced a kind of fight it has never encountered in New Brunswick: a citizen-initiated vote to ban clear-cutting and regulate large forestry companies. The state government added a third option, a more moderate set of regulations, to the ballot. This compromise got the most votes, defeating the more radical plan, but was itself rejected a year later in a straight yes-or-no plebiscite. Still, Angus King, the governor at the time, says "there's much less clear-cutting in Maine than there was when this started and there's a more rigorous forest practices act." The industry, Irving included, heeded public opinion.

The company had little choice because it has almost nowhere else to go, and this is where their presence in Maine highlights a fundamental difference between Irving and McCain. For McCain, Maine is just another part of its global empire, another spot on the map where potatoes grew well: it just happens to be close to its home base. The McCains are not interested in being big fish in a small pond: they have moved into new markets, including fast-growing economies such as China, where wages are low and demand is soaring.

The Irvings, by contrast, seem to consider Maine a good fit precisely *because* it is so close to home. They were able to expand, but cautiously, in a jurisdiction that is similar in size to New Brunswick, and perhaps, as easily influenced. In 2008, they looked at adding the struggling *Portland Press-Herald*, the state's largest newspaper, to their New Brunswick media holdings. But J.D. Irving has never bought a mill in Finland or Russia or Asia, where truly global companies see their futures. By playing it safe, the company, paradoxically, left itself vulnerable when the domestic forestry industry was crippled by a rising dollar. Irving has no other place on the globe where it can move its focus. It is pinned down at home, even if "home" is a single swath of forestland straddling the New Brunswick–Maine border.

And that is the final and most striking aspect of the Irvings and the McCains moving into Maine. The potato-growing areas that feed the McCain plant in Easton, and the large tracts of forest owned by Irving on the Aroostook and south of the Saint John, overlap uncannily, almost perfectly, with the disputed territory that Britain claimed in the 1830s but that went to Maine in the treaty of 1842.

This is irony on a grand scale. It may be American territory, but two New Brunswick families dominate its economy. As a globe-trotting merchant, Richard Oswald would surely be relieved that his mistake in Paris in 1783 did not prevent Her Majesty's subjects from plying their trades in Maine. Oswald may have bungled the border, but his imaginary line hardly matters when there are millions of dollars at stake.

10. GIVE ME A BREAK

IT IS TIME TO MOVE ON, to leave the very arbitrary North Line and continue south, where the border is again a river: the St. Croix, the fulcrum of the boundary between Maine and New Brunswick. I want to find the very point where it changes, a place deep in the woods called Monument. For me, it will be the end of the North Line. From the perspective of history, it was its beginning. Either way, a retired customs officer named Bill Boone tells me he knows where to find it.

I found Boone online. In his seventies, he has reinvented himself as a webmaster, a designer, and host of Internet sites, including one devoted to the history and folklore of New Brunswick's York County. He knows the border well. He grew up in Forest City, a tiny community of Americans and Canadians straddling a narrow channel of the St. Croix River. There was rarely any excitement there. "Every once in a while, somebody would try to bring a washing machine over or something of that nature," he tells me as we drive from Woodstock along Hodgdon Road towards the North Line. In fact, Forest City residents often disregarded the line altogether. In 1966, moving to Ontario, Boone decided to drive through Maine, but he wanted to leave at four a.m., before U.S. Customs opened for the day. So he took his car across the bridge the night before. "I parked the car next to the [American] office. At four in the morning, I walked across, we got the car and away we went. That was quite common."

Boone likes to joke that he was recruited as a Customs officer at an early age. In the summer of 1954 he was driving his old '29 Dodge to see his girlfriend when he was stopped by the RCMP. He had no licence, but the cop offered him a deal. "You live right on the border here, right?" he asked. "You see lots of stuff coming across? I'm not talking about cigarettes or beer. I'm talking about washing machines, televisions, power tools. If you were to keep your eyes open and let us know, we might be able to work out a deal." The cop handed him a ten-dollar bill. "This'll show you I'm serious. Anything we get, you'll get a percentage of it."

Boone joined the air force, was posted to CFB Borden in Ontario, and forgot about the Mountie. But six years later, as a Fredericton police officer, he was arriving in Forest City late one night to visit his father when he noticed a black Chrysler with Alberta plates cross the bridge from Maine. Boone made a wide turn in the road as if to back into his father's driveway, then stopped, briefly blocking the Alberta car. The driver said he was lost. Boone advised him to stop and report at the customs officer's home a few houses away. But the man drove on, so Boone gave the plate number to the RCMP. Several months later, he received a letter from the RCMP telling him the black Chrysler had been stopped near Moncton and the driver fined ten dollars. Enclosed with the letter was a cheque for $1.20, the percentage Boone was promised six years earlier.

After two decades as a city cop in Fredericton, and a brief stint as the chief of police in Hartland, Boone became a border officer for real and spent twenty-two years working Customs and Immigration, mostly on the North Line. He never saw much excitement there, either, he tells me at first. Then, after a long pause, he adds, "I did run into a commercial smuggling operation. I was offered a six-figure bribe to turn my head." It is not a case he cares to describe in great detail, but it involved tobacco, and it took place in the early 1990s, when higher cigarette taxes prompted a spike in smuggling.

"It was probably one of the roughest experiences I ever went through in terms of stress, emotion, and the fact that the person who approached me was a fraternal brother that split the organization," Boone tells me as he drives. "Half of them blamed me and half of them blamed him." Boone was offered seventy-five thousand dollars to "turn your head at the border," as the man put it to him at the time. Others were already on the take, the man said. "I thought, 'Holy shit, if he's talking about customs officers, who in the hell can I trust to talk to?'" Eventually he confided in a neighbour, a Mountie, and soon Boone was at the centre of an elaborate sting operation. He wore a wire as he helped the smugglers schedule their crossings. The police and Customs successfully prosecuted them for conspiracy to smuggle and for bribery.

Boone is driving us south on Route 540 past farms, woodlots, and abandoned fields. He turns right onto Monument Road, pointing his car straight towards the border. I have been almost obsessed with finding Monument since my early research. As the source of the St. Croix River, and the reference point for all the negotiations and treaties that created the border, it was so important that it was marked "Monument" on most nineteenth-century maps of New Brunswick. But those maps are badly outdated now. On Google Earth, I spotted a white dot, clearly something manmade, at the precise point where the North Line becomes the jagged boundary following the St. Croix. But it is not clear how to get there. There are only faint brown lines cutting through the forest in the satellite images, and road maps show nothing.

I do know the first small stretch of the St. Croix below Monument is called Monument Brook. Boone is sure he remembers a Customs house and a bridge there. So after about a kilometre, when we cross a small bridge over a narrow stream, we stop, puzzled, and park at the bottom of a long driveway leading up to a farmhouse. We both wonder for a moment if this is the brook and the bridge Boone remembers, and if we have just entered the United States illegally.

Just then, a woman comes down the driveway in her car. We are still in New Brunswick, she tells us. The whole area is called Monument, but it is not *the* Monument we are looking for, and she has no idea where it is. We press on down the winding road, passing logging roads on the left. Soon Boone's car is bouncing awfully hard through deep ruts and puddles. He stops when the road became impassable and admits he is not sure where to go. But we happen to run into a local hunting guide, Mac Ritchie, who tells us he can take us there.

We follow him down one of the logging roads we passed, jolting along, passing thick stands of trees and clear-cuts, until Ritchie stops at a sharp bend in the road. There is a trail leading into the trees, obscured somewhat with long grass but visible thanks to some four-wheeler tracks. Boone and I head in on foot. We walk for about five hundred feet and emerge into a clearing. On the ground in front of us is a small, stubby, white concrete obelisk: Monument 1A.

I am crestfallen. This is the *second* marker on the North Line, not the first.

Then, remembering that each marker is supposed to be within sight of the next one, I look down the cleared vista. In the distance, perhaps half a kilometre to the south, is the tallest border marker I have seen, probably ten feet tall. It is obviously, unmistakably, Monument 1.

Boone and I set out down the vista, neither of us properly dressed for a hike down the final half-kilometre of the North Line, an increasingly wet and overgrown landscape of fallen trees. Branches scratch my face, and my shoes and socks are quickly soaked through. We try to use the thick layer of trunks and branches covering the ground as a kind of net to keep us above the ever more swampy ground. Though Boone's large, solid frame still conveys strength and authority, he is in his seventies, and he did not bargain for this. I tell him he can stop and wait while I press on alone. But the closer we get, the more determined he is. "We've come this far," he says. "We may as well go all the way."

We move up onto a slight hill to our left that offers higher and drier ground, but the trees are thick and we have to push branches out of our way, while staying close enough to the vista to keep the white monument in our sight. When we are directly east of it, we claw our way back into the clearing, then walk like acrobats along fallen trees towards our destination.

The square concrete base is about four feet across and several feet tall. Perched on top of it is the original, cast-iron obelisk from 1843, when the North Line was re-surveyed and cleared in the wake of the Webster-Ashburton Treaty. The obelisk says "Treaty of Washington" on its north side and "August 9th, 1842" on its south. The name of the British surveyor, Lieutenant-Colonel James Estcourt, is on the east side facing

The north-facing side of Monument 1 at Monument Brook dates from 1843.
(Photo: International Boundary Commission)

New Brunswick, and the name of his American counterpart, Albert Smith, is on the west, facing Maine.

Not in the Fort Fairfield blockhouse or the Friends church have I felt the weight of history so powerfully. *Monument.* The location was first marked by surveyors Samuel Titcomb and John Harris in 1797, as a British-American commission debated which of the many headwaters of the St. Croix would be considered the source under the Treaty of Paris. Titcomb and Harris placed some iron hoops around a yellow birch tree and carved "S.T. & J.H. 1797" into a small stake. Two decades later, a joint team of surveyors under Joseph Bouchette and John Johnson, assigned to follow the North Line until they found the highlands, replaced those original markers with a large cedar post bearing their names and the dates.

And a quarter-century later, Estcourt and Smith arrived here, accompanied by large staffs and more than a hundred local axe-men and foremen, bearing an obelisk — the same one shimmering before me now in the midday sun. The large concrete base is newer, installed by the

International Boundary Commission in 1972, but the obelisk is the very same one Estcourt and Smith erected in 1843.

This is where the border turns. Looking north, I can clearly see the vista carved into the woods, the North Line stretching off into the distance. To the south, though, nature itself indicates the boundary. There are no more monuments and no vista, only the swamp around Monument 1 coalescing into a green, mucky channel about four feet wide. It broadens out a few dozen yards to the south, becoming a brook, winding and weaving through the trees, the international border winding and weaving with it.

This is also where my journey, and my story, pivots. Though I am travelling in the reverse order of the border's history, from its newest section towards its oldest, I cannot help but think of the North Line behind me as the crucible for the boundary's contentious, fear-driven present, and of the St. Croix River stretching ahead of me as the place where its future — indeed, its *several* possible futures — waits to be discovered.

I photograph Monument 1, then Boone and I scamper out of the swamp and straight up the small hill through the trees. We emerge on the logging road, about a half-kilometre from his car.

The difficulty of reaching Monument 1, and the apparent ease with which we could have slipped across into Maine once we got there, reinforces Boone's contempt for the American security build-up. "It's laughable because from here on down to St. Croix you can cross there anywhere," he says. "They can't control those lakes. You'd need Marines out there, for God's sake. People are up and down there all summer on boats. The line follows the centre of the lake, but inevitably people, Americans, are in Canadian coves fishing, or vice versa."

That very remoteness, however, is why Inspector Daniel Goodwin, the RCMP officer involved with the Integrated Border Enforcement Team, sympathizes with his American counterparts. "When they are looking at the Canadian border, they are looking at a vast border where they don't have near the same resources that they do in the south. I would submit that when you compare the Canadian border to the Mexican border, there's no problem. But their thought is still that Canada is a haven for terrorists and that they have to do everything in their power so that terrorists don't get into their country."

I tell Goodwin about how Boone and I did not encounter any patrols at Monument Brook. We were careful to remain aware of where the line was, and never crossed it, so I ask Goodwin if one more step to the west would have got us arrested. "It's very possible. The fact of the matter is, without going into great detail, everybody knows scanners are a big part of it. Scanners are a big part of the technology used by law enforcement in apprehending people who illegally cross the border. That day, you could have set off a sensor. You could have been watched. That's common knowledge. The locations, the techniques, we couldn't discuss that."

As part of his work in border enforcement, Goodwin spent two years at U.S. Customs and Border Protection head office in Washington. "There are a lot of myths that I had the obligation, I believe, as an official from Canada to dispel. It's not as bad as they think. I had the opportunity to present to staffers on Capitol Hill. I started off by saying the 9/11 terrorists did not come through Canada. That's how I started it off. There were chuckles."

But Goodwin also feels he has to rebut the skepticism of Bill Boone and others. "I think we have to respect their moves to make their country safer. Coming back into Canada, I would submit, it's not that difficult. People have told me that you used to go over and everybody said hi, and now it's so stern. But it's a byproduct of the times, and the 9/11 incident. And you can feel for them because there was that closeness. The border was just the place you crossed to go see friends. But that doesn't exist anymore, to a certain extent. And you know, people who tell me that they don't have a passport and it's too much hassle — not really. Do it. It takes a day."

Some American officials do grasp the uniqueness of the Maine-New Brunswick line. A diplomatic cable from the U.S. Consulate in Halifax, made public by Wikileaks, described a 2007 trip by American consular officials from the Clair-Fort Kent crossing down to St. Stephen-Calais.

"After visiting these communities along this stretch of the border—where the people feel a closer attachment to each other through family and social ties than they do to either Washington or Ottawa, and where driving across to the other side to visit family or to buy milk and gas or to take in a movie used to be a matter of simply hopping in the car and driving—it is easy to see why they are reluctant to embrace the new reality of this post-9/11 world."

But embrace it they must. From the American point of view, Goodwin said, "'It can happen anywhere,' is what they're saying. But they understand. A lot of the people I worked with in Washington with Border Patrol are from small towns in the northern U.S., and they get it. ...It limits the ability to cross. But they're patriotic. They're taking their orders and they're marching with them. And there's no apology.... You can never guarantee a hundred percent. Canada's here, and we don't want terrorists here either. So we will work with you to try to make the border more secure, and that's exactly what we're doing."

Goodwin's attitude is typical Canadian pragmatism, or realism, at work. No one else, least of all Ottawa, can tell Washington what to do. If the United States is ever going to relax, even a bit, about its border with New Brunswick, the impetus will have to come not from Canadians but from Americans.

Which, it turns out, is precisely what took place in early 2010, fifty kilometres down the St. Croix from Monument Brook, in one of the tiniest border communities of all.

Forty kilometres south of Houlton on Route 1 is Boundary Road, which runs east towards the hamlet of Orient, Maine. There are signs for fishing lodges and boat repairs, and glimpses of a lake behind the trees. And there is a small bridge spanning a narrow channel of the St. Croix River, linking North Lake above and Grand Lake below. Both are part of the St. Croix system, making this trip across the bridge my first crossing of

Signs mark the divide, on the left at Orient, Maine,
and on the right at Fosterville, N.B.

the waterway, other than my brave leap over the four-foot mucky channel
at Monument 1.

At the other end of the bridge is Fosterville, New Brunswick, and a
small Canada Customs office. The guard asks me where I live and how long
I have been in the United States but requests no identification. Just past the
checkpoint, I turn right down an anonymous road — it has no provincially
designated route number — and ascend a high ridge with a breathtaking
view of Grand Lake, twenty-two miles long and covering more than sixteen
thousand acres. Mount Katahdin rises magnificently behind it. I follow the
lake south to my destination, Bill Boone's hometown: Forest City.

Forest City is two communities, one in Maine and one in New
Brunswick, sitting on opposite sides of another narrow channel of the
St. Croix. The little stream was once known locally as the Thoroughfare,
and people here have always considered the place a single entity. "I never
thought of it as 'not a foreign country,' I would have to say," says Blaine
Higgs, who grew up on the Canadian side and returns often to visit his
father, "though I never thought of my buddy in the U.S. as being any
different than I was, or his family, or the people over there."

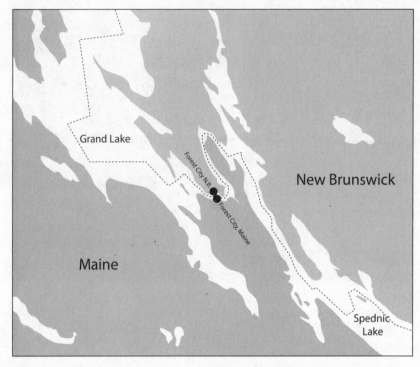

Forest City straddles the border.

Forest City was once a thriving town of more than three thousand people, with three sawmills, a grist mill, and two tanneries. But the tanneries closed more than a century ago, and by 2010 fewer than two dozen people live here year-round, most of them retirees or owners of fishing and hunting lodges. The homes are quaint, the setting bucolic, but the road in from Fosterville is rough. It does not lead anywhere else, at least not within New Brunswick, and is low on the province's road maintenance list.

The Maine side of Forest City is equally isolated. In fact, its odd geographical situation is one reason residents were so alarmed in 2003, when the U.S. government, citing tight budgets, decided to lock down the border at night and on weekends by installing and closing an imposing metal gate.

One arm of Grand Lake, gouged thousands of years ago by glaciers, stretches far south of Forest City on the American side, meaning the road out to U.S. Route 1 is a long arc. The trip to Houlton is a sixty-mile drive. But residents can shorten it by one-third if they cross to Forest City, New Brunswick, drive up to Fosterville, and cross back into Maine at Orient. It is a potentially life-saving margin for someone having a heart attack; closing the gate would have eliminated that and would also prevent Fosterville's volunteer fire department from answering calls in Forest City, Maine. "To a family of four living in Omaha, when the customs service can say 'We have locked down the border with Canada,' they probably feel a little more secure," Bob Parker, the owner of a fishing lodge in Forest City, Maine, told me in 2003. "But they don't know what they mean by 'lock down the border with Canada.' They haven't secured it any more. They've just made it inconvenient, and possibly more dangerous, for those of us living here."

The lockdown could have been justified if it had an impact on terrorism, but Jane Johnson, another American resident, pointed out there was so much wild space along the border, so many rivers, lakes, and forests, that "you're still going to have the ability for terrorists or whomever to come through wherever they wish. The only thing they can't do is cross on the road. The only people being penalized are those of us who try to cross legally."

Canadians in the area shook their heads in tandem with their American cousins. "We've all been investigated for CANPASS and PortPass by the FBI and the Royal Canadian Mounted Police," Chris Farrell, a volunteer firefighter in Fosterville, said of two cancelled programs for frequent crossers. "I don't see where we're an issue." Carl Higgs, a retired Customs officer on the New Brunswick side of Forest City, said closing the gate was futile if it was meant to stop a terrorist. "Get on the end of my snowmobile and I'll have him over across in ten or five minutes," he laughed.

I return to Forest City as part of my border journey to see what has become of the uprising against the gate. Things have worked out just fine, Jane Johnson tells me when I arrive at her house, on a small wedge-shaped piece of land between the main road and the St. Croix. "In the event of an emergency, everyone's been told they can go," she says. "You call and report that you're going to go through, if you can, if you have time, and

Jane Johnson stands at the edge of her property on the St. Croix River.
The New Brunswick shore is in the background.

if not, you call as soon as you get to the other end. And if an RCMP or
Border Patrol follows you and you're going straight to a hospital, they're
not going to question that. They may stop and ask, 'Did you cross at Forest
City?' but I don't feel that is a danger to us at all."

What allows the Americans to "go through" is a small plastic card, not
a revival of Nexus or Canpass but a new program — and a discreet one
at that. "It requires a little more investigation," Johnson tells me. "It was
intended for local year-round residents only. *You* can't get one. And it's
to facilitate getting to doctors, lawyers, you know what I mean, at eight
o'clock in the morning. We're facilitated to go through that way. It's a
special thing. You apply for it and you're quite well vetted."

"I haven't even heard of that," I tell her. "It must be —"

"It is," she says, smiling, but wary.

"It's official, obviously. It exists."

"It's official," she confirms.

"But it's not well-publicized," I say.

"Correct. Our theory is it's so the little old lady in Des Moines will feel safe, so that there's no such thing as people crossing after hours. We use that as our example. The little old lady there can fall asleep at night and know there's no way anyone can cross the border. Which is a total farce, but anyway."[11]

Bob Parker arrives at Johnson's and she pours him a coffee. "Going out of the United States, we can open the gates with a sticker that's on the car," he says. "Coming back in, you swipe your card in front of a reader and it calls Houlton and they ask you if you have any goods to declare, and they open it. The interim period between the time the gates went up and when we got our passes — it was a short period, and really, they haven't been a problem."

But a new problem emerged in 2009. The American government had piles of stimulus money it needed to spend building things, anything, to jump-start the economy out of a recession. And when the Department of Homeland Security got some of the money, it went looking for border crossings in need of upgrades and zoomed in on the tiny wedge of land down from Jane Johnson's house, where the U.S. Customs office sits near the bridge. "They wanted to take her land from here all the way to the border," Bob Parker says. The design plan for the new building would have required the expropriation of Johnson's property and the demolition of her house, a beautiful wood home of high ceilings and large, airy rooms.

What Washington did not count on was Johnson's connections. She once worked for William Cohen, a Maine senator and one of the most influential Republicans on Capitol Hill in Washington. Cohen was a mentor to Susan Collins, another Republican, who replaced Cohen in the Senate in 1996. So Johnson knew whom to call. "She fought it with the help of the senators and everyone else and they finally backed off," Bob Parker says. "So she thought she'd won the game. Then this phone call came."

Johnson pushes a button on her answering machine. She has kept two

---

11 Canada and the United States have revived the Nexus pass system, which now relies on biometric data such as retina scans, but it is in use at airports and major land crossings, not at minor ports of entry such as Forest City.

messages from March 2010. "Customs and Border Protection in the region are reconsidering Forest City and my instructions have been to contact you and request again a right of entry," says the woman, from the Army Corp of Engineers. "The area we'd be looking at, Mrs. Johnson, does not include your house." The women left her number, but Johnson did not call her. The next day, the woman left a new message. "We'd like permission to do some engineering, surveying, and evaluation of some of your land — not your house — and I'll be sending you out a package on Monday."

The Department of Homeland Security still had money to burn, and it was again determined to burn some of it in Forest City.

The new building would have been an eight-million-dollar monstrosity — some estimates put the cost at double that amount — complete with a four-lane approach road, detention cells, and an impound lot for seized commercial vehicles, all for a crossing that averages five cars a day entering the United States.

"People come up here to get away from the city and fish. Sometimes in the fall they hunt," Parker says. "If they had to come up and hunt and fish next to Wal-Mart, which is what you'd have with this phenomenal paved-in area, well, they wouldn't come. And it might take a few years, but pretty soon the sporting camps would be gone. Does it need to be modernized? Yes. Does it need to be bigger? Yes. Does it need to be as big as they wanted? No. Does it need all this truck-handling facility? No. What would a truck come to Forest City for? A moving van may come once every twenty years to move somebody's furniture. Other than that, trucks don't come here."

It is a short walk from Johnson's home to the bridge. Under the 2010 redesign, the house would survive, but, she says, pointing to some lawn, "this was going to be a truck rotary in my side yard." So Johnson dug in. She refused to return phone calls. She refused to sign documents. She refused to meet with Homeland Security officials, unless staffers from the offices of Maine's two senators were there too. "They called one day saying they'd like to come up and meet with me and allay any fears I might have," she snorts. "How the hell do you allay fears of taking most of your land?" And when they did arrange to come, Johnson told them she would not let them on her property. They had to meet down at the Customs office. "They thought they could beat me down," she says.

They were wrong. "I love to think about this because of the expression on their faces. I wish I'd had a camera. I can remember saying, 'So what if I don't sign this? What's going to happen?' 'Well we've never thought of that.' I said, 'Well, it's a fact. What would you do?' I was waiting for her to say 'We're going to haul you away.' They had not considered this option. So I said, 'You take the money and you save it, like anybody else would.'" But this was stimulus money, Johnson was told. "'Oh no no, we have to spend this, to commit it, by September 30.'"

Johnson did not budge. The bureaucrats from Washington felt their hearts sink further when they finally took a look around. "They do cookie-cutter ports," Parker explains to me. "There were three types, and only three types. 'This is a big port, this is a tiny mini-port, and this is a micro-port.' And there is no way that anybody can think any differently. The original program was probably a full-sized port. This year they come back with a micro-port. But nobody came out here. Nobody looked at the canal. Nobody saw anything. On a flat map, they say, 'Let's go to Forest City. Let's put in a micro-port.' When they came out here, they said, 'What's this big ditch?'"

The ditch is an old canal once used by the tanneries. It was long ago blocked off, but when the St. Croix is high, it still fills with water, directly underneath where the new building would go. "On their maps down in Washington, it's just a little squiggly line," Parker says. "They could have saved millions of dollars by just sending someone up here." There were other complications. The new building would have occupied the entire wedge of land between the road and the St. Croix River, right down to the bank. "They were talking about building two houses down in the marshy wetland area," Parker says. But each spring the river level rises considerably, meaning engineers would have to divert the stream near where it ran under the bridge, and the stream, of course, is part of an international waterway governed by a joint commission. "They realized they couldn't possibly do this because of wetlands, but they didn't admit it at the time," Johnson says.

Johnson tipped off several news organizations, who sent reporters to Forest City the day the bureaucrats were there. The journalists cast it as a David-and-Goliath struggle, not a national security issue. No one invoked a 9/11-style threat arriving via Forest City. Rather, it was framed as an example of wasteful, big-government spending. And at a time of rising discontent with Washington, the controversy inevitably went national.

John Stossel, the flamboyant celebrity-journalist from Fox News in New York, dispatched a crew to Maine. "Stossel's big deal, his main thing, is wasting money," Parker says. "His famous line is 'Give me a break.' The fact that it was a border issue was secondary." Stossel excoriated the federal government for trying to foist what he called a "pointless" project on Forest City. "Ten million dollars to expand a barely used Customs station?" he asked on national television. "Give me a break."

"That was pretty close to the turning point," Johnson says. "I think they were getting hit, and they didn't like it. And I think too they knew locally that this idea was half-baked."

Johnson and Parker take me down to Parker's fishing lodge, which sits on a spit of land where the waters of the St. Croix narrow from Grand Lake into the stream running under the Forest City bridge. There is a small dam there to regulate water levels at Domtar's pulp-and-paper mill downriver at Baileyville. Once, local kids from both sides of the border hung out here in the summer. "We'd gather at the dam, have a bonfire, whatever," Blaine Higgs tells me. "During the day, too — jumping off the dam into the river." Now it is off-limits. A U.S. Border Patrol SUV is parked in the trees nearby. Higgs, who became New Brunswick's finance minister in 2010, favours the idea of a security-perimeter agreement for North America, if only to make places like Forest City function the way they once did. "The lake, the restrictions, the obvious presence of border security, it's taken away the coziness of the village," Higgs says. "And having friends on both sides of the border, we really are separated now."

Jane Johnson has no objections to more patrols. But Washington's determination to spend and build beyond what is needed has now gone beyond what people will tolerate. When Johnson worked for William Cohen at his office in Presque Isle, which was responsible for all of northern Maine, she never saw a border concern cross her desk. But Collins's assistant told her he had complaints about fourteen of Maine's eighteen border crossings in a single year. And Washington's inflexibility holds out no hope of fewer headaches in years to come. "I don't think there's any way to get around it," Johnson says.

On a Friday evening in April 2010, however, the Department of Homeland Security, the sprawling bureaucratic behemoth that accumulated vast powers and received virtually everything it wanted in the nine years since 9/11, cried uncle. It surrendered at last, to a retired political aide and a white-haired fishing lodge owner in a tiny community on the edge of the United States.

This is one of the possible futures for the border: ordinary citizens who understand the absurdity of lockdowns and crackdowns finally telling their representatives that enough is enough.

It was a small victory, but it was a start. In one little corner of Fortress America, there was a setback for the culture of fear, and a glimmer of sanity.

PART THREE
BLURRING THE LINE

Sur des milliers de milles, la frontière entre nos deux pays ne peut être découverte qu'en consultant les étoiles.

— Wilfrid Laurier, Boston, November 17, 1891

All frontier people must be like each other!

— George Featherstonhaugh, 1839

11. "WE FRATERNIZE ON THIS ROAD"

JUST AS THE QUICKEST TRIP from Houlton to Forest City is through Canada, the shortest route from Forest City to the New Brunswick village of McAdam, thirteen miles to the southeast, is through Maine. The large, jagged shape of Spednic Lake, part of the St. Croix River system, has blocked any notion of a New Brunswick road. So I drive out to U.S. Route 1, follow it down to Topsfield, and turn east on Route 6 towards Vanceboro and the next border crossing on the St. Croix.

Vanceboro has seen better days. There is no downtown, just a scattering of small homes and a few businesses. In the heart of the community is a sprawling, seemingly abandoned rail yard, the last vestige of the good years. Thanks to the border, the boldly named European and North American Railway opened here on October 19, 1871 — called "Vanceboro's greatest day" — with an arch erected over the track: *Great International Railroad Opening* on one side, *San Francisco-New York-Bangor-Saint John-Halifax*. On the other side were two slogans: *The West Salutes the East* and *We fraternize on this Road*. Past is present: it was an earlier version of Stephen Harper's Atlantic Gateway, the promise of trade and prosperity that would flow from spending public funds on transportation links between the Maritime Provinces and New England.

"Never will this part of the Maine-New Brunswick border witness such a day as that of October 19, 1871," an observer commented at the time. And they were right: within three decades the optimism was gone.

A tannery and two wooden product manufacturers, lured by the rail links, shut down before 1900.

I drive down to Water Street and along the river. This is the outlet of the Chiputneticook Lakes, where the St. Croix narrows for the last time and begins its long, meandering run to Passamaquoddy Bay and the Gulf of Maine. There are two spans here: the railroad bridge (made famous in 1915 when a German soldier tried to blow it up) and, half a kilometre upstream, a road bridge. I cross it into New Brunswick, pass through the tiny community called St. Croix, and speed on to McAdam, five minutes down the road.

McAdam is not a border community in the strictest sense, but the village was created by the boundary and the railroad running across it. It, too, feels a little ragged around the edges. There are few signs of recent construction, and one of the village's main employers in 2010 is a nursing home, hardly a portent of future growth. But McAdam has one asset that Vanceboro lacks: a magnificent architectural remnant of its own glory days. A stone train station, one of the historic rail hotels of old, dominates the village, and in the evenings its entire length, two hundred and eighty-five feet, glows in the setting sun.

The mayor of McAdam, Frank Carroll, is inside, finishing a tour for a three-person television crew from CTV. They are filming an installment in a series on summer tourism destinations around the Maritimes. Carroll could give the tour with his eyes closed: the station is McAdam's calling card, and he promotes it relentlessly. He shows visitors everything from the restored dining room, remade as a 1950s diner with requisite jukebox, to long corridors of still-abandoned hotel rooms upstairs. Bit by bit, section by section, Carroll has been gathering funds, mostly from governments and corporate sponsors, to completely restore the building. "The architectural, conceptual drawings are all done," he tells me. "The idea is to be able to market two things: it's a niche hotel, special amenities, special features, that you'd want to come and stay at. And second thing, it's a conference centre where you can come with twenty-five or thirty people, where we can accommodate you with meals and meeting rooms."

The station, and thus the village, cannot rely on its past alone, Carroll

Frank Campbell (left) and Frank Carroll stand on what was once known as the Western Extension of the European and North American Railway in McAdam.

acknowledges. "It's got to make money to survive. It could never survive just as a museum." Like other small, isolated, rural communities, McAdam is desperately searching for a viable future. The mayor's plan is to create one by leveraging the two pillars of McAdam's history: its rail link and its location near the border.

"The only reason McAdam is here is because the Saint Andrews-Québec line was narrow-gauge railroad, and the one that came from

Graffiti points towards the United States near McAdam, N.B.

Saint John was standard-gauge," Frank Campbell, a member of the local historical society, tells me when he joins Carroll and me at the station. "And they crossed right here, and freight had to be hand-loaded from one to the other, because the cars couldn't be shifted on the narrow gauge. So there started to be some economic activity, and that put McAdam here."

The "one that came from Saint John" was the European & North American, the line crossing the border to Vanceboro, and it was built here for one reason: this was the way to the United States. In 1889, eighteen years after it opened, the E&NA was bought by the Canadian Pacific Railway, which used it and other lines to create a "short line" connecting Saint John to Montréal. Eventually sixteen trains a day stopped in McAdam, requiring a proper train station with a hotel. In 1900 the first section opened with the CPR design, including a steeply pitched roof and prominent dormer windows.

The railroad brought McAdam and Vanceboro together. Local residents used handcars to pump across the border for groceries or to fetch a doctor when one was needed. American Customs officers posted in Vanceboro came to McAdam to board trains heading into the United States. "They would walk through and check the ticket roster the conductor had," Campbell says. But, he adds, "there was no real inquiry in those days. It was pretty slack." Even in the 1980s, when Via Rail trains carried passengers on the old CPR route between New Brunswick and Montréal, there was little border enforcement, an unthinkable approach after 2001.

By 9/11, however, passenger trains were no longer using the short line through Maine. "The CPR snuck away," Carroll tells me. "It was little dribbles, little dribbles. Two jobs, four jobs, five jobs. They never really closed and left. They just really faded away, or tried to fade away. The passenger service got sloppier and sloppier because the company didn't want it, so the people who worked here didn't care anymore. It was very depressing."

And yet Carroll and Campbell believe the railroad, and the border, can give McAdam a future again. "We talk about tourism in this province and the biggest market in the world economically is just eight hours south of us," Campbell says, gesturing down the track towards Vanceboro. "Someone gets on the train Friday night in Boston and they can be in Moncton at 10 o'clock the next morning, right at the centre of the Maritimes. This line is still the only line into the U.S. in the southern Maritimes. This is still the major north-south line right here, and we hope that it will be feasible again." He shakes his head. "The Maritimes have always thrived when there was a north-south trade. It got screwed on the east-west Confederation."

Living in McAdam, Campbell has a good understanding of broader historical forces. And the political and geographical influences at work in 2010 have not changed all that much since April 9, 1864, when the New Brunswick Assembly passed a bill authorizing the construction of a railroad from Saint John to a location "not far from the outlet of the Chiputneticook Lakes," a place in the woods known first as City Camp, then as McAdam Brook (for the St. Stephen businessman who had logging rights in the area) and finally as McAdam.

Roads, whether rail or asphalt, are a long-standing predilection of New Brunswick politicians. Other governments build them when the evidence mounts that they are, or soon will be, needed. But elected officials in Fredericton authorize them seemingly on the presumption that their very existence will magically spur trade, growth, and employment.

The first stirring of grand railroad ambitions in New Brunswick was in Saint Andrews, on the Bay of Fundy, in 1828, when local leaders began agitating for a connection to Québec. The two colonial legislatures endorsed the idea, and engineers chose a route following the St. Croix River north, then continuing via Woodstock to Mars Hill, where it would turn west towards Québec. This meant the route would pass through territory in dispute at the time, and when the Americans objected, the line was put on hold. A competing proposal from Maine developers, to link Saint John to Québec via New England, also failed to materialize. Historian Alan Bailey speculates that had it been built, the Maritimes might have joined New England in a commercial union, "which would have made the political union of British North America an improbability to say the least." The temptation to connect by rail to Maine, and the implications of such a move, would shape New Brunswick politics for the next four decades.

By mid-century, the notion was gaining favour. New Brunswick's trade was shrinking and thousands of its people were emigrating. The Reciprocity Treaty of 1854 was still several years in the future, and when New Brunswick officials attended an intercolonial conference in Halifax in 1849, they said publicly that the poor economy might soon "impel the public mind to seek for relief by incorporation with the neighbouring republic." Britain responded by proposing to stimulate economic growth with a railroad connecting the Maritimes to other North American colonies, Upper and Lower Canada.

In Saint John, the merchant class cheered the news. Their city, they were certain, would be the terminus and main port for this great railroad. After all, it was the third-largest city in all of British North America, and its thriving port gave it a strong entrepreneurial streak. A reporter from Halifax wrote at the time that his own city's businessmen were "often indolent, always easy," while their competitors in Saint John were "eager, ardent, and untiring." London, however, favoured Halifax as the terminus for the intercolonial, in part to link Nova Scotia to the other colonies, and in part to have the rail route avoid Saint John altogether. In the event of another war with the United States, a line that close to the border could easily be seized and severed. A line skirting New Brunswick's eastern and northern shores would be less vulnerable.

In Saint John, however, this was taken as more evidence that the political class in Fredericton and London did not appreciate the city's greatness. There was more outrage at the subsequent rejection of a rail link between Saint John and Shediac. This was a viable project in its own right, given the need to get Northumberland Strait fish to market, but it could also be part of a future Halifax-Québec intercolonial route, provided, of course, that route passed through Saint John. After the rejection of the Shediac line, the city "was prepared to mutiny not only against the British government but against the province," W.S. MacNutt writes. Instead, it turned its rail ambitions where logic dictated, west towards Maine.

John A. Poor welcomed Saint John's interest. Poor, a Bangor lawyer, businessman, newspaper editor, amateur historian, and railroad developer, had viewed the Webster-Ashburton Treaty as a betrayal of Maine's interests. All was forgiven in 1850, however, when Poor welcomed business and political leaders from the Maritimes and New England to Portland to discuss regional rail cooperation. And now Halifax's port was a boon to Saint John. Halifax, Poor argued, was a better port for produce from northern Maine than New York or Boston. The shipping distance was shorter by one-third. But for Maine to ship through Halifax, a railroad would be required from Portland or Bangor through New Brunswick to Nova Scotia. And even better, this route could incorporate Saint John's desired line to Shediac. Poor called it "the European and North American Railway."

The New Brunswick delegation in Portland could hardly refuse, even with no guarantee of financial support from London. "To gain entrance to that [American] market and to be joined to it by a railway appeared as the object to be most greatly desired by the people of New Brunswick,"

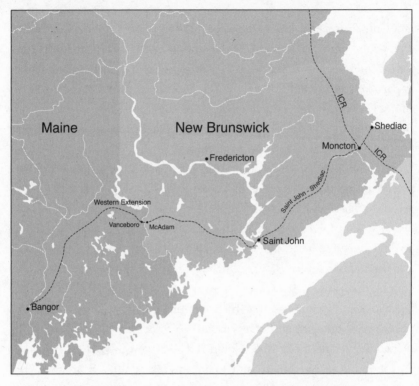

The New Brunswick government was torn between the ICR
and the Western Extension, linking Saint John to Bangor.

MacNutt writes. "Pressures that would cause the province to gravitate
more rapidly to the United States had triumphed." In 1853, a sod-turning
ceremony was held in Saint John for the section of the E&NA to Shediac.
The city celebrated with a parade and a ball attended by New Brunswick's
Lieutenant-Governor. "For Saint John," MacNutt writes, "the millennium
had arrived."

Among those attending the festivities was Samuel Leonard Tilley,
a druggist and temperance advocate. Tilley had been elected to the
Assembly as a reformer in 1850, and was named provincial secretary, the
most powerful cabinet position in the government after that of leader,
when the reformers took power in 1855. He would spend more than a
decade balancing his support for a union of British North America and
an intercolonial railroad, with his sympathies for Saint John's commercial

orientation towards New England and its push for a rail link south. When the E&NA ran into financial problems in 1856, for example, Tilley saw to it that the province took over the project.

The line between Saint John and Shediac, more than a hundred miles long, was finished in four years. But Tilley's balancing act was growing more difficult. New Brunswick's political obsession with railroads had become entangled in the broader debate about Confederation. Canada's Grand Trunk Railroad had reached Rivière-du-Loup, seventy miles from Edmundston. The Saint Andrews-Québec proposal had been revived and was under construction near the St. Croix, but was faltering. It was time for a decision about an intercolonial railroad.

In 1862 Tilley attended a conference of colonial governments in Québec to discuss the issue. He still wanted any intercolonial route to include Saint John, but he was a pragmatist. He would accept the route through northeastern New Brunswick if London insisted. When the conference endorsed London's choice, however, Tilley's Attorney-General, Albert J. Smith, a skeptic of union with the other colonies, resigned. "This scheme is, in my opinion, fraught with consequences most injurious to the best interests and welfare of the Province," he said. "It involves a heavy charge upon the revenue, which, added to the present indebtedness, will impose a financial burden . . . our population and resources will not justify."

The pressure on Tilley was intense. The Saint John merchants, alarmed about being bypassed by the intercolonial, began lobbying for the next phase of the E&NA, the so-called "Western Extension" to the Maine border. Poor told Tilley that without Western Extension, Maine entrepreneurs would soon extend their own lines north into Aroostook County and carry all the trade from the Upper Saint John through the state. But building a rail link to the United States, in the absence of an agreement on Confederation, carried its own risks. Annexationist sentiment in Saint John had been stoked by the earlier slights and persisted beneath the surface.

In Maine, too, there was talk of the Maritimes joining the United States. "The people of these colonies, like our own in their social habits and tastes, are more in sympathy with our institutions, than with those of the old world," said an address of the Maine Legislature sent to the Secretary of War in Washington in 1863. "Change from their institutions to ours, would produce very little shock to their social system." It emerged later that the author of the address was none other than John A. Poor, who would later tell a congressional committee in Washington, "The principles of our Constitution are of universal application, and our Government is capable of indefinite expansion. It must gradually cover the continent, or at any rate all portions of it where the people speak a common language."

The pressure for Western Extension grew even stronger when London imposed financial conditions on the intercolonial plan and Canada balked at the cost, throwing the whole scheme in doubt. In February 1864 a petition signed by virtually every merchant in Saint John was delivered to the Assembly in Fredericton, urging action on Western Extension. It may be going too far to say Confederation hung in the balance at that moment. But it was not as inevitable as it may seem now, from the perspective of the twenty-first century.

Nor was annexation the only other possible outcome, but it was plausible, as a Halifax newspaper commented: "In laying down the rails to the boundaries [New Brunswick] would be forging link after link of a chain which would bind them inevitably to the Chariot wheels of the North, commercially and socially at first, and probably politically afterwards." And the province was the hub of British North America. "Without New Brunswick, the geographical keystone, federal union could not proceed," observed the province's lieutenant-governor, Arthur Hamilton Gordon, A Fredericton newspaper expressed the dilemma succinctly in January 1864: "Duty and interest lead two different ways."

In April 1864, Tilley unveiled his attempt at a grand compromise, a package of legislation to appease Saint John without alienating the rest of the province. Subsidies were offered to any companies that extended the existing E&NA in any number of directions — so many directions that opponents dubbed it "the Lobster Act." Among the approved routes were two from Saint John to two locations on the Maine border, one of them "not far from the outlet of the Chiputneticook Lakes." It was left to the Maine developers to choose which one to link to. Their choice would become the Western Extension.

If Tilley believed he had engineered a successful compromise, he was mistaken. In late 1864 he helped draft the agreements on Confederation at Charlottetown and Québec. But the railroad issue, and particularly the question of Western Extension, had so consumed the political scene in New Brunswick that the agreement was immediately attacked. A new anti-Confederation coalition in the Assembly, led by Tilley's former colleague, Albert J. Smith, argued that if union were to proceed, the rail line to Maine would never come to pass nor the prosperity it promised. Tilley, on the defensive, promised to hold elections before introducing resolutions on Confederation.

Tilley dissolved the Assembly on January 30, 1865. The next night, he and Smith confronted each other at the Mechanics' Institute Hall in Saint John. "New Brunswick is likely to [become] ... a mere municipality," Smith told the crowd, "while Upper Canada with its 194 members will assume the right of taxing the whole," he said. When Tilley took the stage to rebut, he was shouted down. He managed to invite the crowd to return two nights later, but was greeted then by a dismaying mix of cheers, hisses, and groans. Denying Smith's predictions only lent them validity. Pointing out that construction of the Western Extension was guaranteed by the 1864 legislation only reminded the crowd that the law was a year old, and construction had yet to begin. Tilley also insisted, weakly, that the intercolonial's route could still be changed. "The power is yours," he said. "You are the jury, by whom the cause is to be decided."

Decide they did, sweeping Smith's anti-Confederation party to power. Tilley lost his seat, as did every other member who attended the Québec conference. Watching from afar, John A. Macdonald suspected American money had quietly funded Smith's campaign. His ambitions now seemed in ruins. Charles Tupper wrote from Halifax that had Tilley prevailed, he might have got Confederation through the Nova Scotia Legislature; now there was little chance. The entire project appeared doomed because of New Brunswick's wish for closer ties with the United States. "The people of Saint John have been so wild about this Western Extension question," Tilley would explain to one of Macdonald's ministers, "that any member showing indifference upon it, was almost certain of defeat—the opposition took advantage of this state of things, made many of the people believe that in Confederation there would be no Railway Westward."

John A. Poor quickly reappeared in Saint John to promote Western Extension, and both Albert Smith's new government and the city of Saint John bought stock in a new company formed to build the line. The sod was turned November 10, and Tilley joined Smith at a celebratory banquet to praise the project. But the decision to invest public funds split the new government, and when a need for even more capital stalled it completely, and Smith failed to persuade London to help, those internal divisions grew.

Smith's coalition was soon exposed as lacking any unifying principle other than opposition to Confederation. "This point having been disposed of," the journalist and author James Hannay writes tartly, "left them free to differ upon all other points which might arise." Tilley, meanwhile, freed from his duties in Fredericton, toured the province, speaking to crowds to promote Confederation. "We will watch the moment," he had told John A. Macdonald, "and be ready to strike a blow if there appears to be a chance for success."

The moment came in November 1866, when a by-election was held in York County. Tilley estimated the cost of a proper campaign at eight to ten thousand dollars, and persuaded Macdonald to pay half of it. Smith's candidate, John Pickard, a popular local lumberman, faced Charles Fisher, Tilley's man. The eyes of the British Empire were on the contest, for everyone knew that Confederation was at stake—even if Fisher chose not to emphasize it. "The question is not now confederation or no confederation (I consider that question virtually settled at the last election);" he wrote in a letter to voters, "but who is the best man to represent the interests of the county of York?" When he won handily, however, with a seven-hundred-vote margin out of three thousand ballots cast, everyone understood the tide had turned.

The pro-union forces now pressed their advantage. At London's urging, Lieutenant-Governor Gordon stepped in, working behind the scenes for Confederation. As a teenager, Gordon had written that he felt "an excessive desire to be eminent. I believe it is wrong and . . . I have tried to subdue it but in vain, and though I feel that it can never make me happy I still most earnestly desire greatness and power." As the son of Lord Aberdeen, a British prime minister, he easily landed work in the colonial service, and developed a love for hunting, fishing, and canoeing in New Brunswick's vast wilderness. But he was contemptuous of its politicians. "As a rule, to be a member of the Assembly is a proof that a man is uneducated and is not a gentleman," he wrote. Part of his motive for pushing Confederation, according to a biographer, was "the prospect of the abolition of his office which the coming of the federation would ensure" so that he could move to another posting "that would give more scope to his talents."

Gordon now nudged Smith's wobbling government to declare for some form of colonial union. With Fenian agitators active on the border near St. Stephen, Smith suggested perhaps he could, as long as it was not the Québec plan. Then he vacillated. Gordon responded by orchestrating an address to the Queen from New Brunswick's unelected upper chamber, the Legislative Council. It asked the British government to implement the Québec resolutions. Gordon pressed Smith to have his cabinet pronounce on the address, but Smith refused, and after a brief stand-off, his government resigned. In the subsequent election, Tilley's pro-Confederation party triumphed, and the union of British North America, with an Intercolonial Railway to bind the provinces together, was assured.

Gordon was not in New Brunswick to see it. His heavy-handed move against Smith persuaded London he was ill-suited to a colony with responsible government, and in most of his later postings—Trinidad, Mauritius, Fiji, the Western Pacific Islands, and Ceylon—unruly elected members were not a concern. In 1888, near the end of his career, he wrote that his diaries were "a record of a wandering and to a great extent a wasted life; and are full from end to end of unfulfilled intentions, disappointed hopes, unrealized projects, and unsatisfied ambitions. Few have started on a career with greater advantages than I did. Few have more wasted them, and thrown them away."

He was too hard on himself. Gordon's maneuvers were inappropriate, undemocratic, and likely unconstitutional. But they allowed Confederation to take place before Western Extension was built, perhaps preempting annexation. "Who will say that it would not have succeeded," asks Tilley's biographer, James Hannay, "if the several Provinces, which now form Confederation, had been disunited and unharmonious in their relations and pursued different lines of policy?"

In New Brunswick, Confederation was Tilley's triumph as much as anyone's. But on one count, he remained a continentalist. Among the final acts of the New Brunswick Assembly, on June 17, 1867, just two weeks before Confederation, was legislation to buy three hundred thousand dollars in stock in the European and North American Railway. This infusion of capital allowed work to advance rapidly on the Western Extension to Maine. The ninety-one-mile line from Saint John to the St. Croix was completed in 1869. Two years later, Bangor was connected to Vanceboro, and New Brunswick and Maine were linked by rail for the first time, years before the Intercolonial Railway was finished in the province. By then, of course, Western Extension was not an existential threat. "Once the union of the provinces had been accomplished," writes J.K. Chapman, "the cosmopolitan character of the European and North American Railway was sublimated, and it became just another railroad."

Still, its official opening in Vanceboro in October 1871 was not "just another" ribbon-cutting. Governor-General Lord Lisgar and President Ulysses S. Grant both attended. Grant likely had other things on his mind as his train travelled north to Maine: it was during a stop in Boston that he suspended habeas corpus in South Carolina to allow federal troops to capture and prosecute the Ku Klux Klan, which was resisting post-Civil

War Reconstruction. In those circumstances, it was difficult to imagine that he gave much thought to the forty hours of travel time that Europeans bound for New York would now save by landing in Halifax and taking the E&NA.

Yet this president who had seen his own country divided by war must have been struck by the displays of cross-border kinship. Bangor was draped in Star-Spangled Banners and Union Jacks, an estimated fifty thousand people turning out to cheer the new rail link. Lord Lisgar, Tilley, the federal minister of customs, and other Canadian officials had met Grant's train at Portland and joined him for the Bangor celebrations. *Grant and Victoria, Treaty of 1872*, declared a mural. *No fighting on this line.* After a lavish, mile-long parade, Grant told the crowd the railway would help in "fostering and building up a brotherly feeling between two great peoples of the same blood," while Lisgar said he hoped "that such meetings to celebrate the united enterprise of Americans and Englishmen would be of frequent occurrence in the future."

Then it was on to Vanceboro, which the *New York Times* correspondent called "this backwoods village which marks the line between the Republic and the Dominion." Beneath a massive tent, a banquet was held for more than twelve hundred people to mark the official opening of the railway. There were numerous speeches, and some touched on the difficulty Canada and the United States were having in negotiating their first commercial treaty, but the mood was overwhelmingly festive. "It is a pleasure for me to hear and see citizens of this continent belonging to the two nationalities meeting in such friendly communion," Grant said. With the platitudes about brotherhood and the occasional caveats to acknowledge disagreements, it was much like Stephen Harper's official opening of the St. Stephen-Calais bridge in 2010.

The difference was that in Vanceboro, the tableau was playing out for the very first time, among leaders who remembered the Aroostook War. Any lingering political and diplomatic tensions from the Madawaska border dispute were, after three decades, finally, officially, subsumed by the impetus of cross-border commerce and friendship. After the ceremony, the Americans boarded their train for Bangor, and the Canadians theirs for Saint John, and they went their separate ways. But they went on the same railroad.

The Vanceboro ceremony was a milestone in another way. Local players —Poor in Bangor and Tilley in Saint John—had the decisive roles in the railway battle. But Grant and Lisgar opened the line and sealed the connection. The end of the Civil War had given the American federal government a new primacy over the states. In Canada, Confederation had drawn power from the provinces, centralizing it in Ottawa. Maine and New Brunswick would never again have full control over their relationship. It would now be regulated by governments that were distant from the border and its daily realities.

In Ottawa, Tilley continued his effort to bring the Intercolonial to Saint John, but it was in vain. He managed, however, to make the city the terminus of the new CPR line running from Montréal though Maine. Later, as federal minister of finance, he was the chief architect of John A. Macdonald's National Policy. This system of tariffs and duties, designed to resist the pull of the United States by strengthening Canada's east-west economy, defied the logic of Western Extension, which Tilley had always supported despite the political headaches. As a Saint John merchant, Tilley understood that north-south commerce with the United States was vital to New Brunswick's survival. Yet he undercut it with the National Policy. Today, many historians and economists view it as a major error that disrupted historic trade patterns and relegated New Brunswick to the periphery of the Canadian economy.

Tilley might respond that in trying to have it both ways, he was typically Canadian.

"I don't think the north-south trade should have been a victim," Frank Campbell says, a little bitterly, sitting at a table just inside the McAdam train station. "And it was a victim because of tariffs."

After years away, Campbell returned to McAdam in 1994 to manage a

local plant that manufactured gypsum wallboard, used to construct walls
and ceilings. The plant had been trucking the product into the United
States. "The first thing I wanted to do — it was in my blood I guess — was
to reinstitute rail," he tells me. But Canadian Pacific was not interested in
carrying the freight there on its trains. "They didn't want to make money,"
he says. "They wanted out of it." The Irving group eventually bought the
track from CP, and Campbell gave them a call. "The next morning I had
three guys sitting in my office wanting business. And the trains are big
now. Irving's making money now, I tell you. He's mostly carrying his own
things. Oil, lumber, wood chips."

But there were challenges. "The sales staff had pushed people into
just-in-time delivery. So someone from Connecticut would call at four
in the afternoon and we'd have wallboard in New York City or Plainville,
Connecticut, the next morning. That's what they had developed." And that
meant shipping by truck. "If only they could have developed a strategy like,
'If you need wallboard next week, order now, because we can get the rail
here by next week, but we can't get the rail to you tomorrow morning.'"

Still, the wallboard plants employ a lot of local people, and Mayor
Carroll says the village has bounced back after hitting bottom a few years
ago. Like Campbell, Carroll is nostalgic about rail, but he also blames the
community's hard times on its decades-long dependence on the CPR. "The
railway was the Big Daddy in McAdam," he says. "The railway did it all. I
think back when we were kids, this community fought against building a
hospital. No hospital. Because we don't need it. We all have railway passes.
If we get sick, we'll get on the train and the railway will take us and look
after us. We had no fire department for years in McAdam. It was a railway
fire department. And as the railway moved away, suddenly the community
said, we've got no fire department. It was all dependent on Big Daddy."

Perhaps it wasn't the CPR that was Big Daddy, but the border itself. It
was why the railroad came here, after all, and it was immutable. But even
the border does not provide in the way it once did. New Brunswick refuses
to promote McAdam as a convenient crossing for tourists, Campbell
complains. "They only want to drive them through on the superhighway,"
he says. The province's marketing campaigns should instead be encouraging

visitors to use back roads to smaller border crossings like McAdam, Campbell says, to "get them into the real New Brunswick."

Try as they might, the two men cannot convince the province to erect signs on the Trans-Canada. "Out on the highway it should say 'U.S. border 30 miles' or 'U.S. border 100 miles,'" Campbell says. But modern technology is starting to accomplish what road signs cannot. "GPS has helped us a lot because it shows the shortest distance," Campbell says. "Even today," Carroll adds, "we had a lot of Americans here. We're getting them all the time because they're coming across this border because of GPS. They're saying 'Gee, we didn't know this was here.'"

This, too, is a battle already waged and lost. There once was a proposal for a so-called corridor road, from the I-95 at Lincoln, through Vanceboro and McAdam, to the Trans-Canada. "That would have been a good plan," Carroll says. "It would have cost a lot less money. They would have had to build some roads. But it would have been a more direct, short line from the eastern seaboard into New Brunswick. It would have been as feasible as trying to maintain two major border crossings at St. Stephen and Woodstock. They fool a lot of people who are trying to go to Nova Scotia and P.E.I. who go up to Woodstock and then down the Valley again. They wanted to make sure that St. Stephen and Woodstock maintained their borders, and they did. And as a result, we have very little to support getting traffic through this area. It would have made a big difference for us, if [McAdam] had got what should have been one major border crossing."

But the next generation of road is already on the drawing board. In 2008, a Maine-based construction executive, Peter Vigue, unveiled his plan for a high-speed, toll-funded superhighway across north-central Maine, to cut 200 kilometres and two hours off the drive between Montréal and the Maritimes. Vigue said it would be a road of the future, with high-tech "virtual border control" and electronic seals on transport trucks, but the vision behind it was as old as Canada — older, in fact.

"Collaboration is critical," Vigue said, sounding like a modern-day John A. Poor as he addressed an enthusiastic business audience at the Saint John Board of Trade. "We can't separate ourselves as a community, a country, a state, or a province. We've got to look at the big picture. When we improve the economy in our region, we're all going to benefit."

That is hard to imagine as Campbell, Carroll, and I stroll along the tracks of the old E&NA. Vigue's road would start at Calais, bypassing their little rail village on the St. Croix.

It is not just the trains and the border that have left McAdam behind. The future itself is in a hurry to get somewhere else.

12. THE GREAT GAME

I AM LOOKING FOR THE MILLTOWN BORDER CROSSING when I spot the Green Monster.

I have come to Charlotte County, in New Brunswick's southwest corner, by following Route 3 along the Magaguadavic River and then down to St. Stephen. At the edge of town, I join the freshly twinned Route 1 running to the border. These four seemingly ordinary lanes of asphalt leading to the new international bridge are touted by Ottawa as part of the "Atlantic Gateway" to New England, making them a modern-day European and North American Railway. But rather than continue into Maine, I take the last Canadian exit and follow Church Street into Milltown, once a separate municipality but now part of St. Stephen.

I recognize "the Green Monster" immediately when I glimpse it in the large side-yard of a big, rambling house. It is a faithful replica of the iconic, thirty-seven-foot-high left field wall at Fenway Park in Boston. The house belongs to Kathleen Booth, an elderly woman who built the wall with her adult son, Tom. Baseball is big in the Booth household. Kathleen's late husband, Bill, pitched in a local loop called the border league, with teams from New Brunswick and Maine. It was serious ball, but the rivalries ended at the local diamond: everyone shared a fervent devotion for the same major-league team. "When you're in Maine and southern New Brunswick, you're in the Red Sox Nation," says Kathleen's other son, Mike Booth. "This isn't Yankeeville or the Blue Jays. This is

Red Sox country." The Green Monster replica, complete with manual scoreboard, has become a popular backdrop for local Little League teams. From both sides of the border, they come out to the yard to use it as a backdrop for their team photographs.

Mike Booth tells me local people are unfazed by the recent increase in border security. "That doesn't mean anything. Of course people from away, from central New Brunswick or central Maine, they kind of feel it's a hassle. But here on the border, between St. Stephen and Calais, it's more like one single community. We don't think of it as an international border. We think of it as a river that separates one half of the town from the other half."

As if to prove his point, the U.S. customs officer who greets me when I cross from Milltown to Calais is the friendliest I have encountered, cracking jokes about the subject of my research. The small customs office is also a throwback, completely unlike the sterile, modern fortress farther upriver. This one is a small white building the size of a modest bungalow, with a single lane for car traffic. [12]

There had been a bridge at Milltown for three decades by the time the lieutenant-governor of New Brunswick, John Henry Thomas Manners-Sutton, paid a visit to St. Stephen, the largest town on the British side of the St. Croix River, in 1855. During the visit, he also met American residents of Calais. "There was nothing," writes W.S. MacNutt, "to distinguish the mannerisms of the two peoples of the border from one another."

Though the border here is the oldest section of the line separating New Brunswick and Maine, the people have always treated the area as a single community. The first large group of European settlers arrived around the time of the American Revolution, and the first residents of Calais, lacking lawyers and a courthouse, often relied on a St. Stephen justice of the peace to collect debts. During the War of 1812, the lone Methodist minister on the river, Duncan M'Coll, whose congregation was almost

---

12 A U.S. government Web site listing border stations on the National Register of Historic Places explains that Milltown is excluded because it "unfortunately has lost its design integrity."

equally American and British, played a key role in keeping the peace locally. In the era of the sawmills, lumber from both sides of the river was shipped not only to England and the British West Indies but also to New England, and mill owners in Calais worked with counterparts in St. Stephen to run a boom across the river. The communities eventually

Markers in downtown Calais spell out the options.

shared a gas light company, a water utility, trolleys, a telephone exchange, and starting in 1887, a small hydroelectric dam at Milltown.

It is to the dam that I drive, to see a border connection not of the personal kind but of the electrical variety. It is not a new facet of the relationship, but it appears destined to grow in importance in the twenty-first century, perhaps even to redefine the Maine-New Brunswick dynamic.

"It's just poles and lines," Scott Hallowell says, suppressing a laugh, as he points out a pair of wooden poles at the end of a small side street in Calais near the river. From the poles, three ordinary-looking metal cables stretch down the slope leading to the St. Croix River and to the oldest hydroelectric dam in Canada.

For decades it powered a cotton mill on the New Brunswick riverbank as well as the lights of St. Stephen, Milltown, and Calais. In 1946, with demand growing on the Canadian side of the border, Calais pulled out and set up its own utility, the St. Croix Electric Company, though it maintained the connection and continued to occasionally draw some

Scott Hallowell, CEO of the Eastern Maine Electrical Cooperative, stands near the transmission cables that bring power from across the border to New Brunswick.

electricity from the dam. In 1957 the cotton mill closed, and New Brunswick's publicly owned energy utility, NB Power, bought the dam, inheriting the connection to Maine and to the Calais utility, an enterprise run in 2010 by Scott Hallowell.

Hallowell, an affable forty-something wearing a golf shirt and casual pants, is the chief executive officer of the Eastern Maine Electrical Cooperative, the heir to Calais's St. Croix Electric Company. The small, customer-owned, non-profit utility serves most of Washington County and small sections of Hancock, Penobscot, and Aroostook counties. This territory has no cables connecting it to ISO New England, the sprawling regional transmission grid shared by utilities in Maine, Massachusetts, Connecticut, Rhode Island, Vermont, and New Hampshire. With no link, Hallowell's little co-op has to get its electricity from New Brunswick, via the sixty-five kilovolt line running across the St. Croix at the dam. "Electrically we've never been part of the United States," Hallowell tells me. "We're Canadian, electrically."

The link is more than a century old, but the transaction, the buying and selling of electricity, is in a period of flux. In the twenty-first century, at the behest of the United States Federal Energy Regulatory Commission, utilities on both sides of the border treat the generation, transmission, and distribution of electricity as separate functions. They are often handled by separate companies, which compete in the market with others providing the same service. The Eastern Maine co-op does not own generation plants. It merely distributes to its retail customers power that it must buy in bulk from elsewhere. And on the international border, that "elsewhere" is, by necessity, New Brunswick's public power utility.

The co-op also obtains some of the excess electricity from a pulp mill upriver at Baileyville, Maine, which sells excess power onto the grid, a transaction brokered by NB Power. And, in an echo of another part of this story — the search for the highlands — NB Power is also linked to windmills atop Maine's Mars Hill, a hundred miles away, and to the Tinker Dam, a privately owned hydro dam on the Aroostook River, which feeds power to both Maine and New Brunswick through Maine Public Service, another local utility lacking a link to the larger New England grid.

All of this is notional: kilowatts are a measurement of pressure. One cannot follow a given electron from Maine onto the New Brunswick grid and then back into the United States. But the electrons do move back and forth, without regard for the border. The level of integration is, conceptually, dizzying, and it is only a microcosm of the larger regional energy market that seems to have rendered the international boundary irrelevant.

"It is and it isn't," Hallowell says. "It is relevant in that politically there are two different regions. But since the forties and mid-fifties, we have had a tremendously good business relationship with New Brunswick Power, so I don't look at this border as an issue in our relationship with them. We had agreements with them prior to deregulation. What the border does is create more record-keeping. You have to report to the Department of Energy what comes across the border in both directions. It's a different marketplace, not part of the New England marketplace, but that's not a bad thing. It's just different."

Scott Hallowell's little co-op is not the only utility that understands the importance of the New Brunswick-Maine border. The line is the fulcrum for an energy market that encompasses what we think of as Atlantica and beyond. "It's just geography," says Darrell Bishop, a retired vice-president of NB Power. "That's one thing about the electricity market. It's not a global market at all. It's constrained by the evolution of the technology as we know it now." Electricity dissipates as it moves along a transmission cable, so the longer the distance, the less energy gets through. The best market is always the one next door, regardless of political boundaries. "You actually have to constrain it to geography," Bishop says. "Otherwise it's like the turnip truck, and all the turnips fall off the truck before you get to the destination."

This dynamic was brought into sharp relief in the fall of 2009, when officials from Hydro-Québec, the largest electrical utility on the continent, swooped into Fredericton, hungry for a new, virtual transmission link with the state of Maine.

As Shawn Graham, then the premier of New Brunswick, told the story, the discussions began in January 2009, when he and the other Canadian premiers were meeting with Stephen Harper at 24 Sussex Drive, the official residence of the Canadian prime minister. During a break, Graham chatted in the hall with the premier of Québec, Jean Charest, and suggested their two governments look for new areas of cooperation in the energy sector. Graham needed a game-changer. The cost of the Point Lepreau nuclear refurbishment was mounting, and NB Power's debt loomed over the province's long-term financial outlook.

It would later be claimed that the notion of selling NB Power in its entirety to Hydro-Québec did not emerge until the spring. In late June, Graham and Charest issued a joint press release announcing their desire "to step up their discussions with a view to developing partnerships in the energy sector." Officials would discuss "accessibility, supply, transmission, market opportunities, and greenhouse-gas reduction." The wording seemed innocuous, just standard political rhetoric, and the press release passed largely unnoticed by journalists and others. By fall, however, rumours began to circulate that something big was coming. "It'll be the

Québec Premier Jean Charest and New Brunswick Premier Shawn Graham
sign the preliminary sale agreement on October 29, 2009.
(Province of New Brunswick photo)

most important debate we have in the history of New Brunswick in the
Legislature," the province's energy minister, Jack Keir, told reporters.

The Graham government chose an appropriately historic setting to
unveil the deal: Government House, where Arthur Hamilton Gordon
sent the Smith government packing in 1866, clearing the way for
Confederation. Graham's announcement felt no less momentous. Never
before in Canada had one province's publicly owned entity bought
another's. Before a room packed with Liberal operatives, business
people, and other insiders, Graham pitched the deal as one that would
guarantee "lower power rates for New Brunswick residents and New
Brunswick businesses, in every corner of our province." The other main
benefit of the sale was the five-billion-dollar price Québec would pay,
wiping out all of NB Power's debt.

Charest pitched the deal as nation-building, tying Québec more
securely to the rest of Canada and making it more difficult for the
province to separate some day. But his other geopolitical motive was

plain: to acquire NB Power's transmission links to Maine. "The real issue, if we have our eyes on the ball, is to the south of us," he told the crowd at Government House. "That's where things are going to happen. The Americans need clean, renewable, energy, and they need a lot of it. And guess what? We in Canada are the ones who can supply it. But we have to learn to work together. And if you look at New Brunswick and Québec, there is no more natural relationship and agreement than the one we have here. We're maximizing each other's assets."

For Charest, New Brunswick's main asset, plainly, was its border. "What does New Brunswick have?" he asked rhetorically. "It has a geographic position that's fantastic. . . . This allows us to work more closely with our American partners, and to do something that makes sense: link the producer directly with the buyer. And the corridor between the two is now something we can share with New Brunswick, that allows us to efficiently develop these interconnections with our American partners."

It sounded visionary, even historic. And it was. There was one problem. New Brunswickers hated the idea. A report prepared for the government by Toronto-based communications consultants found the agreement was, politically, dead on arrival. "The public appears set to assume they are the losers," according to a summary of one focus-group session. "If it's losing money," one participant said of NB Power, "why would [Québec] want to buy it?"

Danny Williams understood why. Williams, the premier of Newfoundland and Labrador, wanted to develop large-scale hydro dams on the Lower Churchill River in Labrador and export the electricity to the United States. But unlike New Brunswick, his province lacked a border with the Americans. Without a guaranteed route through another province, it was too financially risky to start construction on the Lower Churchill. Québec was the only viable land-only route, and its transmission regulator was taking forever to rule on Newfoundland's bid for space on the Hydro-Québec grid. Williams was convinced this was no coincidence: Québec's 1969 contract for transmission from dams on Labrador's Upper Churchill River gave it most of the profits, and it had since established itself as the lead exporter of hydro power to the

United States. Williams's determination to do it right this time represented a challenge to Québec's dominance of the U.S. hydro market. He was convinced Québec's transmission regulator was stalling.

Williams's government and the provincial utility, Nalcor, went looking for another route to the U.S., by subsea cable from Labrador to the island of Newfoundland, then by another submerged cable to Nova Scotia, and by land into New Brunswick and across the border to Maine. Now, Hydro-Québec's bid to buy NB Power, Williams fumed, was clearly an attempt to block *that* route as well. It was a modern-day, Atlantica version of the Great Game, the nineteenth-century geopolitical chess match between Russia and Britain for control of Central Asia. Richard Oswald would have been awestruck at the billions of dollars at stake in a fight over the line he had drawn.

What Québec was after: three pairs of cables suspended on towers, cables as discreet and unassuming as Calais's little electrical link to New Brunswick. I passed under the cables on my drive from Houlton to Forest City without realizing it. On Google Earth, they are easy to find: they run through a fifty-metre-wide clearing in the woods, stretching from an NB Power substation near Fredericton, across the Saint John River, then over the St. Croix into Maine and on towards Bangor. The cables are known as the MEPCO line, for the Maine Electric Power Company, the consortium that built the American section.

It is this connection that makes New Brunswick part of the regional electricity market covering Atlantica. Unlike the Milltown dam, the Mars Hill wind farm, and the Tinker Dam, the MEPCO line—a 150-mile-long, 345-kilovolt corridor completed in 1969—plugs directly into the main New England grid. From there, you can follow the cables all the way to southern Connecticut, not far from New York City.

The New Brunswickers who supported the construction of the line had a keen sense of geography and of the north-south dynamic running across the border with Maine. "I'll tell you how this all unfolds, because there was a grand scheme in place," Bishop, the former NB Power executive, tells me. "We foresaw Hydro-Québec being interconnected with New Brunswick and recognized that was a route [for their sales to the United States]. And we knew that Churchill Falls was coming on, and Québec had a piece of that, and energy would be available." The Upper Churchill contract gave Québec surplus power, which it sold to New Brunswick via another new transmission link. New Brunswick, in turn, could sell its own surplus generation, at a profit, into the United States via the MEPCO line. The line also allowed NB Power to bring in New England utilities as investors in the construction of new generating stations, in return for a share of the profits and the electricity.

Cross-border sales grew when the United States decided, in 1977, to require its utilities to tender for the generation of power. Utilities that could produce energy cheaply near large markets saw an opportunity. The MEPCO line allowed NB Power to bid on those tenders deeper into the New England market. "That," says David Hay, a former president of NB Power, "was the catalyst for change in the market."

Once again, historic links driven by proximity were trumping notions of domestic sovereignty. "There's this idea of the east-west grid," Hay says. "Well, the power's going to go where the highest-priced market is, and where the biggest demand is. . . . So if Maine is paying ninety-two percent higher rates than what we are in New Brunswick, you can understand why [NB Power is] interested in them as a market. We're just not interested in other provinces. So the idea of going east-west over long lines, with long line losses, is no different than saying to Alberta, during the National Energy Policy, 'See that oil there—make sure it gets to New Brunswick real cheap.' Why would I want to do that when I'm selling it to North Dakota?"

The north-south impetus grew again in 1996, when the Federal Energy Regulatory Commission in Washington ruled that any energy utility selling in the U.S. market had to open itself to the same competition that American utilities faced. The province split NB Power into separate generation, transmission, distribution, and nuclear companies, so that competitors outside the province could, in theory, bid to supplant their roles in New Brunswick's market. The splitting of the company also gave Québec and others the right to bid for use of New Brunswick's transmission grid, to move their own electricity into Maine via the MEPCO line.

By 2007, around twenty percent of the electricity on New Brunswick's lines was generated from outside the province, and an equivalent amount of generation from inside the province was being sent to non-NB Power customers. The province's transmission grid, and its MEPCO connection, was emerging as such a strategic asset that a second link to Maine, known as the Northeast Reliability Interconnect, was built and activated, primarily as a back-up to the aging MEPCO line.

This new cross-border electricity marketplace is constantly changing. Demand moves around the region depending on the time of year. New Brunswick needs extra electricity in winter. In summer, New England, with its appetite for air-conditioned comfort, is seeking deals. This, combined with the open transmission market, created a new opportunity for NB Power to strike short-term supply deals at premium prices. "That's the next incursion into the U.S.," Hay says.

That incursion is plotted, day-by-day, hour-by-hour, from an office on the fourth floor of NB Power headquarters in downtown Fredericton, where a rotating team of energy traders is on duty, around the clock, seven days a week, at a high-tech sales desk. The large open space does resemble a small trading floor, except the people here, a mix of generating-station veterans and young, business-savvy go-getters, trade in electrons.

When I visit the office, Mike Leclerc, a specialist in short-term sales, is watching a bank of computer monitors showing power usage, weather data, the exchange rate on the dollar, the status of the province's large industrial electricity customers, and how various generating stations in New England are running at the moment. Depending on what happens around the region, Leclerc can, with a single call, order a New Brunswick power plant to start generating electricity to be sold into the United States.

A typical summer day for Leclerc is like a carefully choreographed dance. Today he began the morning buying from ISO New England, when its prices were cheap. This allowed NB Power to start building up water behind the idling Mactaquac Dam, New Brunswick's largest hydro dam, near Fredericton. Then Nova Scotia started buying from New England, too, and the price doubled. "So I'm pulling out a bit," he says, "and I know this afternoon the prices are going to be even higher." Sometime after lunch, Leclerc will tell Mactaquac to start running, because by then it will be cheaper than buying from New England. By this evening, his replacement on the night shift will try to sell Mactaquac's power into New England; at that time, it will become the Americans' cheapest option. "It's like a stock market," Leclerc says. "The more you sell, the lower the price. The more you buy, the higher the price."

A few feet away, another trader, Kim McKinley, is watching other streams of data, looking ahead by a day, a week, a month for longer-term deals. She is studying load forecasts, the amount of electricity NB Power's plants expect to generate in coming days, and matching that with weather forecasts to predict how much generation will be needed. The larger strategy is to generate profits so NB Power can keep its own rates low. "It's awesome," she says. "You get a little rush. When you make a good deal you really feel good about yourself."

The team still talks about the colleague who bought five hundred megawatts of power for twelve hours at *zero* dollars. "There was too much energy going into the market in New England," Leclerc says. Plants there were running at night to make sure there was enough load for the next morning, but others were selling into the New England pool at the same time, creating a surplus. "They were just dumping that energy, so the marginal price went down to zero," McKinley says, shaking her head.

Overseeing the group is Kirby O'Donnell, NB Power's director of marketing, who tells me the team could never do what it does without New Brunswick's borders with New England, a voracious consumer of electricity, and with Québec, the continent's biggest producer of clean, low-cost hydroelectricity. "We're kind of the little player in the middle, but that's the key," he says. "We're in the middle." If Nova Scotia wants to put electricity into New England, or if Prince Edward Island's nascent wind-energy farms go looking for American customers, they have to pass through New Brunswick. Under Washington's energy regulations, NB Power must let them through, but it can, and does, charge them. "That's where the value of our transmission system and our geographic location comes in. They're not going to get there unless they come through us, and if they come through us, they're going to pay us and help us keep our rates down."

In the long term, O'Donnell says, transmission through New Brunswick can only grow in importance. "Let's face it. Québec and Newfoundland have an enormous amount of carbon-free energy. And as the New England states mandate more carbon-free energy, where are they going to find it? You can only build so much wind. What's going to happen in Newfoundland with the Lower Churchill? To me it's only a matter of time before that's developed, and that energy will move somewhere."

The cross-border market has, in fact, become a self-fulfilling prophecy. The new Northeast Reliability Interconnect, MEPCO's back-up double, was built to *allow* more trading, but it was viable because NB Power knew there *would* be trading. "We had a high confidence level — with Hydro-Québec around — that there is going to be traffic on this line," Hay says. Québec had generation to sell, its own links to New England at the Vermont border were at full capacity, and building its own new transmission would be expensive and time-consuming. So when the new line was complete, Hydro-Québec bid for the whole thing — all of its capacity. "From our perspective," Hay says, "we don't mind at all because the mortgage is being paid, we have nothing to put on the line, and we've still got the security.

"Not to venture into the Hydro-Québec issue," he adds, "but that's why it was all the more disappointing that, as we were moving down that Hydro-Québec route, somebody didn't say, 'Is there another way to accomplish what we want to do here?' Like, maybe we could sell another line, as opposed to . . ." His voice trails off. What Hay has stopped himself from discussing is a subject he has steadfastly avoided talking about since his departure from NB Power early in 2010: Shawn Graham's proposal to sell off to Québec the utility itself, and in effect, New Brunswick's geographic advantage on the U.S. border.

By the time Jean Charest landed in Fredericton to sign the agreement with Graham, Danny Williams had already accused him of blocking Newfoundland's energy ambitions. "The rule for energy distribution and transport is an open market," Charest responded during the news conference at Government House. "It is in the vital interests of Québec that there be an open market. We want to build more capacity to sell clean and renewable energy to our neighbours, particularly the United States. If there's anybody in this country who believes in open markets, we are it." But polling for the Graham government showed seventy-four percent of New Brunswickers agreed with Williams and his crusade against the deal.

Subsequent polling went from bad to worse. "All messages find less traction in the second week," the consultants reported to the Graham government in early November. "New information is driving negative views of the deal by a three-to-one margin." The premier's promise of "lower rates for residents," it turned out, was actually a *freeze* on rates; they were only "lower" compared to a scheduled three-percent increase that would occur without the sale. Equally damaging, the province's estimate of five billion dollars in rate savings turned out to be drawn from the air, based on no set time period. And the large power rate cut for big industrial plants was soon seen as a favour to J.D. Irving Limited, which had suggested it might move its Saint John paper mill to Québec for lower electricity rates there. "This deal has nothing to do with us," said a focus group participant. "It's all about Shawn and his friends."

Even Graham's Liberal Party was not immune to skepticism. Many delegates to a scheduled party policy convention expressed doubts during a question-and-answer session with the premier and his ministers. "You should stop, slow down, and really study it, even if you have to go to an election," one delegate told them. "They want our transmission lines, that's for sure." In January, Justice Minister Mike Murphy resigned, and Social Development Minister Kelly Lamrock said publicly that he could not vote in favour of the deal and that "a whole bunch of my colleagues" felt the same way. Lamrock did not disclose that the caucus had already endorsed a revised agreement, but the amended deal was not enough to forestall a second resignation in February by another minister, Stuart Jamieson, who wanted a referendum held on the sale.

The second version of the agreement saw New Brunswick maintain nominal ownership of NB Power. Only the hydro dams and the Point Lepreau nuclear generating station would be sold to Hydro-Québec, for a reduced price of $3.2 billion. But it emerged that Québec was also given transmission rights to go with those plants. "You don't need to *own* the transmission lines to be able to use the transmission lines," said Hydro-Québec CEO Thierry Vandal. Added Jean Charest: "We continue to meet the objectives we had set for ourselves from the outset." Now the opponents could attack the deal for still giving Québec the asset it coveted most — *de facto* control of transmission access to the United States — but for less money than New Brunswick would have received under the original agreement.

The pressure continued, with protests at the Legislature and with elected members being harassed at their constituency offices and community events. The Liberals pushed back the deadline for a final contract to make time for public hearings, but nothing, it seemed, could satisfy the public short of cancelling the deal altogether. It finally happened in March, though Graham told the Legislature that he was not giving in to protests. He said Hydro-Québec, one of the world's foremost builders of hydro dams, had, at the last minute, discovered some technical concerns with the Mactaquac hydro dam, prompting it to ask for further financial concessions from New Brunswick. "Our government could not accept that," Graham told the Legislature.

The reasoning left the premier in an awkward position. Graham claimed to have learned a lesson about listening to voters, even though he insisted he was not caving in to public opinion. Six months later, he was defeated at the polls in a Progressive Conservative landslide. Graham's government became the first to lose power after a single term since Albert Smith's anti-Confederation party was defeated in 1866.

The antipathy to the Québec deal appeared largely based on a straightforward impulse to keep a Crown utility public, or to lash out at a government seen as catering to the province's wealthiest industrial family. Most voters understood only in the vaguest terms that, for Québec, the *border*, and transmission access to it, had been the big prize. In the new electricity marketplace, New Brunswick's historic connection to Maine, built first by rail and road, then by power cables, is coveted by other governments.

In defeating Graham, voters unknowingly preserved that special relationship. Standing on the banks of the St. Croix in Calais, I cannot help but wonder if, in border communities and in Saint John, where one commercial eye is always fixed on New England, the sale of NB Power might have been more palatable if the buyer had been a private company from Maine or Boston. In St. Stephen, it would at least have been the devil they knew, though the people here would probably tell you that it is really no devil at all.

The death of the Hydro-Québec deal did not slow the pace of the cross-border energy trade. Before losing the election, Graham's government invited the French nuclear company AREVA to look at building a second reactor at Point Lepreau, specifically to sell electricity across the line into the United States. Irving Oil, rebranding itself as a modern energy company, was exploring whether to build its own "energy corridor" of transmission lines and pipelines into Maine. And in November 2010, Danny Williams announced that Newfoundland and Labrador had found its way around Québec, signing a deal with Nova Scotia's Emera to develop one of the smaller Lower Churchill sites. This revived the idea of transmitting its electricity by subsea cable to the Nova Scotia mainland and potentially through New Brunswick and into Maine — though given the enormous distances, many observers doubted the project was financially viable.

Other deals were afoot in Maine. Emera has owned Bangor Hydro since 2001; in 2010 it announced it would buy Maine Public Service, the transmission company that carries electricity from the Tinker Dam on the Aroostook and the Mars Hill windmills. Hallowell believes the company wants to link the dam and the windmills to the larger New England grid, a hugely lucrative move that might, in the process, disrupt a smaller pooling arrangement between his co-op and Maine Public Service. Suddenly his own small-is-beautiful arrangement with New Brunswick is threatened by the large-scale power game unfolding on the border.

The game, though, is simply a new, higher-stakes version of a commercial impetus dating back centuries, one that centres on the border while helping erase it. "People talk about a regional energy market," Darrell Bishop says. "And it just occurs to me that when you've got a marketing desk in Nova Scotia, you've got a marketing desk in New Brunswick, and you've got a marketing desk sitting in New England, you know, we've already got a regional market. Because the minute there's a one-cent differential, somebody's on it like a fly on cowshit. They're there. And they make the deal. We've got so close to the regional market that we envisioned back in the eighties that I don't think we can do better."

In this constantly changing business climate, there is one constant that Scott Hallowell can rely on. His members, he says, have no qualms about where their electricity comes from. "I have not really heard about any real complaints or concerns about being served from New Brunswick," he says. "Historically we've always been served from there. Particularly the local people who have generations of family here, they have relatives on the other side of the border, so it's just a way of life.

"There's been some political issues with LNG here," he adds, almost as an afterthought, "and that's where you see a little backlash on the U.S. side towards the Canadian side. What you hear on the street here is, 'They're building LNG in Canada, but they're trying to block us.' I'm not saying that's my view, but yet they're saying that's not right."

Another fight over another source of energy, LNG — liquefied natural gas — is being fought across the same border. It is time to move on. I head back to New Brunswick.

13. COLLISIONS ON THE BAY

WITH ITS NEATLY LAID-OUT DOWNTOWN GRID of perfectly square blocks, its narrow side streets dotted with white clapboard houses, and its sophisticated restaurants and boutiques full of tony knick-knacks, Saint Andrews, New Brunswick, could pass for coastal New England. The resemblance is no coincidence. The town began as a transplanted community of American Loyalists, who first fled the Revolution to Castine, on Penobscot Bay.

The British had seized and were holding the area in the hopes of creating the colony of New Ireland.[13] From the safety of Castine, the small community of traders, calling themselves the Penobscot Association, petitioned London first to be designated neutrals, and failing that, to have the new border drawn on the Penobscot River so that Castine would remain British. When Britain agreed instead to the St. Croix as the boundary, the settlers were forced to move again, and they chose a site farther up the coast, on a point of land extending into Passamaquoddy Bay. "Their houses at Castine were taken down and placed on schooners with furniture, dishes, silver, tools, and livestock for transport to the new home," writes Guy Murchie in his history of the region. A few of the Loyalists headed upriver and founded St. Stephen, but most remained on the peninsula and began building Saint Andrews.

Many of the houses shipped or towed by boat still grace the town,

---

13 See map on page 46.

which, infused with the entrepreneurial spirit of those early traders, grew into a seafaring community and, later, a getaway resort for members of the Canadian élite. It also became an escape for expatriate Americans, though these days, they are not refugees from revolution but tend to be well-heeled New Englanders and others anxious to embrace the natural beauty of the bay. In 2004, a threat emerged to the bay, provoking an unlikely grassroots movement of Americans, Canadians, and aboriginal people — a "three-nation alliance," they called themselves — who discovered that the border they had long regarded as a bureaucratic nuisance had suddenly become their best defence.

"Really, if you're in New Brunswick or Maine, it's very similar," Jessie Davies tells me as I settle into a chair on the front porch of her large modern home, located down a winding road away from the tourist hubbub of Water Street. "So I would say I mentally play down the border. It isn't that important. But that's just from coming in from outside."

Davies, earthy and elegant, is American, a retired professor at the University of New Brunswick and a year-round resident of Saint Andrews. She tells me she has lived "all over," including in Seattle, where she saw north-south connections between Washington State and British Columbia that reminded her of those on the St. Croix. "I think a lot of people who live here have relations on both sides of the border, and it's sort of an affront when people ask you to say who you are, one way or the another. For me, it's there, and it's obviously more there than it used to be, but it's just a line on a map."

Fog is quietly moving out of the bay in front of us to reveal its blue splendour. "When we look at the Gulf of Maine Council maps, there's no border between Canada and the U.S. because it's just showing an ecosystem," Davies says. "None of the critters out there recognize the border. So I guess I think of it as less important. Crossing is not the same as driving just to St. Stephen, but it's not terribly different."

"Jessie is so much a Canadian now that she's nicer than I am," says the man sitting next to me, another American. "I see it a little bit differently." Carl Sapers, dressed in a crisp pink shirt and beige corduroys, one of the "summer people," as they are known, is a lawyer in a top Boston law firm and a former mentor to two Massachusetts governors, and his analysis reflects his Democratic politics. "I think there is a class issue which Saint Andrews is more sensitive to than other border towns. Washington County is quite depressed, and it has very few employment opportunities. Here, we have people of substantial wealth, some of whom, very few of whom, flaunt it." A neighbour, he says, has just given seventy-five thousand dollars to a marine centre in town. "And I doubt there are very many on the other side in Washington County, even the summer folk, who can do that. There is money here, and children of privilege growing up here in the summer, and not incidentally, a kind of cosmopolitan community that is really extraordinary anywhere. There are lots of people living in Europe who come here. It makes the place much more interesting than most places people go for the summer. But Washington County lacks this to a great extent. And that has led to a kind of contrast."

That contrast usually remains below the surface, but it has been more pronounced since 2004, when Davies, Sapers, and others began organizing residents of Saint Andrews to fight proposals for not one, not two, but three enormous liquefied natural gas terminals on the Maine side of the bay. In Saint Andrews, where the dire economic conditions of Washington County, Maine, were not an immediate concern, the activists focused on possible contamination of the bay and the potential safety hazard created by massive freighters moving between islands to their destinations. But at a public meeting he attended near Calais, Sapers discovered an entirely different reaction. "I would say that forty to fifty people got up, and almost to a man, the argument was, 'We want our children to have the opportunity to stay and live with us on our homestead or nearby, and there are no jobs, and we've got to have these facilities so we have jobs.' And the elected politicians, to a man, got up and supported this plea. There were only two people who spoke on the other side. You had a sense that these were not people of great means. These were people who managed to get by, but it was a struggle for them, and it would be a struggle for their children if they stayed here."

There are opponents in Maine, Sapers says, but they are badly outnumbered and have few resources. "They've had very little success.

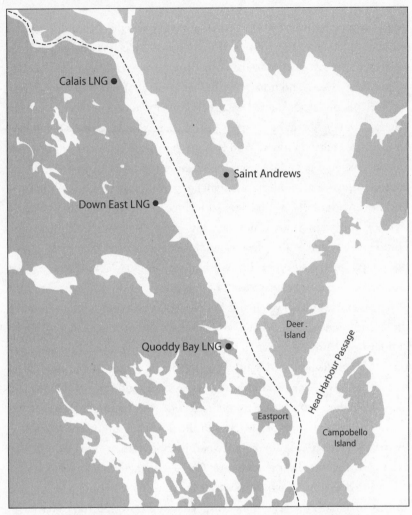

The three proposed LNG sites sit on the New Brunswick-Maine border.

We on the other hand have set out several targets, and without being too euphoric about the thing, we have hit every one of them." One was to convince the Canadian government to oppose the LNG terminals and to declare that Head Harbour Passage, a channel between two New Brunswick islands and the only feasible route to the terminals, is Canadian waters and off-limits to tankers. Stephen Harper said precisely that just months after becoming prime minister in 2006, and his government has repeated it ever since. They also persuaded the New Brunswick government to fight the LNG plans at American regulatory hearings. "In Canada, you have much easier ways of making the system work for you," Sapers says. "We were able to do it."

The fight has become an irritant between the governments of New Brunswick and Maine, which normally enjoy good relations. The premier and the governor meet often to discuss regional issues, but LNG grew into a point of contention between Shawn Graham and John Baldacci. "It is not appropriate for the Canadian government to hold control over commerce in Maine and the United States," Baldacci said in 2009. "We cannot cede control of commerce in Maine to another country, no matter how well we are able to cooperate on other issues."

Baldacci's frustration was personal. He encouraged LNG terminal developers to look at Maine for potential locations. But community after community rejected the idea: in Harpswell, near Freeport, residents blocked one bid in a referendum; when the governor conceded that any community ought to have the right to vote on LNG, the population of Searsport, farther up the coast, voted down a proposed terminal for Penobscot Bay, not far from Castine. "All the way along the coast, they have turned it down," Davies says, "and they just kept going up, further away, until they found a place where people were desperate enough that they'll take anything." But when they reached Passamaquoddy Bay, Baldacci and the developers had literally run out of Maine coastline. On the very edge of the state, they inevitably collided with Canada, whose border created a whole new set of headaches.

From Saint Andrews I head back to Maine, this time following New Brunswick Route 1 straight to the St. Croix. The new U.S. inspection station sprawls out like a Wal-Mart, and that is not the only contrast to the smaller Milltown checkpoint. At the end of a maze of roads and merge lanes, the officer on duty is all business. He never cracks a smile.

Then it is along the St. Croix to downtown Calais, where one of

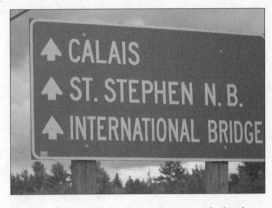

A sign on U.S. Route 1 points the way to the border.

the project companies, Calais LNG, has a storefront office with American and Canadian flags. "A clean, secure energy future for Maine and the Maritimes," the company's resolutely cross-border slogan proclaims. I continue down U.S. Route 1 as the river opens up into the bay. In less than an hour, I am crossing a causeway to Moose Island and pulling into the faded, once-thriving downtown of Eastport, the easternmost city in the United States. There is no question I am at the periphery of America as I step out onto a balcony on the back of Bob Godfrey's souvenir shop. In front of us are two Canadian islands, Deer Island and Campobello. Between them is the narrow channel where LNG tankers would have to execute a turn of more than ninety degrees, directly in front of Eastport, to head up towards their terminals.

Bob asks me how I fared crossing the border. Like most residents, he laments the impact of post-9/11 security measures on this international community. "Prior to the LNG, the relationship has been pretty convivial. We moved out here because of the closeness and the friendship. . . .You can go back and forth without much hassle, or you used to. Still can, for the most part. And of course there was and probably still is a strong smuggling industry between the two places. If LNG hadn't come along, things would be a lot friendlier than they are, and they're still friendly among most people."

Many American residents along the bay still resent Canada for using similar sovereignty arguments to scuttle a proposed oil refinery for Eastport in the 1970s. Though there was homegrown opposition to the plant — some saw its eventual defeat as the beginning of Maine's "environmental imagination" and its self-image as a "post-industrial

Bob Godfrey of Eastport, Maine, is one of the opponents of proposed LNG
terminals. Deer Island, New Brunswick, is visible across the bay.

sanctuary"—Canada got the blame. "There's still people mad about
that and who wish that it had happened: 'It's Canada keeping us from
having our economic development,'" Godfrey says. Others see the hand
of the Irvings, who have just built their own LNG terminal in Saint John
and, so the theory goes, have persuaded Ottawa to block competitors.
"It's toxic is what it is," Godfrey says of the atmosphere. "It's bad for
the intercommunity and interpersonal relationships."

Even at the border, the war on terror has become a pretext for
Americans to take out their local anger on Canadians, Godfrey suggests.
He knew of three cases when New Brunswickers crossing at Calais to
attend public LNG meetings were "hassled" at the checkpoint.

But the crackdown at the border and the culture of state-sanctioned
fear—the chance, however remote, of a terrorist attack on an LNG
tanker—is also a boon to the opponents of LNG.

In early 2009, in a waterway suitability report prepared as part of the
regulatory approval process, the U.S. Coast Guard noted "a significant
portion of the transit route" for tankers heading to the Downeast LNG
site, one of the three proposed terminals, was in Canadian waters.
"The eventual involvement and cooperation of Canada's maritime,

environmental, and public safety authorities are paramount to ensure the safety and security of the waterway," the report said. Given Ottawa's opposition to the terminals, that cooperation was unlikely.

"And this," Godfrey says, "is a U.S. agency saying you have to do that. This is Homeland Security saying, 'We can't take our escorts into Canadian waters. We can't board it with armed personnel in Canadian waters.' So once that tanker comes through Head Harbour Passage, it's right on top of Eastport — it's three-quarters of a mile from Eastport — before [U.S. security personnel] can get on board."The American regulators, he says, "can't ignore the issue from a Homeland Security point of view. So they're going to have to deal with it some way, and it may be that they say, 'Since we cannot take Canada into account, we can't assure that this will be the best security we can provide, so we're going to recommend against the project.' That could happen. And that would kill it, in a sense."

Godfrey, who came to Eastport from Indiana with his wife Linda in search of a simpler lifestyle, now finds himself trying to become an expert on marine law, energy regulation, industry standards, and security guidelines. As we sit and watch boats plod through the waters of the bay, he rattles off a series of problems touching on hazard zones, emergency response plan requirements, and the United Nations Convention on the Law of the Sea, which would allow the United States to claim the right of "innocent passage" through Canadian waters, except the U.S. has not ratified it. The story here on Passamaquoddy Bay is, on a much larger scale, similar to the one in Forest City, where the presence of the St. Croix, an international river, helped stymie Washington's plans for a new customs complex. The LNG proposals, Godfrey says, are "absolutely full of obstacles" — the biggest being the border itself.

Vera Francis, a performance artist, was working on a play when she became one such obstacle. It was June 22, 2004, and word was getting out that proponents of an LNG terminal had arrived in her community, the Pleasant Point Indian reservation just outside Eastport, to make a presentation to the tribal council. "It started behind closed doors and they tried to keep it behind closed doors for the greater part of the process," Francis says. "It was fast-tracked from the beginning."

Francis quickly rallied like-minded members of Pleasant Point, known in the Maliseet-Passamaquoddy language by its original name, Sipayik. She launched a group called Nulankeyutomonen Nkihtahkomikumon (We Take Care of our Land) to fight the fifty-year lease the tribal council had approved for Quoddy Bay LNG. The group pointed out that, by law, only the Bureau of Indian Affairs could sign such a lease. "And they're supposed to do this with transparency," Francis tells me, "and within the federal laws, they have a mandate to follow when they lease tribal land." Nulankeyutomonen Nkihtahkomikumon argued there had not been a proper environmental assessment and that other federal agencies had not been consulted—both legal requirements. The group succeeded in pushing regulators to demand more supporting information from Quoddy Bay LNG on its safety measures. When the company did not provide them, the Federal Energy Regulatory Commission (FERC) suspended the application process. The deal between the company and the tribal government began to unravel, and in the spring of 2010, the federal Bureau of Indian Affairs officially cancelled the lease.

"I think what killed it was that it was never really a good idea, and it was never really a good idea to keep us in the dark," Francis says as we sit on the banks of the Saint John River in Fredericton, where she is attending university. Now she hopes the Passamaquoddy people will join the fight against the other two proposed terminals, Downeast LNG, to be located about halfway between Calais and Eastport, almost directly across from Saint Andrews, and Calais LNG, which hopes to build less than ten miles from the centre of Calais. The Passamaquoddy people consider the whole bay, on both sides of the border, to be their home. That and the border itself make for a powerful combination. "Those two things should be what stop the projects." If the Canadian government could only see it, Francis says, "it would be a stranglehold on these projects. It's a missed opportunity when they don't come together."

The problem, she says, lies with Canada's attitude towards the

Passamaquoddy, one of the Abenaki people that inhabited present-day Maine, New Brunswick, and Nova Scotia long before colonial borders were drawn. When the Loyalists from Castine arrived at the point of land that later became Saint Andrews, it was not uninhabited. It was the largest of the Passamaquoddy settlements, whose territory included the St. Croix and land stretching towards the Saint John, where they overlapped with those of the Maliseet, to whom they were related. "It's a good expanse of land," says Francis. Her grandmother, the daughter of a Maliseet from the St. Mary's reserve in Fredericton and a Mi'kmaq from the Bear Island reserve in Nova Scotia, went to live on one of three reserves on the Canadian side of the St. Croix. But those reserves were eventually eliminated by Ottawa, and the Passamaquoddy were pushed out. They relocated to Indian Island, just south of Deer Island. When conditions there proved too difficult, the United States government let them come ashore at Pleasant Point.

The result is that while the United States recognizes the Passamaquoddy, Canada does not. "We were told, 'We can't talk to you, because you don't have an entity,'" Hugh Akagi, the traditional chief of the Passamaquoddy, explains as we sit on his deck in Saint Andrews. "Without a reserve, how do you dialogue with Indian Affairs? Because they deal with reserves exclusively." This has made land claim discussions difficult. Akagi himself, chosen by the Passamaquoddy as their chief for the unofficial discussions with Ottawa, has dual citizenship, but only the United States recognizes his native status.

Nor does Canadian law reflect the 1794 Jay Treaty, which says native people have the right "freely to pass and repass by land or inland navigation, into the respective territories and countries of the two parties." While the United States incorporated that right into its Immigration and Naturalization Act, and requires only a status card from an aboriginal person entering the country, Canada has left it to the courts to interpret how the treaty applies. "There's more respect there [in the U.S.] for the border not being an issue when it comes to dividing our people," Akagi says. "That's where Canada falls down." Vera Francis tells me she never has problems entering the United States, but when she enters Canada,

Passamaquoddy Chief Hugh Agaki says the border divides his people.

she has to adopt a conceit that she is merely visiting family. "'Don't come live here. Don't stake any ground here. Don't stay long. Don't stay long in your homeland' is the message," she says. "I can't say I'm going home. Once I say that, they stop me. The first time I said I was going home, I was pulled into Immigration."

From the beach across from Akagi's house in Saint Andrews, the water tower at Pleasant Point is visible across the bay. The wider panorama before us—bay, islands, sky—was all Passamaquoddy territory, but the border is an artificial construct to Akagi, an imposed barrier. "We are people of the Schoodic river," he tells me, using the Passamaquoddy word for the St. Croix. "We occupied both sides of the river. When we look at the river, it binds us as a people and defines us. That river was everything. And then, when the new society comes along, this European thinking, you use mountain ranges where our people lived, and rivers where our people lived, as borders and boundaries. All of a sudden you draw a line through it and you divide people. This destroys our communities and our capacity to be native peoples.

"I remember when, after forty years, the Berlin Wall came down and people celebrated. It had divided a people for forty years. This line has divided my people for two hundred and fifty years. Nobody will look at that. Nobody's taking that down for us. Just recognize the Jay Treaty. That would help a lot. But instead we've got to go into their [Canadian] courts, their system, just in order to get together as family and people. It's a terribly destructive line."

It is a constant frustration, but given the heightened security, Akagi is careful not to show it when crossing into the U.S., treaty or no treaty. "You don't approach these people like you're cocky: 'Let me in or else.' It doesn't work that way. You just don't upset them. As much as I know my rights and understand my rights, I can't jeopardize my rights. One of the things I need to be able to do is go in and out of the States. I can't afford to have them blacklist me."

Though Akagi's status is recognized by the United States, as a resident of New Brunswick he had no formal role in the Pleasant Point tribal council as it grappled with the LNG issue. But he watched Vera Francis with admiration as she rallied members of the community. "The guys are great, but the women know how to fight," he laughs.

Akagi never bought the line that Quoddy Bay LNG would bring prosperity to his people. "We've been there and done that, and I don't believe what I'm told anymore. We've been sold too many bills of goods where the truth wasn't part of the equation.... So LNG, when they tell us all the jobs it's going to bring us, when they tell us it's a fail-proof system and they can come through the most dangerous waters in the world, and nothing can go wrong, I don't believe any of this any more. We don't have a lot of land, so you don't part with it, you don't jeopardize it, you don't put it in the hands of someone who says, 'We're only going to be here for twenty-five years and we're going to give you a lot of money.' We have to be stupid if we keep taking things like land, water, resources, fisheries, and keep saying that it can be replaced by money.

"It's like the definition of a home. People think of home as a house. But to us, a home is where you live, it's what you live with, it's everything around you, it's the ancestors in the soil. It means so much more. We can't possibly describe to you what our home is. It's not a place where you live, it's not a place you go back to, but it's a place where your people have always been. We've been here for twelve thousand years. That's home. Can you imagine that as your home? Your people have been here four hundred years. You still celebrate it as home. So how do you understand that connection, and what it means, and the spirituality of being part of all this?

"But for us to fight LNG, we're supposed to go in and identify specific locations that are important to us. And they don't seem to like the idea that we've used this bay for twelve thousand years and we want to protect it. They need to know, why? What area? They keep pounding on these questions: show us where you need to protect it. That's not being native. [Being native is] about wholeness, it's about everything, and it's all connected."

With Quoddy Bay LNG just about dead in the summer of 2010, Akagi, Francis, Godfrey, Davies, and Sapers are pressing the fight against the two other proposed terminals. Downeast LNG looked finished in 2007, when there were objections to its pipeline route through the Moosehorn National Wildlife Refuge, southwest of Calais. But the company was allowed to withdraw its applications and can reapply later. "I don't like that they can do that," Akagi tells me. "It's amazing how many times you have to kill something. It's just like a Stephen King novel. It's got so much money that feeds it, this animal, it keeps coming back to life . . . When they come to the hearings, they fly in on Lear jets. We have to carpool."

Against such powerful forces, I suggest, there is always a chance that Canada will compromise, perhaps as part of a trade-off with Washington on some other issue. But Jessie Davies cannot see it happening. "Harper appears to connect this with the sovereignty of the Northwest Passage. So throwing down the gauntlet here helps him over there." Godfrey agrees that compromising on Passamaquoddy Bay would undercut the prime minister's assertion of Canadian sovereignty over the Arctic and its potentially lucrative oil and gas reserves. "If Canada relents here, it has less of an argument up there. It's not going to do it."

There is an irony here, of course. Davies and Godfrey are counting on the lure of Arctic oil to stiffen Canada's spine on enforcing its border, while Hugh Akagi is lamenting the overzealous exploitation of nature and dreaming of a world without borders. He was in Europe last summer on a motorcycle trip. "It was wonderful to go through seven countries, four thousand kilometres, and the only border I had to deal with was Switzerland. I think Europe is getting it right. I think what the Americans are actually doing is they're helping the terrorists win because they're terrorizing their own people. In Europe they're getting rid of borders and putting people back together. It's a wonderful feeling to just weave in and out of countries, and know it's not 'them and us,' 'one or the other.'"

It reminds him of what he has learned about the era before colonization, when the Mi'kmaq, Maliseet, Passamaquoddy, and Penobscot peoples had no firm boundaries and travelled into each other's territories, respectfully, to hunt and fish. Some of Akagi's people used to row large canoes out past Grand Manan Island and ride a gyre, a rotating ocean current, across the Bay of Fundy to what is now Nova Scotia, where they would trade with the Mi'kmaq. But in 2010, the Canadian government is enforcing boundaries it claims once existed for native hunting and fishing grounds, prosecuting natives who harvest outside what the government considers their people's traditional territories.

In Europe, Akagi drove his bike through Alsace-Lorraine, a piece of territory that France and Germany fought over for decades, mainly for its iron mines. "It was the energy hub of its day," Akagi says, borrowing a government slogan for Saint John's energy sector. "That's what they fought for. Now French and Germans speak each other's languages and they get married. It's going to be hard for them go to war now. When you become one family — and here we go back to the native concept of our community, which is family — if we can put that back together again, I think your borders are more secure than ever because they're bonded by a common people, instead of a line that's holding people behind it."

More irony, I think to myself as I leave Saint Andrews to return to Maine: Akagi views the border as an intrusion. But as I drive back to Route 1, I glimpse an island that will forever be associated with another man, the one who began the process of imposing those borders on the Passamaquoddy people. He, too, has been enlisted as an ally of the three-nation alliance and as an opponent of LNG. He is not the most important or powerful foe of the projects, but in a dispute connected so intimately to land, sovereignty, and boundaries, there is a certain symmetry, even poetry, to his role in the battle.

He first came here four centuries ago. His island is in American territory, yet he is considered the founder of Canada. And the choice he made in 1604 is poised, four centuries later, to pound yet another nail in the coffin of LNG on Passamaquoddy Bay.

14. SAVING CHAMPLAIN

THE BOAT TURNS BACK FOR ME. I am early, and Meg Scheid has already set out to ferry two others to the island when she spots me and circles back. I slip on my rubber boots at the small launch as she brings the motorized aluminum boat ashore. Shaking my hand warmly, Scheid, a ranger with the U.S. National Park Service, hands me a bright red flotation jacket, and I climb in with her, along with Lindsay Clowe, a student working as a park ranger for the summer, and Patricia Bernier, a volunteer. It is cloudy, and the St. Croix River is a dull grey as we travel half a mile, and four centuries, in less than five minutes.

A small beach connects the south end of the main island to a small outcropping of rock. We land there and use a set of wooden steps to climb up the rocky hill. At the top is a flat, grassy plateau, and beyond it, a small ridge and a second plateau. To our left is Maine. To our right, just slightly more distant, is New Brunswick.

As we walk into the centre of the island, I feel the same thrill I experienced at Monument Brook, for this, too, is a place where history pivoted. It is, in fact, where Canada was born. This is Île-Sainte-Croix, Saint Croix Island, where Samuel de Champlain came ashore in 1604, four years before he founded Québec. I am walking in his footsteps. "Take a minute and soak it up," Scheid says softly, "because you're standing in a place where a hundred and twenty men came from France and built a

U.S. Park Ranger Meg Scheid, oversees Saint Croix Island, visible in the background.

settlement"—the first European settlement north of Florida and the first French habitation on the continent.

It lasted precisely one winter, one disastrously severe winter. The seven-acre island is not just the birthplace of a country; it is also a graveyard. "They learned lessons that winter," Scheid says in a hushed, reverent tone. "Fresh water was on the mainland. There was no fresh water on the island. Parts of this island are more sandy than soil, so the gardens they planted sprouted, but the sun scorched a lot of their gardens. And they cut the trees for their firewood, so when an unexpected early winter, extra cold, arrived—what we know today as our mini-ice age—it caught them off guard. They weren't ready. And they weren't ready with their supplies in terms of food. They had ship's biscuits, presumably they had lots of meat, they had Spanish wine, probably a little wine from France, no doubt, but what they didn't have was the fresh fruit and vegetables they needed in their diets to prevent scurvy."

Near the northern tip of the island is a large tablet on an enormous rock. The tablet was installed relatively recently, in 1904, to mark the three-hundredth anniversary of Champlain's arrival. We see two other small, engraved stones on the island, explaining Champlain's story. But there is nothing to mark the precise location of the thirty-five skeletons, removed during an early archaeological dig and reburied by the park service ahead of the four-hundredth anniversary in 2004.

"We do know where the cemetery is," Scheid says, "but we don't want that made known to the public for obvious reasons. And we know where the settlement was. And what we generally say is on the north side of the island is where the settlement was located, and on the south side of the island is where the cemetery was. And we've promised to keep the details of where things are located general, and give people as much wonderful interpretive information as we can, but we don't give them enough to get in trouble or encourage anything."

In fact, the island itself is closed to the public. On the mainland, a short drive south of Calais, tourists can look at statues and read display panels as they walk a short interpretive trail to a viewing platform to see the island. Another park on the Canadian side overlooks the site from a higher elevation. Scheid hopes to eventually arrange boat tours to circle the island, but no landings will be allowed. "It's fragile archeologically. There are thirty-five graves on the island out of seventy-nine men who wintered here. And it's fragile geologically. Take a walk over here and you'll see the erosion on the south shore. So if we invited the public — not just the American public, the world is invited to visit our crown jewels — we would have a problem. We would have issues with erosion. We would have issues with people who might perhaps want trophies, archeological pieces of value."

We are returning to the boat at the southern end of the island when Scheid stops abruptly and points out a fist-sized clump of organic matter sitting on the top of a small rock. "Lots of berries," she concludes quickly. "Raccoon? Owl?" she asks aloud, though neither is known to frequent the island. "I don't know. It tells me we've got something." Perhaps they were droppings, she offers, reconsidering her first guess. "It's too early for berries, isn't it?" Finally, she concludes the dark, wet, disgusting chunk of stuff is a large number of flies. "I think you're looking at a regurgitated pellet from a seagull that's been eating insects in flight."

Scheid is the first U.S. park ranger I have ever met. She fits the bill: her long, tightly curled hair, bronze with streaks of brown and grey, is the colour of the Grand Canyon. From her urge to identify the regurgitated bugs, to her request that I photograph a washed-up bottle for her in case it is an artifact, her naturalist and conservationist impulses are obvious. Scheid's first job with the service was at Acadia National Park, down the Maine coast. She later took a sabbatical, moved to Canada, visited all its national parks, and learned French. The job here, as the first full-time ranger at Saint Croix Island International Historic Site, was a logical move, given her ability to speak French alongside her affection for Acadia National Park and for historic Acadia. "Erase all these modern boundaries and you're in it," she says.

Scheid's fellow ranger for the summer, Lindsay Clowes, is a nineteen-year-old student. In a different way, she is also a perfect hire for an American park commemorating the founder of Canada. She was born in Fredericton but moved to Calais when her mother was remarried to an American. Lindsay received special permission to go to school in St. Stephen to finish the New Brunswick French immersion program. "We crossed the border every morning and she drove me to school, because obviously there's no school bus that would cross the border," says Lindsay, who gained dual citizenship. "I like being dual. I can work wherever I want when I'm older because I'm dual. I can work here because I'm dual." Her ability to speak French, not a consideration at most U.S. national parks, is a vital asset at the park, where many French-speaking tourists come to stroll amid the statues and look out at the island.

At Lindsay's house in Calais, the clocks in her room, and on her mother's side of the bed, are set to New Brunswick's Atlantic time zone, while the one on her stepfather's side of the bed is on Maine's Eastern time. "I love living in Calais, and I love living in the United States — my father still lives on the Canadian side so I kind of get to live in both — but I still feel very Canadian. I feel like I talk Canadian. When tourists come

The tablet installed on Saint Croix Island in 1904 marked the tricentennial of Champlain's landing.

down here, they somehow know I'm Canadian by the way I talk. I don't feel like I live in two countries. I mean, Canada's right there," she says, pointing off the island's eastern side to New Brunswick. "It doesn't seem like a whole other country. It's kind of like our own little community of both. It would be hard for one to live without the other."

Meg Scheid and Lindsay Clowes are the most recent stewards of Saint Croix Island. The person who made perhaps the greatest contribution to documenting its history, and reviving its place in the Canadian imagination, was William Francis Ganong, one of the "Chocolate Ganongs" of nearby St. Stephen. But William, born in 1864, was never that interested in the family business. After studying at the University of New Brunswick, Harvard, and Munich University, he became a professor of botany at a small college in Massachusetts. He spent his summers back home in New Brunswick, researching the province's natural and human history, an effort that placed him, according to one admirer, "at the centre of the Maritime region's historical reawakening." In 1902 he published a detailed study of Saint Croix Island and two years later spoke at the ceremony marking the tricentennial of Champlain's arrival.

"On a fair mid-summer day just three centuries ago, a tiny vessel came sailing along the lonely Fundy coast from the eastward," he recounted, "and turned her prow to the river on whose historic banks we now are standing. She was a tiny craft that thus appeared out of the unknown, for she was no larger than the fishing sloops we know so well in our Quoddy waters today.

"She carried about a dozen men, of whom two bore the unmistakable stamp of leadership. One was a prominent gentleman of France, lofty in spirit, devoted in purpose, trusted of his king, the commander of the company, Sieur de Monts. The other was one of the great men whom France has given to the world, a remarkable combination of dreamer of dreams and man of wise and swift action. The intentness of his gaze as one new feature after another unfolded itself along the coast, and his constant use of compass and pencil, showed him to be the geographer and chronicler of the expedition. He was the first cartographer and historian of Acadia, later, the founder and father of New France, Samuel de Champlain."

Champlain had not wanted to come this way. He and de Monts were agreed that France needed to establish itself in the Americas. De Monts promoted the fertile soil to King Henri IV, while Champlain emphasized the potential for a convenient route to China. But Champlain favoured settling the St. Lawrence Valley. De Monts, the senior of the two, preferred the coast, so the coast it was. They sailed in April, met floating ice as they approached the New World in May, and first dropped anchor at a place Champlain called Cap de la Hève, near the present-day Lunenburg, Nova Scotia.

In the following weeks, leaving behind most of their company in the two larger vessels, Champlain, de Monts, and ten other men used a little barque to explore the coast, first around the southwest tip of what is now Nova Scotia, then up into the Bay of Fundy, looking for "some more suitable place" to settle. On June 24, while working their way back down the bay's northern shore, they came upon "one of the largest and deepest rivers we had yet seen" and called it the "Saint-Jean," because that day was the Catholic Feast of Saint John. Continuing down the coast, they encountered countless islands — Champlain used the Algonquin word for island to name a large one Grand Manan — before sailing into a vast bay and up an estuary, to a place where three rivers came together in the shape of a cross.

De Monts called the river "Sainte-Croix," and he gave the same name to a small island, which appeared ideal for a settlement. "It is by nature very well situated, except on one place, where for about forty paces it is lower than elsewhere," Champlain wrote. "This, however, is easily fortified, the banks of the main land being distant on both sides some nine hundred to a thousand paces. Vessels could pass up the river only at the mercy of the cannon on this island, and we deemed the location the most advantageous."

They sent for the larger ships, and soon the company was clearing the island, erecting wooden houses and a palisade, and establishing a storehouse, meeting room, kitchen, and blacksmith shop. They mounted cannons at both ends of the island, laid out gardens, including on the mainland, and built a small chapel at the southwest tip. Adjacent to it they established a cemetery, which, Ganong writes, "was destined to prove all too necessary before the winter was over."

It was an exceptionally harsh winter for the seventy-nine men chosen to remain. Champlain recorded that the snow began on October 6. "All our liquors froze, except the Spanish wine," he wrote. "Cider was dispensed by the pound. We were obliged to use very bad water, and drink melted snow, as there were no springs nor brooks; for it was not possible to go to the mainland in consequence of the great pieces of ice drifted by the tide. . . . Work on the hand mill was very fatiguing, since the most of us, having slept poorly, and suffering from insufficiency of fuel, which we could not obtain on account of the ice, had scarcely any strength, and also because we ate only salt meat and vegetables during the winter, which produced bad blood."

By spring, thirty-five men had died of scurvy. A vessel from France finally arrived with provisions in mid-June. Within two days, de Monts, unaware that the winter had not been normal, decided to "go in quest of a place better adapted for an abode," Champlain wrote, "and with better temperature than our own." The ill-fated island was abandoned. "Had that first winter been a mild one," Ganong speculates, "the settlement would not have been removed to Port Royal; and the Saint Croix valley, if not the island itself, would have become the centre of French settlement and power in Acadia. In this case, the subsequent history and in some small degree the present status, of the Ste. Croix valley would have been very different. Upon such small accidents does the course of history often turn!"

Yet even with events unfolding as they did, it was not clear, almost two centuries later, which river Richard Oswald, Benjamin Franklin, and John Adams were referring to when they agreed the St. Croix would be the border.

Marc L'Escarbot, another of de Monts's company, had written, "We must need say that the isle of St. Croix is difficult to find on one's first visit." They were prophetic words.

The Loyalists from Castine who settled at Saint Andrews learned rather quickly after their arrival in 1783 that the river named in the treaty was, as Ganong described it, "an abstract, a legal St. Croix, for the identity of the real St. Croix of Champlain had been forgotten." Before Britain and the United States could sort out the location of the highlands, they would have to settle what had been meant by the St. Croix River, the reference point for the North Line and thus the key to the entire border.

The Castine refugees had encountered an American colonel while sailing into the bay. "I passed by the ships and cautioned them at their peril not to land any inhabitants," Colonel John Allan told John Hancock, the governor of Massachusetts. The following year, Hancock wrote to John Parr, the governor of Nova Scotia, to tell him the Magaguadavic River, east of Saint Andrews, was the St. Croix of the treaty, meaning

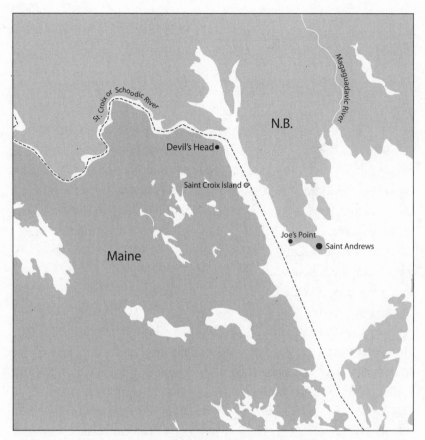

The United States claimed the Magaguadavic River was
the St. Croix referred to in the Treaty of Paris.

the Castine Loyalists had settled in American territory. By then, New
Brunswick had been carved out of Nova Scotia, and its first governor,
Thomas Carleton, replied to Hancock that the Paris negotiators were
referring to the Schoodic River, which emptied into Passamaquoddy Bay
to the *west* of Saint Andrews. "It is the only River on that side of the
Province of either such magnitude or extent as could have led to the
idea of proposing it as a limit between two large and spacious countries,"
Carleton argued. The settlers, therefore, were safety in British territory.

In the Jay Treaty of 1794 — the same agreement that allowed
aboriginal people to cross the new border without harassment — Britain
and the United States appointed a commission to decide whether the

Schoodic or the Magaguadavic was the St. Croix. Much hinged on the deliberations. The border would run south from the chosen river into the bay, perhaps determining which islands belonged to which country. More importantly, the North Line would run north from the river's source and determine the size and shape of New Brunswick and Massachusetts. In fact, American surveyors had already appeared in Meductic, on the Saint John River, to mark a line running north from the source of the Magaguadavic, which would reduce New Brunswick's land mass by almost one-third. "Evidently the Government of Massachusetts was going on the principle," writes James Hannay, "that by making extreme claims, more might be obtained than by a moderate statement of their case." After their first meeting at Saint Andrews in 1796, the commissioners went to see the Schoodic and the Magaguadavic, and took testimony from local residents, including members of the Passamaquoddy tribe. "They thereupon gave the following information: that two or three hundred years ago, the French came in three or four ships to Passamaquoddy Bay, entered at the Letete Passage and erected a cross at the entrance of the Magaguadavic River," according to an account by Ward Chipman, the British agent to the commission.

Chipman realized immediately that the Americans would exploit this aboriginal testimony to their advantage. He had read accounts of Champlain's voyages, and was convinced that Dochet Island, a small island in the Schoodic River, was the site of the French settlement. When he shared the accounts of 1604 with Robert Pagan, a judge and one of the original Castine refugees to Saint Andrews, Pagan "at once said, to my great surprise, that he knew from the description tho' he had never before heard it, what Island it must be," Chipman told Carleton. Pagan also reported that the Passamaquoddy tribal chief, Francis Joseph, had spoken to him of "a tradition among the Indians, that the Island, which from the description, thus suddenly occurred to him, as the Ile Ste. Croix, was the first place the French resorted to, upon their first coming to this Country." Chipman went out to the Schoodic to see the island, and the surrounding scenery appeared to match the descriptions from 1604. He wrote to Governor Carleton suggesting that copies of Champlain's own writings and drawings of Saint Croix Island be sent to him.

Meanwhile, the commission went about its business. The Americans based their case on a map drawn three decades earlier by John Mitchell, the British cartographer, which was used by the Paris negotiators. It identified the Magaguadavic as the St. Croix. Two of the Paris negotiators, John Jay and John Adams, told the commission that, in their minds, the St. Croix boundary of their treaty was the traditional boundary of Massachusetts Bay, which they assumed to be the one on Mitchell's map. But, they acknowledged, no thought had been given to the possibility that Mitchell had been mistaken.

The breakthrough came in the summer of 1797 when Chipman received his copies of Champlain's writings and maps. He sent them to Pagan, who hurried to the Schoodic River and Dochet Island. What he found there, he said in his deposition, was "a most striking agreement between every part of these shores, coves and points and that plan," referring to Champlain's drawing. "Where in the plan above mentioned the French buildings are laid down, he found four distant Piles of ruins agreeing in their situation and distances from each other with the spot at A." Continuing to dig, Pagan found more ruins, matching perfectly Champlain's description, and also a spoon, a musket ball, a piece of pottery, and a spike.

This clinched the matter. Once the commission learned of Pagan's findings, it ruled for the British. The Schoodic was Champlain's St. Croix River, and it would form the boundary.

And so Dochet Island returned to history as Saint Croix Island, and helped settle the earliest of many border disputes between New Brunswick and what would later become Maine. "It is too much to say that upon it alone depended the identification of the river and hence its selection as the boundary," Ganong concluded, "for there was probably enough other evidence to have produced the same result. But, on the other hand, it is very probable, since one of the commissioners is known to have held at first strongly for the Magaguadavic, that without the evidence drawn

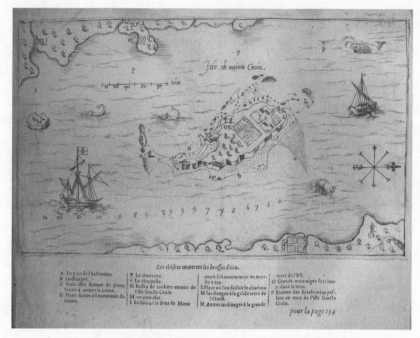

Champlain's map of his island was used by Ward Chipman in 1797 to settle the
dispute over the true St. Croix River and the location of the border.
(Courtesy New Brunswick Museum)

from the island, the commissioners would have been divided in opinion
instead of unanimous. In this case their decision would have been received
with reserved acquiescence and some feeling of injustice, rather than with
general approbation and satisfaction as it was.

"Dochet Island, therefore, has contributed something to the peace
between nations."

The confirmation of Dochet Island as Champlain's Saint Croix did
not quite end the commission's work. The treaty of 1783 said that the
boundary was to be drawn north from the source of the St. Croix, and
the Schoodic (now accepted as that river) had two major tributaries: the
Schoodic Lakes to the west, and the Chiputneticook, a stream flowing in
from other lakes to the north. After long negotiations in which various

choices proved inconvenient to both the Americans and the British, the commissioners compromised by selecting the western headwaters of the Chiputneticook. This decision led to the first survey of the site, which became known as Monument Brook, and the erection of the first monument there. It was the beginning of the North Line and the root of the dispute over the highlands.

The American agent to the commission also suggested to the members that they set the boundary from the mouth of the St. Croix into the sea, to settle the nationality of the various islands in Passamaquoddy Bay. But the commissioners decided that they had fulfilled their mandate and left the ownership of the islands for another day, which would arrive soon enough.

As for Champlain's little island, the birthplace of Canada, it became part of the United States because of a seemingly inconsequential detail in the commission's decision. For reasons unknown, the members identified Joe's Point, near Saint Andrews, as the mouth of the St. Croix. In geographical terms, the real mouth is seven miles to the north, at Devil's Head, where the river flows into a long waterway that is salt water and tidal, and thus clearly an arm of Passamaquoddy Bay. Saint Croix Island sits roughly halfway between the two, geographically in that arm of the bay, but legally and politically in the river.

And that meant the island was subject to the clause of the 1783 treaty that said the border would run down the *middle* of the river. Saint Croix Island, slightly to the west of that middle, was thus on the American side of the imaginary line. Had the commission correctly chosen Devil's Head as the mouth of the river, the island would legally have been in the Bay of Fundy, and subject to a clause saying islands once "within the limits of the said Province of Nova Scotia," as Saint Croix Island had been, would remain British.[14]

Whether the Americans who squatted on the island in 1799 understood these niceties is unknown but move onto it they did. Chipman and Carleton briefly discussed mounting a claim to the island, but Chipman

---

14 A 1908 treaty updated the location of the border in the St. Croix, shifting it from the middle of the river to the thalweg, the line that follows the deepest point of its main channel. This did not affect U.S. ownership of Saint Croix Island, which sits to the west of the channel.

reluctantly concluded they had no case. As recently as 1896, the New Brunswick Legislature mistakenly included the island within provincial boundaries. "However much we may regret that this island does not belong to the country with whose history it is so closely connected," Ganong writes, "we must all agree that the title of the United States to it is perfectly clear and just."

In 1820, the island was officially granted to John Brewer, of nearby Robbinston, and there were other residents over the years. The United States government bought most of it in 1856 and built a lighthouse, but the remaining section was still in private hands in 1902, when William Francis Ganong wrote his monograph. He hoped that the entire island would be acquired by the Maine or U.S. government to be protected and preserved. "It is a good thing for a people to take pride in their history," he writes, "and this they do the more if they can study it freely upon the actual sites of their historic events, and surrounded by the charm which always hovers over places which have witnessed historic scenes." His wish was fulfilled in 1949, eight years after his death, when the U.S. National Park Service took over the island and declared it a national monument.

Though the declaration recognized Saint Croix's historical legacy, its ecological survival has taken on equal importance for the park service. Even in 1902, Ganong predicted that, without human intervention, the island's soil would be entirely washed away in the future. This is why Scheid cringes just a little every time a large boat sails by. "Erosion is our number one concern and it happens regardless, and it particularly happens at high tide when we have storm surges, weather events, or we have high wake situations. Even a simple motorboat passing by is enough to take a few grains of sand from the bottom, and once you've got grains of sand removed from down here, you get this." She points up to chunks of soil and grass that have slid halfway down the hill. "It's a huge responsibility for the Parks Service to protect an area like this of such huge importance."

In this way, Saint Croix Island is returning to history yet again. Champlain's arrival in 1604, the 1797 commission ruling, Ganong's effort to reawaken awareness of the site — all these are part of a chain of events leading to the U.S. National Parks Service's decision to "express its

William F. Ganong photographed Saint Croix Island from
the Canadian shore for his 1902 study.
(Courtesy New Brunswick Museum)

concerns" about liquefied natural gas terminals. Calais LNG's proposed
site is less than two miles up the shore, and the massive tankers would
surely hasten the erosion of the island.

"We don't take a position on Calais LNG," Scheid insists. "We don't
take a position on LNG. The only position we have is the mission we have
to uphold, and that mission is to protect and preserve Saint Croix Island,
and the resources that are there, into perpetuity. Our concern is the
vessels that would pass in the channel: the LNG carriers, their engines,
diesel engines, and the four associated tugboats, their engines, all four of
them. That has never happened before in the history of this river, passing
through that channel at high tide. That's when the island's shoreline is
most vulnerable. It has to do with the impact of wave action on the island
at high tide.

"We need to express what our concerns are. Erosion is one of our
concerns. Visitor experience is another concern. Visual impact is another
concern. And noise is another concern. And finally the night sky. So
we're looking at impacts more than just erosion."

Samuel de Champlain experienced something of a rebirth leading up to 2004, when people gathered here to mark the four hundredth anniversary of his arrival, now considered the founding of Acadia and of Canada. There were symposia and documentaries. A major new biography by American historian David Hackett Fischer recast Champlain as a humanist, a renaissance man, and a friend of aboriginal people, a man whose values of fairness and tolerance live on in present-day Canada. The journalist Andrew Coyne noted in 2010 that Champlain has become part of the Canadian government's strategy to rebut Québec nationalism. By referring to him as "Canada's first governor," Coyne said, the government is appropriating his founding of Québec in 1608 as an integral part of the Canadian story, a milestone not just for a single province or ethnicity, or its separatist movement, but for the country as a whole.

And on the St. Croix, he offers yet another argument against massive industrial development on the river. Champlain, I reflect as Scheid steers us back to shore, is still blazing new trails.

15. NEW BRUNSWICK ON THE PENOBSCOT

EASTPORT WEARS ITS HISTORY WELL. Downtown, Water Street is lined with three- and four-storey buildings from a more prosperous time. Some of the old sardine canneries are still here, facing Passamaquoddy Bay, a blanket of blue wrapped securely around the island on which the city sits. The large, stately homes, once owned by the seafaring merchants, stand proudly along narrow streets leading up the hill. The solid, red-brick public buildings speak of an expansive civic optimism.

But a closer look reveals empty storefronts, and the streets are almost free of traffic, even at the start of the workday. There is a low rumble of activity coming from the water, but overall the city is far quieter than its history would lead one to expect. The canneries closed long ago. The population, more than five thousand a century ago, was one-third of that in the last census. Eastport retains its charm, but it is a ghost of a city clinging to tourism, an industry on the edge of the modern economy, for its economic hopes.

A small clutch of men, all of them with greying or white hair, has gathered at the counter of the Waco Diner. They lean in, perched on stools, like they own the place. They are the morning regulars. "I'm going to the border," one announces.

"You got your passport?" a friend asks, with mock earnestness.

"I got my passport," he answers.

"This might be the time to get dual citizenship," another offers, and there are knowing noises and chuckles of agreement from the others.

This easy-going wariness of the border is not a surprise. On Passamaquoddy Bay, people seem somehow more relaxed about the line in the water. There is, after all, a long history of circumventing it, on a much larger scale than even the rum-runners of Madawaska managed. A resident of Charlotte County, New Brunswick, across the bay, once described it as a trade "which some are in the habit of styling contraband — but which we call free trade." And when Passamaquoddy Bay was a smuggler's paradise, Eastport was its hub.

The first commercial centre on the bay was Saint Andrews, where the relocated traders of the Penobscot Association quickly launched themselves back into business. Early settlers on the Maine side of the water bought provisions there and sold their timber, spars, and shingles to Saint Andrews boat-owners, who shipped them on to England. Americans soon established themselves on Moose Island, incorporated Eastport in 1798, and entered the market. In a time of border uncertainty, with trade restrictions imposed as an assertion of national sovereignty, smuggling inevitably took hold. Britain forbade other countries from trading with its colonies, but the Maritimes relied on New England imports. Eastport was where American goods were sent to await a discreet transfer to British jurisdiction out on the water. An unofficial neutral zone between Campobello and Moose Island came into being, where Yankee and British ships exchanged cargoes outside the scrutiny of customs officials.

In the early nineteenth century, New Brunswick's local superintendent of customs, George Leonard, was forever trying to crack down, but his superior in Saint John, William Wanton, knowing the province's reliance on trade with New England, turned a blind eye. Another popular tactic was for ships to land at Eastport and have cooperative customs inspectors "seize" the cargo, then severely undervalue it, so that a bidder acting on behalf of the buyer could post a bond, claim it, and complete the transaction. "Where countries border on each other, it is utterly impossible to put an effectual stop to illicit intercourse between the Inhabitants on each side," Wanton responded when Leonard complained to colonial officials.

Historian Joshua Smith argues that smuggling is a natural consequence of the imposition of artificial borders. Like NB Power's modern sales of electricity, it is a commercial, not ideological, activity, driven by the proximity between buyer and seller. "Borderland residents possessed an attitude that rejected the arbitrary authority of the state, an almost libertarian view that de-emphasized commercial restrictions and borders imposed by distant governments," Smith writes, articulating an argument that must warm the hearts of Atlantica advocates. "Smuggling was the most obvious manifestation of this disregard for governmental interference in the economy. The more government forces attempted to halt unregulated trade, the more apparent it became to locals that the state was an unwelcome and alien force."

In 1807 the renewal of Britain's war with Napoleon prompted London to try to cut off France's trade with other powers, including the United States. When the British began seizing American vessels, Thomas Jefferson responded by imposing an embargo on American vessels sailing to foreign ports, and on foreign vessels shipping U.S. goods. But the embargo proved difficult to enforce on Passamaquoddy Bay, given the fog and the swift-moving tides. "It is, at times, utterly impossible to designate the exact boundary line of the United States," one American naval officer complained.

Britain then undermined the embargo by opening several of its ports, including Saint John, to U.S. ships, and deploying warships to escort them safely to harbour. The Americans came in huge numbers, transforming Saint John into a thriving port[15] and turning Eastport into an even more lucrative smuggling hub, particularly for flour. At its height, Guy Murchie writes, a hundred and sixty thousand barrels of flour passed through Eastport each year. "Flour was piled everywhere," he writes. "Every pile

---

15 The Free Ports Act was such a boon to Saint John that the provincial government commissioned a portrait of its author, Lord Sheffield, which hangs in the New Brunswick Legislature to this day.

of flour was guarded, but the flour somehow disappeared, embargo or no embargo."

When Jefferson's futile embargo was repealed in 1809, there was a grand celebration in Eastport, attended by merchants and customs officials from both sides of the border. The local militia fired salutes, and at a sumptuous banquet, fifty prominent merchants and residents raised sixteen toasts, each punctuated by the firing of the cannon at Fort Sullivan. The commercial impetus to trade had triumphed over the political imperative to enforce the border.

But there was an important consequence of the embargo that was literally echoing across the bay. The fort had been built a year earlier, and troops were stationed there, to enforce the embargo. Their presence alarmed the British, who had never given up their claim to Moose Island.

Within five years, it was back in their hands. The Union Jack flew over Eastport, and New Brunswick's border with Maine shifted a hundred miles west to Penobscot Bay, where Richard Oswald always thought it should be.

The Peavey Memorial Library offers more proof that Eastport values its past. Not only is the building itself, as an example of Romanesque Revival architecture, strikingly well-preserved, but its collection of books on local history was clearly assembled with care by librarians who understood the importance of collective memory. Among the volumes is William Kilby's *Eastport and Passamaquoddy: A Collection of Historical and Biographical Sketches*, the classic work on the first century of the town's history. Thoroughly researched and gracefully written, with a gentle, understated nod to Maine's take on the border — New Brunswick officials "decided for themselves" the Schoodic was the St. Croix, Kilby writes — it is a worthy companion to William Francis Ganong's scholarship on the same subject.

"The people of Eastport were not allowed to forget that the government of Great Britain still claimed jurisdiction over their island," Kilby writes, setting the scene for the drama that unfolded on Passamaquoddy Bay in the second decade of the nineteenth century. In 1786, New Brunswick had included Moose Island in legislation dividing the province into counties and parishes, which the governor of Massachusetts labelled "a most daring insult upon the dignity of Massachusetts and the United States." But Britain argued Moose Island was part of Nova Scotia's historical jurisdiction, covered in the 1621 land grant that included islands within six leagues of a line drawn from St. Mary's Bay, near present-day Digby, to the mouth of the St. Croix. It was therefore exempt under the 1783 clause that gave the United States all islands within twenty leagues of its coast except those that had been part of Nova Scotia.

The issue was more than symbolic: if Britain held Moose Island, the main channel between Campobello and Deer Island leading into Passamaquoddy Bay and the St. Croix would be entirely under British control.

In 1803 American and British negotiators agreed to a treaty ceding Moose Island to the United States. The border would run down the channel between Moose Island and Deer Island, except — unlike its eventual configuration — it would then turn sharply to the northeast and moved up the main channel between Deer Island and Campobello, while still giving both those islands to New Brunswick. The "peculiarity" of this border, as Kilby describes it, would have given the United States access to the shipping passage, while awarding the two major islands on *both* sides of the line to Britain. Whether this would have been workable is unknown. The U.S. Senate refused to ratify the treaty over unrelated provisions. Three years later, Jefferson refused to submit a second attempt at a treaty to the Senate, again because of unrelated elements. And so the matter was left unresolved.

War between the United States and Britain came in 1812. On Passamaquoddy Bay and the St. Croix, there was a collective decision that the conflict would not disrupt good relations. In St. Stephen, the Reverend Duncan M'Coll, who ministered to a congregation of worshippers from both sides of the border, urged that "a Committee should be chosen on both sides, who should consult together and maintain peace and order till such a time as troops from either side should take command on the lines." M'Coll himself discovered he could still cross to Calais without incident.[16] Farther north, Woodstock and Houlton likewise agreed to not permit any hostilities between their communities.

The day after Eastport learned of the war, there was a town meeting where everyone agreed "a good understanding" with New Brunswick had to be maintained. Kilby writes that "inhabitants on both sides of the boundary line, feeling that the injuries which they could inflict upon one another would only embitter their own lives without helping either government, and bound together by ties of business, cosanguinity, and friendship, determined to mutually discourage predatory excursions, and to live on as amicable terms as the state of affairs would allow." Unarmed U.S. ships carrying goods would be allowed to continue landing at Saint John and to leave if the British products they were carrying were of no military use. Smuggling continued, naturally, with boats sailing under Swedish flags to transport provisions between Eastport and Campobello. "Sweden was only a mile or two away," Murchie writes with a wink, "and two entries in a single day were possible."

The war continued for more than two years. Its best-known battles took place in Upper Canada, now Ontario. But in the spring of 1814, with Napoleon defeated in Europe, Britain turned its attention to New England, which it had exempted from its naval blockade, and where it now hoped to strike a decisive blow against the United States. The New Brunswick government and the Halifax Committee of Trade petitioned Britain to correct the mistake of 1783 and re-establish its border at the Penobscot River by seizing eastern Maine, starting with Moose Island and the city of Eastport.

I look up from my reverie at the Peavey. A thin man with glasses has arrived and is making his way over to my seat. As he shakes my hand,

---

16 Harold Davis's definitive history of the St. Croix includes the famous anecdote, cited by Stephen Harper in the introduction to this book, about the British lending gunpowder to Calais for a Fourth of July celebration. Davis situates it "back in the days when there was still fear of an American invasion" but does not say explicitly that this was during the War of 1812. He attributes it to a local historian, Dr. Maud Maxwell Vesey.

Local historian Wayne Wilcox shows off the ruins of
the British powder house in Eastport.

he glances approvingly at the copy of Kilby. His name is Wayne Wilcox,
and he is an amateur historian, an enthusiast of Eastport's rich lore, and
a contributor to the local newspaper, the *Quoddy Tides*. He has come to
show me a relic of the four years Eastport spent under British occupation,
a time when it ceased to be a border town and was, essentially, part of
New Brunswick.

As a member of the Border Historical Society — a telling
name — Wilcox is planning events and raising funds for 2014, when
Eastport will mark the bicentennial of the morning the British navy
came ashore. Wilcox has applied for funding from Washington, surely the
only time, I suggest, when the U.S. government has been asked to help
commemorate the occupation of American soil by a foreign power. Imagine
when Fox News gets hold of *that*. "Here's an idea," Wilcox says. "In 2014,
you celebrate the British coming. Four years later, 2018, you celebrate
the British leaving. Two celebrations. It could work. Unfortunately, I think
the burning of the White House [when British troops reached Washington
in 1814] is going to suck all the air out of that."

Wilcox and I drive through Eastport's small downtown to Washington Street, then up a side street onto a bluff atop the city. We park at a nearby school and walk down McKinley Street to a squat, four-walled stone structure. It is the powder house built by British troops after they seized Fort Sullivan in 1814 and renamed it Fort Sherbrooke. "You've got to envision this without any trees, just a bare rock overlooking the harbour," Wilcox says. "This thing was huge. It had like two hundred barrels of black powder. It had a huge roof on it. And the barracks, the enlisted men's barracks, went down that way."

The fort itself is completely gone. The ruins of the powder house are underwhelming, but it is the only surviving structure directly connected to the British occupation, and Wilcox is determined to save it. "We're trying to get funds to put a roof over it, to prevent it from deteriorating any further," he says. "What we want to do is completely rebuild it again. Hopefully, with grant money, you're probably looking at a hundred and sixty thousand dollars. This is all original stone. It's never been even partially restored."

It was to this spot, on July 11, 1814, that a single British soldier, carrying a flag and trailed by a growing crowd of citizens, walked "at a very rapid pace" to lay claim to Eastport. A fleet of a dozen ships had come up the main passage into the bay that morning. At first they were assumed to be merchant ships, so Eastporters shrugged them off. Even when guns were spotted, the boats were assumed to be heading for Saint Andrews. Instead, they quickly drew up off Eastport and sent a small boat to the wharf, from which Lieutenant Oats of the British Army sprang.

At Fort Sullivan, he handed Major Perley Putnam a written demand for the surrender of the fort and the island. "My orders are imperative," Oats replied when Putnam invited him to sit down. "I cannot stop." He gave Putnam five minutes. The American major replied that he would fire on the ships, but several citizens who had followed Oats up the hill told Putnam resistance was futile and the town might be destroyed if he chose to fight. "Major Putnam finally consented to accept the terms offered to him," Lorenzo Sabine writes in a historical sketch of the occupation included in Kilby's history.

Within the hour, five hundred British soldiers came ashore, and Eastport and Moose Island were under British jurisdiction. It was not an ordinary military occupation, Sabine notes. "As conquered citizens of the United States, they would have been exposed to many injuries, which, as subjects restored to their rightful sovereign, they escaped," he writes. The two-thirds of the population who agreed to swear an oath to the King were allowed to stay and go about their lives; the others had to leave. New schools were established to accommodate the children of the British troops, and balls, theatres, and horse races were organized. Residents with a pass could travel to the American mainland, and farmers and boatmen were allowed to trade. Still, "there were many things to render their situation irksome and extremely unpleasant," Sabine writes. The New Brunswick government refused to grant the Moose Islanders British citizenship, even though no one knew whether they would ever again be part of the United States.

The uncertainty may have been unpleasant, but it was not oppressive. The American Revolution had taken place within living memory and had not yet acquired a sense of permanence. Particularly on the border, Britain was not seen as the enemy. "It was kind of a love-hate type thing," Wilcox tells me. "It was a good thing for Eastport for four years because the British didn't look at it as conquered people. They looked at it as welcoming brothers back into the family. The first year was kind of rough, but once things got ironed out, it was accepted and Eastport really made out well. The British improved roads, they built a lot of infrastructure, they did some amazing things here."

Six weeks after the capture of Eastport, an armada of British ships left Halifax for the next phase of the attack on eastern Maine, with Governor John Sherbrooke of Nova Scotia in command. The plan was to capture Machias, a town down the coast from Eastport that Britain had held during the Revolution. But when an American military ship was seen heading for the mouth of the Penobscot, Sherbrooke gave chase, hoping to capture it. The British landed at Castine, took the town, and secured the Penobscot River as far north as Bangor. Many of the wealthier Americans he met along the river, Sherbrooke wrote, "are really desirous of changing their present form of government." He determined to grant their wish: rather than press on to capture more territory, Sherbrooke consolidated his gains and established a customs house at Castine. He had, in effect, shifted the New Brunswick border to the Penobscot River.

Had Sherbrooke known the weakness of the American defences, he might have pushed down the coast, and history might have been very different. Jefferson's 1807 embargo had so damaged the economy of Massachusetts, particularly in its District of Maine, that citizens began electing Federalists to Washington. As punishment, Jefferson refused to fund defensive fortifications in those areas, leaving much of the Massachusetts coast vulnerable. Had Sherbrooke known, he might have tried to take Portland.

Washington's neglect further inflamed the anti-war sentiment in New England, where state officials were more concerned with maintaining trade ties to Britain than with fighting what they viewed as someone else's war. By late 1814, the five New England states convened the Hartford Convention, where they discussed seceding. Instead, they drew up demands including constitutional amendments to limit trade embargoes to sixty days, and to require a two-thirds majority of Congress to declare war. A Massachusetts delegation had arrived in Washington in February 1815 to press these demands when word arrived that British and American negotiators in the Flemish city of Ghent had signed a treaty to end the war. Unaware of the vulnerability of coastal Massachusetts, Britain agreed to return eastern Maine to the United States, and its troops left Castine, Bangor and other towns. "New Brunswick's brief expansion westward, to the old boundaries of Acadia, was over," historian Barry Lohnes writes in a study of the occupation.

The British had by then collected eleven thousand pounds in duties at the customs house on the Penobscot. The money was placed in what was called the Castine Fund and was used by Lord Dalhousie, Sherbrooke's successor as governor of Nova Scotia, to establish a new non-denominational college in Halifax. Today it is Dalhousie University. "New Brunswick," notes Lohnes, "at whose new 'border' these monies had been collected and at whose instigation the expedition had been mounted, received nothing."

The Treaty of Ghent restored all territory captured during the war to its previous owners, with one exception. The British would not leave Moose Island. The negotiators agreed that a commission should finally fix the water boundary in Passamaquoddy Bay. Until that task was completed, Eastport would remain under the Union Jack.

Britain's commissioner was again Thomas Barclay, who had sat on the St. Croix commission, and its agent was Ward Chipman, whose use of Champlain's writings and maps had produced the breakthrough at Dochet Island. The American commissioner was John Holmes of Maine, and when work finally began in 1816, he aggressively claimed all the islands of Passamaquoddy Bay. The British argued they had all been within the limits of Nova Scotia as it was granted to William Alexander in 1621, exempting them from the 1783 treaty that gave the United States any islands within twenty leagues of its shore. The Americans argued that the Nova Scotia of 1621 had ceased to exist when it was annexed to Massachusetts seven decades later and that the islands were not explicitly included when it became a separate colony again.

The commission seemed headed for a stalemate, but Barclay exploited a weakness on the American side. Holmes, the American commissioner, had been elected to Congress in 1816 and would be seated in December 1817. But the American Constitution barred members of Congress from holding other government appointments. Holmes had to finish his work by the fall or resign one of the two positions. If Holmes opted to be a congressman, Barclay hinted he would feel entitled to rule himself as a one-man commission. And there was little doubt how he would rule.

In a private meeting in October, Barclay presented Holmes with an ultimatum. Britain would give up Moose Island and two other smaller islands nearby if the United States ceded Grand Manan and all the others.

The trade-off made sense. Americans were firmly established at Eastport on Moose Island, while Loyalists had settled Grand Manan. Holmes tried to get Campobello for the U.S. in exchange for giving up Grand Manan, but to no avail. "I told him he had my ultimatum," Barclay recalled. With time running out, Holmes folded his cards. The deal was done.

The British made plans to leave Eastport. A remarkable period in the city's history drew to an end, a period that continues to resonate in 2010 as a historical novelty. "A lot of the new people who've joined the historical society are fascinated by it," Wayne Wilcox says. "Russ Terry, he's from California, he and his wife retired here, and they love it. They can't believe the British occupied the island. Eastport has the designation of being the last piece of American territory given up from the War of 1812, and actually, until the Japanese occupied two of the Aleutian Islands in World War Two, this was the last piece of American territory occupied by a foreign power."

A lawn mower is buzzing around the outside of the powder house. Russ Terry is cutting the lawn. Terry is one of those Americans who has roamed and rambled across the breadth of his country, farming in California, working in a national park, and building cabinets in Arkansas before coming to Eastport for a visit and deciding to stay. Now he chairs the Border Historical Society's powder house committee. His interest is not the conflict it represents but the connections. "I think it's fascinating, the interrelationships, the families on both sides of the border," he says when he quiets the mower. "It's a community, is what it is. The bay makes it a community. It was easy to cross. A lot of people traded in Eastport from those areas because it was so easy. The international boundary is more on paper than a reality among the people."

In the decades following the War of 1812, the Webster-Ashburton Treaty, and Confederation, the connection endured, even as that local, libertarian impulse to disregard the border became more difficult to obey. Smuggling continued, but reciprocity treaties and, eventually, tougher enforcement sapped much of the incentive to continue on a large scale. A lax approach to cross-border hiring gave way to stricter regulation, putting an end to Canadian islanders working unofficially in Eastport's sardine factories. More recently, there was 9/11 and the security crackdown. The locals blame it all on distant national governments that apparently cannot grasp that an international community is capable of managing its local cross-border affairs on its own.

"No matter what Washington or Ottawa does, there's always going to be that tie," Wilcox says. "Especially with the fisheries, the sardine plants, marriages, and families on both sides of the border. You had that strong bond here, even after the British left. You still have that today."

On the sunny afternoon of June 18, 1818, American soldiers set foot in Eastport for the first time in almost four years. A large crowd greeted them and cheered, and they marched in a column to a vacant lot where they pitched their tents and waited. Twelve days later, the arrangements were set, and hundreds of Eastport residents gathered at Fort Sherbrooke's parade ground to watch the handover. The British and American troops marched in and formed ranks around the flagpole, and General James Miller, the senior American officer, and Captain Richard Gibbon, the British commander of Moose Island, exchanged a few words. Then the order was read returning the fort, and the island, to the United States. A twenty-gun salute was fired, a band played "Yankee Doodle Dandy," the Union Jack was lowered, and the Star-Spangled Banner was raised. As it caught the breeze, the crowd cheered heartily. Fort Sherbrooke was Fort Sullivan again, and the British soldiers, after exchanging salutes with the Americans, formed a double column and marched down the hill to the wharf, where they boarded boats that took them to a ship waiting offshore.

The symbolism suited the importance of the day. But the most telling moments had taken place in the twelve days between the arrival of the American troops and the departure of the British. A group of forty-two prominent Eastport residents wrote to Gibbon, the British commander, to express their "high respect and esteem" for his effort, during his command, "to conserve the interests of the inhabitants; to unite moderation with firmness; and prudence with decision." He and his officers, they said, "have had the magnanimity and uprightness to refrain from all oppression, and to overcome the temptation *to feel power and forget right.*" The letter went on to praise the "prompt and friendly attention to the interests of the inhabitants" of another officer, and the garrison doctor's "many charitable and kind offices towards many of the inhabitants of this place."

It could only have happened here. Citizens who had lived under martial law for four years were writing *thank-you notes* to their captors. Gibbon responded in kind: "We sincerely hope," he wrote, "that the amity and good understanding so happily re-established between nations, of the same language and feelings, may be so strongly cemented by a reciprocity of interests and advantages, as never to meet with interruption or disunion."

Gibbon's hope was granted, and continues to be granted, on Passamaquoddy Bay. "I grew up here and the border community is still here," Wilcox says. "Campobello, Deer Island — I don't think of them as foreigners. If it wasn't for the Canadians, we wouldn't have a Fourth of July, seriously. They generally send the bands over. We get the Canadian bagpipes and the Shriners. We get some from the American side, but it always seems to be the Canadians who are more willing to send them. There's a cultural bond here to begin with."

There is a symmetry to Canada helping make Eastport's Fourth of July one of the biggest in Maine. It explains why it is *not* so strange that Eastport would seek to commemorate its occupation by a foreign power: because the occupiers were not truly *foreign*.

16. BELOVED ISOLATION

THERE IS ONE LAST BORDER "MARKER" TO SEE. It is not an official monument. The last genuine one I saw was at Monument Brook, and there are none below it, only reference markers on the shores of the St. Croix and small plaques or discs on the international bridges. This final marker is informal and does not sit precisely on the border, but it, too, connects the New Brunswick-Maine boundary to the much longer line running across the continent to the Pacific Ocean. I have set out on foot from Liberty Point, the southeastern tip of Campobello Island, to hike a narrow but well-maintained trail along the cliffs facing the Bay of Fundy and Grand Manan Island.

The trail follows the curve of Liberty Cove to Ragged Point, and as I march up the hill towards the rocky tip pointing southeast, a view of Grand Manan Channel opens wide before me. Somewhere out there in the water, Canada's border with the United States executes a right turn before heading out to sea.

At Ragged Point I find the SunSweep sculpture, or more precisely, one of them. Installed by the artist David Barr in 1985, the piece, a five-feet-tall arch of black granite, is one of three that forms a larger, symbolic work stretching to Lighthouse Park at Point Roberts, Washington, where a companion piece, another arch, is located. Barr's third piece, at American Point Island in Lake-of-the-Woods, Minnesota, comprises two wedge-shaped slabs, representing the keystones for the continent-spanning work.

The SunSweep sculpture at Ragged Point, Campobello, is part of a work that ends near the Pacific.

Barr chose the sites deliberately. They are all geopolitical enclaves, part of their respective countries yet isolated from them by the Canada-U.S. border. Point Roberts, south of Vancouver, British Columbia, is at the tip of the Tsawwassen peninsula on the Georgia Strait, just below the forty-ninth parallel; when that line was chosen as the boundary, negotiators did not notice that it would create a five-square-mile patch of American territory reachable by land only via Canada. The piece in Minnesota, on a peninsula cut off from the rest of the state because of an error in the Treaty of Paris, is also accessible by land only through Canada. And Campobello Island, though part of New Brunswick, has its only bridge link to the mainland at Lubec, Maine, a consequence of the trade-off in 1818 that awarded the island to Britain. The only all-Canadian route between Campobello and the rest of the province involves a two-ferry trip via Deer Island.

Britain's bid for Campobello made sense at the time. Loyalists had settled there after the Revolution, and its location so close to the American mainland was not a concern when boats were still the primary mode of travel around Passamaquoddy Bay. One could easily move between Eastport, Lubec, Deer Island, Saint Andrews, and Campobello. "People were coming and going all the time," Alice Gough, one of the island's oldest residents, recalls as she sits in her living room in Welshpool. "If I wanted to go to Eastport, I went down to the wharf, and maybe somebody would be going, and I'd get aboard their boat. With a mail boat, you paid. If you went with a fisherman or anybody else, you didn't have to pay them. They were very obliging when they'd take you."

Gough was born in 1918 and raised as an American in Eastport but met her husband at a dance on Campobello when she was sixteen years old. "A friend of mine had been coming over to the dances. Mama wouldn't let us get a boat and go over, but she took my sister, who was training to be a nurse, down to Bath, Maine, and while she was gone, we took advantage of it. My friend knew when the boat was coming in. I sort of went along with the flow."

Lubec, founded by merchants who chose to leave Eastport during the British occupation rather than pay duty to the King, is separated from Campobello by a narrow channel eight hundred feet wide. When Alice Gough was young, no one gave a second thought to the fact that crossing the Narrows meant crossing the border. "I had mom and dad over in Eastport for years after I got married, and I went over probably three or four times a week at least, sometimes oftener," Gough says. "I used to go almost every day after the kids went to school. Ran down, got the mail boat, stayed all the day. There was a customs office at Eastport but they weren't always there after hours. I can't ever remember reporting to customs." Canada later posted an officer at Campobello, but "if we came back late, we didn't wake him up."

First settled by the French when it was part of Acadia, Campobello was granted by the British to Captain William Owen in 1770, as a reward for his military exploits in the Seven Years' War, and remained in his family until its paradoxical location — isolated, yet accessible from coastal Maine — caught the eye of a group of wealthy Americans. In 1881 they formed the Campobello Company, bought out the Owenses, and set about turning the island into a getaway for the élite of the northeast United States. "The islanders, without participating in the decision, were about to see an enormous social change take place on Campobello," writes Jonas Klein. The locals, seen by the new arrivals as rugged and industrious but hardly their equals, faded deferentially into the background. "Wealth, style and privilege were to dominate their island in a manner that was to them unknown. Overnight, Campobello became a playground for American gentility of the Gilded Age."

Part of the appeal was the island's cool temperatures, which, in the days before refrigeration and air-conditioning, offered relief from the sweltering summers of Boston and New York. James Roosevelt, part of the wealthy Roosevelt family of New York, visited in 1883 with his wife Sara and their one-year-old son Franklin, and James commissioned a "cottage" to be built near Welshpool, facing Eastport. The cottage was, in fact, a fifteen-room house closer in style to a large Victorian home, designed to accommodate guests and servants. This grand summer home became an important touchstone for young Franklin as he learned to sail the family yacht *New Moon*, befriended local fishermen, and hiked a good part of the island.

Campobello's heyday as a summer resort would be relatively brief, as modern conveniences — particularly automobiles and air-conditioning — made its far-flung location less appealing. But it remained a "beloved island" to Franklin and Eleanor Roosevelt. His growing involvement in politics was the only thing that prevented him from spending full summers there with his wife and their children. In 1921, it was the scene of a turning point in his life: after a fall into the cold waters of the Bay of Fundy, followed by a day of strenuous outdoor activity, Roosevelt experienced the first symptoms of polio, which would confine him to a wheelchair. "I'd never felt anything as cold as that water," he would remember. "Walking and running couldn't overcome the chill. . . . I'd never felt quite that way before." He soon lost the ability to walk, making visits to the island considerably more difficult.

Roosevelt returned three times during his presidency. The first, in 1933, saw him sail from Massachusetts up the coast for a two-day visit, including public festivities in Eastport, Lubec, and Campobello. Landing at Welshpool, the president addressed the gathered crowd from the back of a touring car. "I was thinking," he told them, "as I came through the Narrows and saw the line of fishing boats and the people on the wharves, both here at Welshpool and also at Eastport, that this reception here is probably the finest example of friendship between nations — permanent

President Franklin Delano Roosevelt (second from right) chats with
New Brunswick Premier Allison Dysart on a Campobello Island beach in
1936. Canadian Senator Neil McLean is at the left and N.B. Attorney-
General John McNair is next to Roosevelt.
(Provincial Archives of New Brunswick Department of Supply and Services photographs: P158-1)

friendship between nations — that we can possibly have. . . . I hope and
am very confident that if peace continues in this world and that if the
other nations of the world follow the very good example of the United
States and Canada, I will be able to come back here for a holiday during
the next three years."

His next trip, in 1936, was for only one night, though he took the
time to share a picnic lunch with the premier of New Brunswick, Allison
Dysart. His last visit, in 1939, was even briefer. "I think people on the
island were very proud that Roosevelt came here, and everybody had a
good word for him," says Alice Gough, who went to Eastport in 1933 to
see him. "But I would say on the American side, there's always politics,
you know, and he was a Democrat. My father was a staunch Republican
and he had not too much use for Roosevelt. He would call him 'that idiot'
in the White House. And I would listen to Dad and felt the same way.
But I had a friend, Amy, whose mother was a staunch Democrat. Talking
to her, I was sort of on the fence. I could see things that Roosevelt did

that I thought were fine. In fact, now I think the two people who have made the most changes in the lives of people were Franklin Roosevelt and Louis Robichaud," she says, referring to the modernizing premier of New Brunswick during the 1960s. "I think God sent Roosevelt at exactly the time he was needed."

After Roosevelt's death at the end of the war, Eleanor returned often to Campobello, including in 1946 to attend the unveiling of a red granite cairn and bronze tablet installed at Welshpool by the Historic Sites and Monuments Board of Canada. It was the first memorial to her husband on foreign soil. She later gave the cottage to their fourth child, Elliot, who sold it in 1952 to the industrialist Armand Hammer and his two brothers. The Hammers restored the house, adding electricity and a telephone, and invited Eleanor to use it whenever she wished. Her final visit was in 1962, at the age of seventy-seven, for the official opening of the Franklin Delano Roosevelt International Memorial Bridge, which finally linked the island to the mainland at Lubec. But she was too ill to attend the ceremony, and she died later the same year.

When the Hammers failed to find a buyer for the cottage, they offered it to the United States government as a memorial to the president. Because it is on Canadian soil, the site is designated an international park, administered by a commission with members appointed by the two governments. "It is the only park in the world owned by the people of two countries," its Web site says. Besides the original cottage, the park now includes a visitor centre, three other historic summer homes, and a 2,800-acre protected natural area. It comprises ponds where Roosevelt canoed as a young man and rocky coasts where he hiked, including that trail along Liberty Cove to Ragged Point.

And so a park dedicated to an American president became a premier tourist attraction for a small Canadian province, and an economic lifeline for an island that taught him about a broader world beyond his life of privilege: a fitting tribute to Roosevelt and to the friendship he spoke of in Welshpool in 1933.

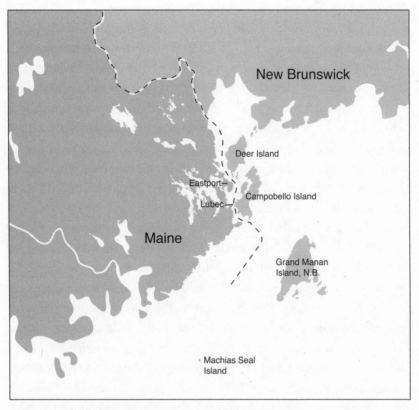

Though ownership of the islands was settled in 1818, the route of the border
into Grand Manan Channel wasn't established until almost a century later.

I linger at the SunSweep sculpture, imagining Franklin Roosevelt standing
there as a boy, looking out at Grand Manan Island and the Bay of Fundy
beyond. Little has changed, with one invisible exception: when Roosevelt
was at Ragged Point, no invisible line ran through the waters out there.

In 1818, the British and the Americans had resolved who owned the
islands of the bay, but not *where* exactly the border ran as it emerged from
the St. Croix. Only in 1910, when Roosevelt was already twenty-eight
years old, did Canada and the United States agree on how to extend it
into the Bay of Fundy. This new treaty, one of eight signed over a period
of seven years to resolve outstanding boundary issues, drew the line from
the bottom of Head Harbour Passage, between Treat Island and Friar Head
on Campobello, through the Lubec Narrows, then southeast into Grand

Manan Channel, where—halfway between Ragged Point and Grand Manan Island—it turns sharply southwest towards the Gulf of Maine.

The 1818 commission left other loose ends. When Maine's John Holmes agreed, under pressure, to give Campobello and Grand Manan to Britain, he and Thomas Barclay struck a gentleman's agreement, which they described in letters to their governments. "In making this decision it became necessary that each of the commissioners should yield a part of his individual opinion," they wrote. "Several reasons induced them to adopt this measure; one of which was the impression and belief that the navigable waters of the Bay of Passamaquoddy, which, by the Treaty of Ghent, is said to be part of the Bay of Fundy, are common to both parties for the purpose of all lawful and direct communication with their own territories and foreign ports." This was a reference to Head Harbour Passage, and it appears to give the United States transit rights, including for LNG tankers.

Bob Godfrey thinks not. For one thing, the letters amounted to an informal handshake and were not legally binding. He also says that the United Nations Convention on the Law of the Sea gives signatory nations the power to pass regulations on what kind of ships could transit their passages, and if all other objections fail, and American regulators approve one of the LNG terminals for construction, Canada can block the ships with little more than the stroke of a pen.

It is early 2011 when I check in with Godfrey, and he does not believe there will need to be a regulatory showdown on LNG. By now, all three projects are looking shaky. The market for natural gas is questionable, he says. "North America is in a hundred-year natural gas glut, mooting the need even for some of the now-existing terminals, much less additional construction," he tells me. The head of Quoddy Bay LNG, Don Smith, said in April, when Washington cancelled his lease with the Passamaquoddy tribe, that "the financial circumstances of the country have made it impractical to build it now." And in July, GS Power Holdings LLC, a subsidiary of the global giant Goldman Sachs, pulled out as the major investor in Calais LNG.

The Calais partnership scrambled to find new backers and asked Maine's Board of Environmental Protection to postpone public hearings on its permit application. But there were more troubles. In September, the U.S. Coast Guard, as it had done earlier for the Downeast LNG regulatory review, said the waters leading to the Calais LNG site were safe for shipping. But, it added, "the most probable security regime should consist of a mix of U.S. and Canadian federal, state/provincial and local law enforcement, which may require cost-sharing agreements." Calais LNG, it said, had to show "an effective security regime has been established during the Canadian portion of the vessels' planned route"—an impossibility as long as Canada continued to oppose the project.

Calais LNG withdrew its state permit applications just before Christmas 2010, citing the "extreme turbulence" of the financial markets. The company made noises about refiling when the economy rebounds, but only Downeast LNG, the proposed terminal across from Saint Andrews, was left in the hunt. But its federal and state regulatory applications were both stalled, and if it revives them, it, too, will have to contend with the Coast Guard's insistence on Canadian cooperation.

There is always a chance of a political trade-off. Nothing about the border exists in isolation, particularly when it comes to energy. In 2009, looking for ways to pressure Canada to back off on LNG, the Maine Legislature imposed a moratorium on energy transmission corridors, aimed at the one Irving Oil wanted to build in the state. "They've been willing to play hardball," said Kevin Raye, a Republican representative from near Eastport. "We should, too." The moratorium was lifted in the spring of 2010, raising fears of a backroom deal. And in August, there were indications Prime Minister Stephen Harper was looking to resolve Arctic boundary disputes with the United States, which might eliminate his most important strategic reason for standing firm on LNG.

Everything is interconnected on the line. The Passamaquoddy tribe, their flirtation with LNG behind them, was working with a company called Tidewalker Associates to look at generating tidal electricity, a concept once espoused by no less than President Franklin Roosevelt. He first heard of the idea from his Campobello neighbour Dexter Cooper, an engineer and another of the American "summer people." Roosevelt backed it in part to help Democratic Party fortunes in Maine, which leaned Republican at the time. When construction began in 1935, "the depression, indeed, appeared over in northern Maine," writes historian Walter Lowrie. "The sleepy villages resounded to the noise of construction and made room for the influx of workers, administrators, and reporters." But influential private power utilities in Maine pressured the state government to stall their role in the project, and as costs at the site soared beyond projections, Congress grew restive. When war loomed, Roosevelt let the project die.

President John F. Kennedy tried to revive the idea in the early 1960s, linking it to a proposal for a hydroelectric dam at Dickey, Maine, on the Upper Saint John River. Tidal power again proved unworkable, but the Dickey Dam, upstream from Fort Kent and the Saint-François, received preliminary funding from Congress in 1965. Studies and preparations on the river were halted in 1976, however, after the discovery of Furbish's lousewort near the site. The odd-looking herb grows only along the banks of the Saint John River and had been considered extinct. The Dickey Dam would have flooded eighty-eight thousand acres of its habitat, one reason — a "downright silly" one, according to *Time* Magazine — that Congress finally killed the project in 1986.

Furbish's lousewort, it goes without saying, does not respect borders. It grows on both the American and Canadian sides of the Saint John, making it an international obstacle to the hydro dam. The border may be an imaginary line, but it is a *single* line from the Upper Saint John to Passamaquoddy Bay, and it connects all the stories that unfold along it.

Energy is one constant narrative along the border. Security remains the other. "It's a nuisance but you've got to live with it," Alice Gough tells me. "I think everybody's beginning to realize that they can't go as freely as they did years ago. It doesn't bother me too much. They're pretty quick about it, taking your passports." The impetus to cross remains the same, she says. "Some things we can get here, and some things we can't. I buy groceries on both sides. Now some of the people over there are coming

A highway sign on the road leading to St. Stephen and the border
points to the anomaly of Campobello.

over here. We have a drugstore and they don't have a drugstore in Lubec.
And also the drugs are cheaper."

The crackdown is particularly difficult for Campobello, given its
anomalous location. "This is an island fifty miles — in winter — from
the nearest Canadian town, and two minutes from the nearest American
town," says Joyce Morrell, a co-owner of The Owen House, the island's
best-known inn. "We are physically attached to Maine and physically
removed from Canada. That's not true of most of the other border towns.
So this is a really strange situation. This is the door to the rest of the world,
so everything is affected by that border, constantly. That border is a big
part of our lives. And it's just a huge presence because you can't escape it
no matter what you do. You can't hide from it. You can't work around it."

Morrell's inn was built in 1835 by William Owen, the son of the soldier
who was granted Campobello in 1770. It sits on a cliff at Welshpool with
a commanding view of the bay. From the porch we can see the Roosevelt

property down the shore and Eastport across the water. Morrell's co-owner, Jan Meiners, brings us tea and tells a typical Campobello story, about the inn's washer and dryer. "We bought it at Sears in Machias, Maine, because the Sears store in St. Stephen told us they would not send a service person here to honour the warranty, because of the border. Sears in Machias said they would deliver and they'd take the old machines. I said, 'Will you send your service truck to Campobello?' They said 'We're sorry, we can't do that because the Canadian side won't let us in to do warranty work, and on the American side when we come back through, it takes too much time because they want to search the whole truck. We just can't justify it.' So even though there's a warranty that's part of the purchase price, they will not honour it." When the pipes froze on the washer the following winter, a serviceman from Machias, about half an hour away, came over on his own time, in his own truck, and took the machine back to fix it. "You have to learn how to work around the problems," Meiners says. "You have to be creative."

The odd political geography causes people on Campobello to see the whole *concept* of connections differently. For Alice Gough's generation, the border did not matter nearly as much as the physical separation created by the eight-hundred-foot Lubec Narrows, a separation that finally ended in 1962. "The bridge changed our lives," she says. "The car ferry would only run until six o'clock. After a while, in the summertime, it ran until nine. So we were pretty limited. If we went over and went to Calais, we had to hurry back. And sometimes we missed it, and then we would have to go get somebody with a boat to row us across the Narrows, and then you wouldn't have your car. I used to speed coming home, but once we had that bridge, I said I would never go over the speed limit again, and I don't think I ever did. I'd gone too many times — not if I had anyone with me, but if I was alone — when I'd step on it and just fly. And the road wasn't as good then.

"Everything you gain, you lose something," she adds, suddenly seeing the bridge from a different perspective. "It was kind of a social thing, the boat, lining up. When you would go up in order to get, maybe, the one o'clock ferry, maybe to go over to Machias and come back, there'd be a lineup of maybe fifty cars, and you'd have to wait because they only took a few. And then coming back, the whole Front Street in Lubec would be lined up with cars, and you could get out of your car and do your shopping. You went back and forth between cars talking to people. If Joe was driving and there was a friend of mine in another car, I might get in and go across with them."

In early 2011, Prime Minister Stephen Harper and President Barack Obama announced negotiations that may lead to the line being restored to something like its pre-9/11 state. "We commit to expanding our management of the border to the concept of a North American perimeter, not to replace or eliminate the border but where possible, to streamline and decongest it," Harper said during a visit to the White House. There were immediate and predictable reactions that Harper was giving up sovereignty; on that issue, Obama's popularity with Canadians may prove decisive in selling an eventual agreement. "I have great confidence that Prime Minister Harper's going to be very protective of certain core values of Canada, just as I would be very protective of the core values of the United States," Obama said. "And those won't always match up perfectly."

I expect the idea of a looser line will be embraced along the New Brunswick-Maine border. But Joyce Morrell is no longer sure that the best border is a soft border. "You ask anybody on this island when they complain about the border if they'd like to have no border, and be U.S. territory, and you'll get a very different answer. They'll come up short. 'Well, no. That's not what I meant.' No, they wouldn't want that."

Morrell is the first border person to directly, squarely, challenge my developing thesis that the line is an unwelcome, unnatural intrusion. The LNG fight, she tells me, has given her a new appreciation for clear-cut boundaries. "I like the Canadian political system, because fighting LNG, we've had wonderful responses, personal, committed responses, and on the American side you'd never even get anyone to talk to. It's such a huge bureaucracy. It's much different over here."

This is not knee-jerk Canadian nationalism: Morrell is American. She was eleven years old when she first came to Campobello with her parents from New Jersey, "one of the first transplants here," she says, referring to year-round expats, not the "old guard" upper-crust Americans of the summer colony.

The island was wilder when Morrell arrived as a child, with more moose roaming the woods, more whales in the water, and more birds in the air. "The bay would be totally white with birds and they'd sing like a symphony all night long. I used to sleep on the front porch as a kid to hear it. This is a little bastion of old-world peace and we really would like to keep it that way because it's so valuable and special. It's valuable for us and it's valuable to the tourists. I can't tell you how many come and the troubles just sort of fade and they say it's just not like this anywhere in the cities: 'We can't find this kind of quiet. It doesn't exist anymore.' . . . So we'd like to hold onto it if possible."

The border was never a concern when Morrell was young. "Since my mother didn't work and my father was retired, it didn't seem a problem. I know the border was much looser. There was hardly any border security. There was a little bit, but it was certainly leaky. There was no thought of terrorism on either side. It was a much kinder, much calmer situation."

Now, because of LNG, it does matter, profoundly, to the point that she plans to pay her adopted country the highest possible tribute. "After going through this fight for five years, I'm going to make it a point to become Canadian because the differences are unbelievable."

"We've got the applications on the kitchen table," Meiners says.

"I told Jan, Canada's been so good to us and we appreciate it so much," Morrell adds. "Why don't we just become Canadian citizens?" It would be, she said, a fitting celebration of victory over LNG. "I'm gradually getting more optimistic. The weight is going off my shoulders. I've been carrying this leaden weight around for five years and I've noticed that it's lightening, so I must have sort of a feeling that it's less likely to happen than it was. It's been like David and Goliath, three of these heavily funded, immense projects. Two of them are pretty well done in. There's only the third one now. As long as the Canadians stick to their guns, it won't happen, because they hold the trump card."

In 1987, scholars from both sides of the line met at the University of
Maine at Orono, home of the Canadian-American Centre, to discuss what
they called the "borderlands" region of New England and the Maritimes.
John G. Reid, a professor at St. Mary's University in Halifax, described
the constantly shifting and ever-ambiguous border between the British
colonies and Acadia during the seventeenth and eighteenth centuries, and
the resulting conflicts and commercial ties. Graeme Wynn, a professor
of historical geography, sketched "a greater New England of experience"
from Boston to Passamaquoddy Bay to Halifax. Margaret Conrad, of the
University of New Brunswick, saw emigration from the Maritimes to New
England in the late nineteenth century as part of the same continuum.

But P.A. Buckner, another professor at UNB, disputed the concept
itself. The theory of "borderlands," he said, suggested that national
boundaries hinder the understanding of shared experiences of people on
the border. Fine, he said, but he disputed the implication that what those
people have in common is more important than what divides them, and
that the border is "therefore either meaningless or an undesirable barrier
to the free flow of people, goods, and ideas." The border is "more than an
artificial line along a map," he argued, and if people choose to shop where
goods were cheaper, and emigrate when the economy was bad, that does
not mean they are uncertain about their national identity. "Whether they
realize it or not," he said, "those who deny the validity of the international
boundary are promoting continentalism."

This is what Joyce Morrell is talking about on the porch of the inn on
Campobello. The border is an arbitrary line, but a line that brings a very
powerful country up against another nation, with which it has no choice
but to contend. The United States and Canada are not equal powers in
the world, but being pressed together creates a relationship in which the
smaller of the two has some leverage. The border diffuses power, allowing
more people to grasp a share of it. It is a check on unilateral action. "I
think it's a sovereignty issue," Morrell says of the LNG fight. "I'm all for
Canadian sovereignty. Go for it."

Not long before she died, Eleanor Roosevelt reflected in her newspaper
column about the meaning of connections, and of isolation, ideas she

understood well from her summers on Campobello. "Now there will be a bridge from Lubec to the island instead of the little ferry which always took our cars across in the later years. People will cross with ease, and there will be less and less division between the U.S. and Canada. Still, those of us who remember the past will have a nostalgic feeling for the days when you could spend a month or six weeks, virtually cut off from the world and all its troubles, enjoying to the full the 'beloved island.'"

That isolation is what Morrell cherishes, and if it takes an international boundary to maintain it, so be it. At the same time, "the border is a problem," she acknowledges. "It's a problem living here. It's a little island, surrounded by Maine. It's hard to do anything.

"The fact that it's so difficult also means that it hasn't been exploited. It's not full of condos. It's still peaceful and quiet. It hasn't got a lot of the pressures that people are trying to escape. It's got plenty of wildlife. It hasn't changed a lot, and that to me is a very valuable asset. Very, very valuable. Far more than opening the border and letting it all flow in. So I love to see the border there. I'll put up with the problems. Of course some people have more difficulty than we do, and there are problems, real problems, to having the border the way it is, but there are real benefits as well. The fact that that border is there is keeping those LNG people at bay. So I'm happy with the border."

EPILOGUE
ÎSLES AUX PERROQUETS

THERE IS NO DAWN ALONG THE MAINE COAST this morning, only a gradual change from night to murky grey. The drizzle is turning to steady rain as a woman with a clipboard circulates between the parked cars at Cutler Harbour, checking off names. I see the older couple from North Carolina — he is a rocket scientist, she a sociologist — whom I met at breakfast at the inn in East Machias. There is a younger couple from Indiana, and a group of Chinese-Americans, and a man from Illinois with a thoroughly drenched handlebar moustache. And there is a Department of Homeland Security bureaucrat from Virginia, who tells me that he, like all the others, has come to see the birds, though I wonder later if he is doing a different kind of field research.

There are fifteen of us in all. I put on my rubber boots and shuffle down to the skiff, which takes us out in groups of five to Andy Patterson's boat, the *Barbara Cross*, anchored in the fog-obscured harbour. The rain is picking up. It is not a great day to go looking at birds.

Soon we are heading out into the Gulf of Maine. Patterson, a broad-shouldered captain who resembles the comic-book superhero Thor, is taking us to Machias Seal Island, a fifteen-acre, low-lying piece of rock that his Web site calls the largest puffin colony on the Maine coast. "We get people from all over, around the world, foreign countries," he says later. "It definitely has wide appeal. If you're a birder in the know or you talk to someone in the serious birder community, a trip to Machias Seal Island is kind of like a pilgrimage, a must-do in your birding career."

On the way out, Patterson talks constantly about the marine environment, the various species of birds on the island, and their migratory patterns. He also explains the logistics of getting the birders ashore: he will take us in the skiff, which he is towing behind his boat; the lighthouse keeper and some bird biologists will meet us at the ramp and take the birders to special viewing blinds. The only detail Patterson does not mention is who owns the lighthouse and who the keeper works for.

Forty-five minutes after leaving Cutler, we catch glimpses of puffins racing across the surface of the water, ahead of the boat. Then we hear a foghorn, and gradually we see it emerge from the mist: an expanse of rock, a lighthouse, a handful of small buildings. The tide is coming in on the east side of the island, where the ramp is, making it too rough to go ashore there. "I can get you onto the island," Patterson says, "but I may not be able to get you off." A collective mood of resignation descends on the boat. Most of Patterson's tours only circle the island to observe the birds from the boat. This group has chosen this date, and paid extra, because it is supposed to include landing.

Patterson steers the *Barbara Cross* around to the other side of the island, where the waters are slightly calmer, and goes out in the skiff himself to take a close look at a small area of seaweed-covered rocks below the lighthouse. "It's doable," he announces to his young first mate when he returns. And so in groups of five, we pile into the skiff — except one woman, who is too scared — and are ferried over to the rocky shore, where Patterson wedges the boat between two large rocks and guns the motor to keep it there. Then, as he promised, a couple of men appear to grab our hands and pull us over the wet rocks and the seaweed. When everyone is ashore, more people appear and escort the group up a wooden walkway sitting a few inches above the ground.

As we pass between the lighthouse and a small shed, several of the birders look up, notice a Canadian flag flapping in the wind, and appear suddenly puzzled.

They thought they were still in the United States, and according to the

State Department in Washington, they are. But Ottawa's view is that they have just arrived in Canada. The island is disputed territory. More than two centuries after the Treaty of Paris, it is the last piece of land still claimed by both countries. The United States lists it as belonging to Maine; Canada considers it part of New Brunswick. I have come to Machias Seal Island not to find the end of the border, but to see a place where it does not exist.

"A lot of people get off the boat and see the bird sanctuary sign and they say, 'Canada?' And the first thing they do is turn to us and ask us," says Catherine Jardine, a biology student from the University of New Brunswick and one of the people who escorted the birders to small huts where they are watching the puffins discreetly at close range. "They get here and they see the Canadian flag and they ask, 'Do we need our passports? Where are we?' They generally ask what's going on. We say it's claimed by both countries, and they usually just shrug it off."

We are sitting at the kitchen table in the small prefab house used by biologists and students from the University of New Brunswick and the University of Maine at Orono, who spend summers on Machias Seal Island documenting the bird life. From inside, it looks like a typical house shared by students. As I sip tea, I mention that Patterson told his passengers about the lighthouse but not about who owns it. "He leaves it fairly ambiguous, and because it is ambiguous, Andy acknowledges possession is nine-tenths of the law," Kevin Kelly, another of the UNB biologists, tells me. "But at the same time, he's totally aware that he's not really under our jurisdiction. It's a little weird, and we kind of hold our tongues because we don't really have any official status here as government or anything else. When people ask us, we say as far as we're concerned, it's ours."

There is a second house along the wooden walkway, used by the lighthouse keepers, and I call on them as well. Ralph Eldridge, a burly man with a thick beard and plaid jacket, is the senior keeper of the two on duty, and his first task is to disabuse me of the romantic clichés about his line of work: the quiet contemplation, the complete lack of things to do, the isolation, the inconvenience. "Do you know how many people in the world can't drive into town, or don't have a town to drive into?" he says. "Groceries? Big deal. Lots of people buy their groceries a month at

Ralph Eldridge has worked on Machias Seal Island since 1996.

a time. I don't know where people even get this idea. From the media, mostly. 'There's nothing to do.' What do you mean, there's nothing to do? There's always something to do. If you're alive, there's something to do. When you're home, you can sit on your ass, or you can fix the cupboard hinge. There's no limit to what you can do. It's not necessarily stuff that has to be done. But there's no such thing as nothing to do."

Eldridge has worked "on the lights," as he puts it, for almost forty years, first at a lighthouse on the mainland and then, when that light was automated in 1996, on Machias Seal Island. Every eight weeks, he hops on a Canadian Coast Guard helicopter in Saint John, which deposits him at the landing pad down the walkway for a twenty-eight-day rotation. The house is comfortably equipped with large leather reclining chairs and satellite TV—a guy's house, with the large console of radio equipment the only giveaway that it is not a normal home. "The only difference is the rotation," Eldridge says. "Well, it's a little different because there's a seabird colony too." Eldridge helps out with the birder tours: there is one per day from Grand Manan Island in New Brunswick and two from Maine, including Patterson's. It is not part of his job, but he has the time and the inclination.

"It's just another location," he shrugs. "There's a little difference here from the other ones, but the rotation's the only real difference."

The only reason there *is* a rotation at all, of course, is because of Machias Seal Island's disputed status. The lighthouse would have been automated long ago if not for the fact that a human presence helps Canada's claim to the island. International law refers to "acts of interest," assertions of *de facto* sovereignty, such as the staffing and maintaining of a lighthouse, that can bolster a claim when treaties are not clear. And the treaties are anything but clear about this hunk of rock.

The media relations people at the Department of Fisheries and Oceans, who arranged my interview with Eldridge, told me he would not be able to discuss the dispute. But during our chat, he waves me over to a large marine chart showing the island, along with Grand Manan, Passamaquoddy Bay, and the coast of Maine. "There is no boundary," Eldridge says. "You're at a non-existent border. There is no boundary and there never has been." He traces the 1910 line down from Grand Manan Channel to a point about fifteen miles northeast of Machias Seal Island—the agreed-upon maritime boundary or fishing zone limit. Then his finger leaps over our location, to another agreed-upon point southwest of us. "It ends up here somewhere. [This] is also established border now." Then he moves his finger back to circle the island. "You have this gap in between where there is no border."

Perhaps more accurately, you have *two* borders: the maritime boundaries, unilaterally established by both countries, overlap here. The island is included in both. "There's the contention right there," Eldridge says, pointing to the overlap. "It has nothing to do with the island whatsoever. The result is you have a thing like a pointy football here, about twenty-five miles long, eight miles wide at its widest point, and it's a he-said she-said: 'It should be here.' 'No, it should be here.' There are also arguments about occupation, and some of them are talking about geology, and you can take the old treaties and stuff, and I can come up with legitimate arguments for both sides."

Machias Seal Island's status has never been resolved because it has never been of any consequence to either country. In early September 1604, with the St. Croix settlement under construction, Samuel de Champlain

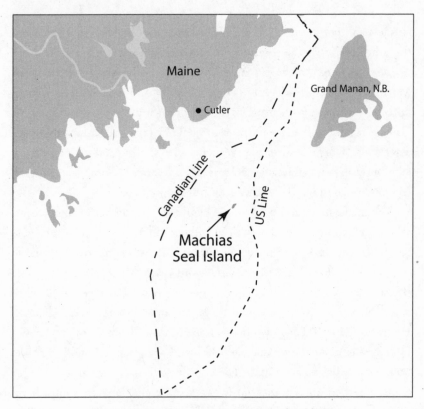

The Canadian and American marine boundary claims
overlap, both taking in Machias Seal Island.

sailed past it while exploring the coast of present-day Maine. He named
it, together with the smaller, nearby North Rock, Îsles aux Perroquets,
after the thousands of puffins he saw, but decided it was not worth a stop.
And in 1818, when the commission appointed under the Treaty of Ghent
settled the ownership of Grand Manan, Campobello, Moose Island, and
all the others, it did not occur to anyone to clarify the status of Machias
Seal Island.

Still, in 1832, New Brunswick erected a lighthouse, which the federal
government took over at Confederation. Ottawa built the current one
in 1915, and in 1944 designated the island a migratory bird sanctuary.
None of this was protested by the United States. It was only in 1971, when
Canada decided to close its fishing zones to foreign fleets and used Machias
Seal Island as a reference point to define those zones, that Washington

sat up and took notice. The Americans denounced it as a violation of international law and suggested referring the issue to the International Court of Justice in The Hague. Canada refused, saying that it had exercised undisputed sovereignty over the island. If it suddenly agreed to a hearing, Ottawa reasoned, it would undermine its case. The Canadians were, in short, disputing that there was a dispute. Eventually, however, they would have to deal with the American claims.

The disagreement revived that centuries-old argument over the King's 1621 grant of Nova Scotia to William Alexander, which had been cited in 1817 to sort out the islands of Passamaquoddy Bay. The document said all islands "near to, or within" six leagues of a line drawn from St. Mary's Bay to the St. Croix River were part of the Nova Scotia grant and any "questions, or doubts" should be resolved "in the most extensive sense" in favour of the grantee. This, Canada said, clearly covered Machias Seal Island. The Americans have argued, as they did two centuries before, that the 1621 definition of Nova Scotia was extinguished by subsequent treaties. The island, they said, was within twenty leagues of the U.S. coast and was therefore among those awarded to the United States by the 1783 treaty. And, the Americans pointed out, though Canada had occupied the island for more than a century, the United States had never explicitly ceded it.

Canada had other arguments. Geologically, Machias Seal Island could be considered part of a Grand Manan archipelago. And there were the "acts of interest"— not just the presence of lighthouse keepers but their inclusion, back when they lived there year-round, on voter lists in Canadian and New Brunswick elections. None of those arguments would trump a treaty, however, and Washington insisted that its interpretation of the treaties was correct.

The disagreement simmered for more than a decade as each country unilaterally expanded its fishing zones in the Gulf of Maine. In 1984, they agreed to send their competing maritime boundary claims to The Hague for a ruling, but, surprisingly, excluded Machias Seal Island from their arguments. Each country apparently worried that if it won the island, the International Court might feel obliged to balance that victory by ruling against its more important claim to the lucrative Georges Bank fishery—the same notion of "splitting the difference" that shaped the diplomacy over the Madawaska Settlement. So they marked one point northeast of the island and another southwest, and asked the court to *not* rule on the boundary between those two points. This created the "football," the twenty-five-mile long grey zone that Ralph Eldridge showed me on the map: an anomaly, a diplomatic loose end, and for two distant federal governments, clearly not a priority.

At the local level, it proved difficult to ignore the practical implications. For years, two tour-boat operators—Preston Wilcox from Grand Manan and Barna Norton from Jonesport, near Cutler—brought birders to the island; under a gentlemen's agreement, each captain brought half of the maximum daily visitors allowed under Canada's bird sanctuary laws. In 1986, with a letter from the U.S. State Department declaring the island U.S. territory, Norton began bringing more birders, anchoring his boat off the island overnight so he could land first. This put Canada in a Catch-22: once the daily cap on visitors was exceeded by the Maine tours, no more birders were allowed. Wilcox risked prosecution if he landed his Canadian tours. But Ottawa could not prosecute Norton without creating an international incident.

Eventually there was a compromise, with the two captains landing on alternating days. After Andy Patterson began his tours from Cutler, another dispute arose: Canadian officials decided the landing ramp for visitors was unsafe and that tours should not be allowed to come ashore. "The captains felt that was a rush to judgment," Patterson says, and he continued to bring birders to the island, knowing that, again, Ottawa could not enforce its ruling without provoking a serious diplomatic problem. The U.S. government also permitted landings by Preston Wilcox's son Peter, who had taken over the Canadian tours. "Eventually they decided they couldn't prevent us from landing," Patterson says, "so they'd better do what they could to make it safer." With Washington pondering the construction of its own landing structure, Ottawa quickly built a new concrete ramp, the one still in use in 2010.

In 2002, there was another crisis, this time not over the island but the original point of contention: the overlapping fishing zones. The waters around the island had always been fished by lobstermen out of Cutler. "A fisherman can only keep secrets for so long, and Canadian fishermen started hearing reports of some pretty good catches," Patterson says. "And they decided they wanted a slice of that pie." They successfully lobbied Ottawa to give Grand Manan lobstermen a seasonal fishery in the summer, so they could catch some lobster before they were all fished out by the Americans, who are free to work year-round.

There were conflicts between the two fleets, marked by angry exchanges and vandalized gear. "There's been no real movement between the governments, no effort to determine a boundary once and for all," Patterson tells me, "and it just ain't going to happen. The fishermen reconciled themselves to that, and worked it out themselves, as fishermen often do. Some Canadians still come down, but they work out their differences and try to stay out of each other's way. Because by and large, you know, we're neighbours. Both sides recognize these are working-class guys who are just trying to earn a living and raise families. So the conflict is still there, but it's on a low ebb at this point."

None of the irritants is large enough to force Canada and the United States to resolve the status of the island. The only thing that might, people joke, would be the discovery of oil. After all, on the St. Croix River and Passamaquoddy Bay, it is large-scale energy development that is prompting Canadians and Americans to reexamine what national sovereignty means on the border. And, I learn on Machias Seal Island, the jokes may not be that wide off the mark. Becky Holberton, a University of Maine biologist, tells me Cutler was one of seven proposed test sites for offshore wind turbines. It did not made the final cut, but the proposal may be revived someday. And the construction of hundreds of turbines in the water would have an obvious impact on marine traffic and, perhaps, the maritime boundary. "I have some interesting maps for wind development," Holberton says, "and the boundaries don't look like anything on the Canadian maps."

In the meantime, Machias Seal Island seems likely to remain a fifteen-acre piece of unfinished business between the two countries. "When I give talks about our work here, I feature the Canadian flag large," Holberton tells me. "I guess I'm like the birds. I don't see a geographical boundary. I consider this Canadian and I just don't need a passport to come here. That's how I've always viewed it. I think it's a mentality out on the island. It's not the mainland so you have this disconnect to begin with. But I firmly believe possession is nine-tenths of the law."

"It's like the highlands," Eldridge, the lighthouse keeper, tells me. "What's the highlands? Is that the highest point of land, or the highest point you can see? There's a lot of high ground before you get to the St. Lawrence. It's the same sort of stuff."

As I speak to Eldridge, his two-way radio crackles to life. It is Patterson, out on the *Barbara Cross*, calling to discuss when to attempt to get the birders back to the boat. "Is it still looking pretty bumpy and frothy down the ramp?" Patterson asks. Eldridge looks out the large window. "It's nothing special," he answers. "It's one of those situations where you're going to have to go look at it yourself." There is a pause. "Yeah, right, well," Patterson answers. "I've been watching it and there's just a little bit of tide roll, but it's just enough that it would be a little tricky when the bigger ones come along there. It may be a case where we have to wait until just after the high water, which is a little under an hour from now. Yup, I made my bed and I've got to sleep in it now."

As Patterson predicted, getting us off the island proves more difficult than getting us on to it. The morning gives way to afternoon, and as the sun comes out, finally drying everyone's clothes, our departure is pushed back. I briefly ponder the notion of being stranded overnight on Machias Seal Island with a group of earnest American birders, a gruff Canadian lighthouse keeper, and a team of biologists from both countries: a small, borderless international community, forced together by circumstance and geography.

Eventually, however, the ocean calms enough and we grope our way down the concrete ramp to the skiff, then clamber aboard the *Barbara Cross*. "It's a topic that comes up on every tour," Patterson says as we sail for Cutler. "Who owns Machias Seal Island? And I just grin and say the birds own it. We need to treasure and protect the island. We need to look after it, be it Canadians, Americans, I don't care who. If we value this opportunity to get out and see this slice of nature that's fairly hard to come by — it's not that these birds are rare, but they're hard to get to — by looking after this island and minimizing what goes on on the island, we're giving these birds a place of their own.

"Canada has done a good job of maintaining the island as a sanctuary, and I certainly support all the efforts towards that end. Those of us who are on the front lines, if you will — the boat captains, the lighthouse keepers, the researchers — we're not looking at nationality. It's meaningless, right? It's insignificant. We're most concerned about the birds and ensuring that their needs and their setting out here are not unduly or negatively impacted.

"The reality is it's a small little speck of land, a fifteen, sixteen-acre speck of land. We're never going to do anything about it. We're never going to go to war over it or cause any kind of diplomatic incident over it. It's too insignificant. After doing tours for twenty-three years and being out on the water for thirty-some years, to me it's a dead issue. The two countries will never take the time or undertake the energy or effort required to finally settle where the boundary is. See, that's the issue at its essence. The island's sovereignty is disputed because the two countries have never clearly established an imaginary line."

Perhaps Patterson is right and there is no compelling reason to settle the island's status once and for all. If Saint Croix Island, a touchstone of Canadian history, can be managed by the United States, and if the Roosevelt Cottage, beloved by one of America's greatest presidents, can exist within Canada, Machias Seal Island can probably remain in geopolitical limbo. Let it be a part of both Maine and New Brunswick, an example of what is possible when two countries realize the stakes are not really that high.

The idea brings me back to Yves Carrier's dream of an international park on the Upper Saint John: a protected, natural area, with only a limited number of entry points — a charmed place where the international border can truly be imaginary and where local wisdom can resolve any complications.

The island, I reflect, is the park that Carrier has envisioned.

It is also an argument for letting New Brunswick and Maine manage their relationship themselves, along the lines of what Robert Kaplan predicted in *An Empire Wilderness*. Kaplan's thesis, that history and geography are such powerful forces that they roll right over arbitrary boundaries, is borne out by the smuggling, the pressure for the Western Extension, the cross-border energy trade, and even by the compromises struck by the lobstermen of Cutler and Grand Manan. In each of these cases, local relationships and local imperatives trumped artificial barriers.

But James Laxer's argument in *The Border* has a place here too. There may be little traction for his critique of American exceptionalism — border-oriented Mainers are an exception to that exceptionalism — and his fear of deep integration seems misplaced along a line that is already deeply integrated. But his defence of the border as a vital expression of sovereignty resonates in the LNG fight.

The common thread is that, along a border between a small province and a small state, citizens understand the need to keep money and goods moving across the line but are also determined to take their rightful place at the centre of border affairs. LNG has taken a back seat to national sovereignty, a sovereignty expressed through the activism of Canadian citizens who "own" the line as much as their American neighbours. Electrical utilities are racing to get their clean hydroelectric power over the border into the United States, but people — New Brunswick voters and member-owners of the Eastern Maine Electrical Cooperative — insist on having a say.

Cross-border traffic by individuals has started to rebound between New Brunswick and Maine. People are voting with their feet to keep the border open. This is an important reminder that nothing on the line is immutable, even in the post-9/11 era.

In 1865, just days before dissolving the Assembly for an election campaign fought over the Western Extension, Arthur Hamilton Gordon, the lieutenant-governor of New Brunswick, wrote to an American diplomat about reports the United States would soon require travellers crossing the border to carry passports countersigned at a U.S. consulate.

This, Gordon wrote, would mean someone crossing from Woodstock (where there was a New Brunswick colonial passport office) to Houlton would first have to travel all the way to Saint John to have their papers signed by the American consul there. "This is by no means an idle question," Gordon wrote. "The strict requirement of the countersignature of the Consul at St. John to every passport issued by me will practically put an end to the intercourse at present happily prevailing between the citizens of the two states along the boundary line, a result which I should greatly deplore and which would I doubt not also be regretted by the government of the United States."

The requirement was eventually lifted, but Gordon's logic, so similar to Canada's position on the U.S. passport requirements of 2007, reminds us of the ebb and flow along the line. As surely as the impulses of the moment try to close it, human nature forces it open it again.

"The border is not finished," the International Boundary Commission proclaimed in its centennial report. Nor should we want it to be: like the people of New Brunswick and Maine, it is imperfect, occasionally infuriating, yet constantly evolving — and always irresistible.

We are drawn to it as surely as we are drawn to each other.

ACKNOWLEDGEMENTS

THIS BOOK REALLY WAS A JOURNEY, and along the way I relied on the kindness of many guides. Professor Margaret Conrad has been very supportive of my work in general and has let me bounce ideas off her. Professor Chip Gagnon encouraged me to explore the history of the border. The late David Folster's interest in this project boosted my morale. Professor George Findlen also helpfully responded to my queries and urged me on.

For tips, suggestions, contacts, and favours, I thank Harry Bagley, Jeannot Volpé, Janice Harvey, Jesse Robichaud, Joyce Pedersen, Anne Marie Murphy, Cathy St. Pierre, Paul Greene, Nathalie Godbout, Tony Diamond, Stephen Bornais, Phyllis Siebert, Lyle Skinner, Mike Tipping, Cyrille Simard, Karen Grey, Norm DeMerchant, and Carole Savage. Kevin Bagwell of the International Boundary Commission's Houlton office sent me reports and photographs, and answered many, many questions. Professors Ted McDorman and Denis Roy both sent me excerpts of their legal studies on the disputed status of Machias Seal Island. And a special thanks to my dear friend Chantal Poulin, who welcomed me as a houseguest during my travels in the former Madawaska Settlement.

I also extend my sincere thanks to all the people along the border who agreed to be interviewed for this book. I will not list them all here because their names appear in the text, but I want to give special thanks to four people who helped me visit hard-to-reach locations along the border:

Dr. Yves Carrier (Beau Lake and Glazier Lake), Bill Boone (Monument Brook), Ranger Meg Scheid (Saint Croix Island), and Captain Andy Patterson (Machias Seal Island). Seeing these places first-hand brought their stories to life; the book would not feel complete had I not been there.

Researching also means spending time in libraries and archives, always a delight. I am grateful to Kenda Clark-Gorey and the staff at the New Brunswick Legislative Library, Patricia Belier at the Harriet Irving Library's Archives and Special Collections, Gary Hughes and Jennifer Longon at the New Brunswick Museum, Fred Farrell and Julia Thompson at the Provincial Archives of New Brunswick, Sister Bertille Beaulieu, archivist for Les Religieuses Hospitalières de Saint-Joseph, Guy Lefrançois at the Bibliothèque Rhéa-Larose, Université de Moncton, Edmundston campus, and Pauleena MacDougall at the Maine Folklife Center at the University of Maine at Orono.

Three of the students I have taught in Journalism 2033 at St. Thomas University agreed to do research for me. Lily Boisson, Colin Hood, and Michelle Twomey all delivered beyond my expectations. They are all talented young journalists who are going to do great work in the business.

At the CBC, Mary-Pat Schutta, Dan Goodyear, and Andrew Cochran indulged my latest urge to vanish from my day job for weeks at a time. The interest of my colleagues in this project, particularly Peter Anawati, Julie Clow, Myfanwy Davies, Dan McHardie, Terry Seguin, and Alan White, was a great motivator. Dan also joined me on a return trip to Monument Brook, which I appreciate.

Several current and former colleagues agreed to read some of my chapters and provide feedback: Kathy Kaufield, Julie Clow, Dave Atkinson, and Dan McHardie. Jonathan Dursi also pitched in to read the chapter on railroads, even though it isn't rocket science. Their suggestions and feedback were a great help.

At Goose Lane Editions, Akoulina Connell was the first to show interest in this book, and Susanne Alexander generously agreed to give me the green light to pursue it. I thank Julie Scriver for her work with the maps, the photographs, and the general design, and John Sweet, my editor, for his thoughtful and careful edit. Clare Goulet was a diligent copy editor, and Angela Williams helped get us all over the finish line. I am also grateful to the Canada Council for the Arts for financial support under the Creative Writing Program, which allowed me to take two months off work to travel the border.

My wife, Giselle Goguen, provided the most important support of all. She gave up much of her own time so that I could travel and write. She was a sounding board for ideas, she read several chapters, and she cheered me up and calmed me down as circumstances required. This book would not have happened without her, and I am forever grateful.

SOURCES

I CONDUCTED A NUMBER OF INTERVIEWS as I travelled to various border communities in May, June, and July of 2010. The people I spoke to are quoted by name in the text. In addition, I relied on a range of primary and secondary source materials:

INTRODUCTION: GATEWAYS
Guy Murchie's *Saint Croix* (New York: Duell, Sloan and Pearce, 1947) helped set the scene in St. Stephen. Ideas on the border are from Robert Kaplan, *An Empire Wilderness: Travels Into America's Future* (New York: Random House, 1998) and James Laxer, *The Border* (Toronto: Random House, 2003). The federal roundtable is summarized in *The Emergence of Cross-Border Regions Between Canada and the United States: Roundtables Synthesis Report* (Government of Canada Policy Research Initiative, May 2006).

1 :: WICKED CLOSE
One of the most valuable books during my research was Beatrice Craig and Maxime Dagenais, *The Land In Between: The Upper St. John Valley, Prehistory to World War I* (Gardiner, Maine: Tilbury House, 2009). Census data is from the U.S. Bureau of the Census. I also read Pierre Tristam, "The Quiet Border," *American Impressions, Chapter 12: Maine*, at www.pierretristam.com. Interviews with John Allen Page and Jim Connors were from 1970–71

and were part of an oral history project of the Maine Folklife Center, University of Maine at Orono.

2 :: OSWALD'S FOLLY

Chip Gagnon's remarkable Web site, http://www.upperstjohn.com, which he maintains as a hobby, was an important guide as I traced the history of the border. It includes scanned copies of many original documents. Equally valuable was Francis M. Carroll, *A Good and Wise Measure: The Search for the Canadian-American Boundary, 1783-1842* (Toronto: University of Toronto Press, 2001), the definitive history of the period. For Richard Oswald, I relied on David Hancock, *Citizens of the World: London Merchants and the Integration of the British Atlantic Community, 1735-1785* (Cambridge: Cambridge University Press, 1995) and on W. Stitt Robinson's essay in *Richard Oswald's Memorandum* (Charlottesville: University of Virginia Press, 1953). More general accounts were Samuel Flagg Bemis, *A Diplomatic History of the United States*, Fifth Edition (New York: Holt, Rinehart and Winston Inc., 1965), W.S. MacNutt's *A History of New Brunswick* (Toronto: Macmillan, 1963), and the Web site Nova Scotia's Electronic Attic (http://www.alts.net/ns1625/). This chapter also includes information from Matthew Edney, "The Mitchell Map, 1755-1782: An Irony of Empire" (Portland: University of Southern Maine Osher Map Library, http://usm.maine.edu/maps/web-document/2/home), Charlotte M. Lenentine, *Madawaska: A Chapter in Maine–New Brunswick Relations* (Fredericton: University of New Brunswick MA thesis, 1955), James K. Chapman, *Relations of Maine and New Brunswick, in the Era of Reciprocity, 1849-1867* (Fredericton: University of New Brunswick MA Thesis, 1951), Henry David Thoreau, *The Maine Woods* (Boston: Ticknor and Fields, 1864), Pierre Berton, *Flames Across the Border* (Toronto: McClelland and Stewart Ltd., 1981), and John LeCouteur, *Merry Hearts Make Light Days*, edited by Donald E. Graves (Ottawa: Carleton University Press, 1993). The letter of Colin Campbell to William F. Odell, July 29, 1843, is found in the Odell Family fonds, F32-16, New Brunswick Museum, Saint John, New Brunswick. I also used Murchie in this chapter.

3 :: PARTITION

This chapter relied extensively on Carroll, Gagnon, and MacNutt. I also used James Hannay, *A History of New Brunswick*, Vol. 1 (Saint John: J.A. Bowes, 1909); Geraldine Tidd Scott, *Ties of Common Blood: A History of Maine's Northeast Boundary Dispute with Great Britain* (Bowie, Maryland: Heritage Books, 1992); Winfield Scott, *Memoirs of Lieut.-General Scott, LL.D, Written by Himself* (New York: Sheldon and Company, 1864); J. Chris Arndt, "Maine in the Northeastern Boundary Controversy: States' Rights in Antebellum New England" (in *The New England Quarterly*, Vol. LXII, no. 1, March 1989, pp. 205-223); Doris Kearns-Goodwin, *Team of Rivals* (New York: Simon and Schuster, 2005); Alec McEwan (editor), *In Search of the Highlands: Mapping the Canada-Maine Boundary, 1839* (Fredericton: Acadiensis Press, 1988); and Lawrence Martin and Samuel Flagg Bemis, "Franklin's Red-Line Map Was a Mitchell" in the *New England Quarterly*, Vol. 10, no. 1 (March 1937) pp. 105-111. I also used Bemis, Lenentine, and Berton here.

4 :: GODFATHERS OF THE VALLEY

Rino Albert's 2000 interview with Georges Cyr for the Société Historique de St. Hilaire was a valuable source for this chapter, as was B.J. Grant's *When Rum Was King* (Fredericton: Goose Lane Editions, 1984) and Benoit Long, *Philip Long: An Old Servant Of Government* (self-published, 2009). Accounts of the Estcourt liquor raid and subsequent Edmundston court appearance in 1922 are from two contemporary newspaper articles, "En cours de Police," *Le Madawaska*, November 10, 1922, and "Canadians Arrest Maine Dry Agents," *New York Times*, November 9, 1922. The account of the Dean Michaud case is based on my reporting on his arrest for the New Brunswick *Telegraph-Journal*, on trial coverage by my colleague Gary Dimmock, on an interview with Dean Michaud by another colleague, Alan White, and on State of Maine vs. Dean Michaud (1998 ME 251), Maine Supreme Judicial Court, November 25, 1998.

5 :: "A FEW MISERABLE FRENCHMEN"

Background in this chapter is drawn from Beatrice Craig and from "Notes on the History of Fraser Companies, Limited," an internal company history given to me by Ron Beaulieu. For the story of post-treaty Madawaska, I consulted Perry Garfinkel, "Madawaska: Down East with a French Accent" (*National Geographic*, September 1980); Richard W. Judd, "Timber Down the Saint John: A Study in Maine-New Brunswick Relations" (*Maine Historical Society Quarterly*, Vol. 24, No. 1, Summer 1984); oral history interviews with Marcella Bélanger Violette and Belone Pelletier held at the Maine Folklife Centre; Pam Belluck, "Long scorned in Maine, French has Renaissance" (*New York Times*, June 4, 2006); Barry H. Rodrigue's essay, "French speakers ... not always, but always Franco-Americans!" (University of Southern Maine, 1991); "Acadian Culture in Maine," an essay on the University of Maine at Fort Kent Web site (http://acim. umfk.maine.edu/language.html); Cleo P. Ouellette's term paper "A New Look at French in the Saint John Valley" (University of Maine at Fort Kent, April 1993); Acadian Genealogy Homepage at http://www.acadian.org/ acadcrss.html; Louise Gravel Shea, "L'influence de la frontière Canado-Américaine sur la population de Grande-Rivière Madawaska" (Québec: Université Laval MA thesis, 1999); Mary Lunney, Tom Scott and Tim Doak, "Two-Way French Immersion in Rural Maine" (American Council on Immersion Education newsletter, Vol. 5, No. 1, November 2001, University of Minnesota); and my own reporting for the New Brunswick *Telegraph-Journal* and CBC News.

6 :: REMAINS

This chapter relies extensively on George L. Findlen, "Under His Own Flag: John Baker's Gravestone Memorial in Retrospect," translation of an essay published in *La Revue de la Société historique du Madawaska* 30 (janvier-mars 2002), pp. 5-55. I also consulted Martin and Bemis, Gagnon, Carroll, Edney, and Scott, as well as *Fort Fairfield Register and Town History, 1904* (Fort Fairfield Frontier Heritage Historical Society, republished 2008). An account of Jared Sparks's weaknesses as a historian is included in Jill Lepore, "His Highness" (*The New Yorker*, September 27, 2010). The

1837 Foundation of Northern Maine Web site is at http://www.rootsweb. ancestry.com/~me1837.

7 :: GOOD NEIGHBOURS

This chapter is based on my reporting for the CBC on the Pedersens's farm, as well as on Laxer's chapters on border security and on newspaper reports from *The Washington Post, The Boston Globe, The Aroostook Star-Herald, The Globe and Mail, The Bangor Daily News,* and *The Victoria Star.* The story of Loring Air Force Base soldiers heading to Saint John for love is from Connell Smith and Christina Harnett, "Invasion of the Flyboys" (Maritime Magazine documentary, CBC Radio, November 21, 2010). Allan Gotlieb's op-ed "Proximity, reality, strategy, destiny" appeared in *The Globe and Mail* on June 25, 2009.

8 :: INVASIONS

I drew heavily on Ruth Reed Mraz, "Hiding in Plain Sight: The Friends Church in Fort Fairfield" (unpublished monograph) and on Edith Miller, "New Brunswick Connection with the Underground Railroad" at http:// www.quaker.ca/Publications/cfriend/2001-Mar/CF-MAR-2001-miller. pdf. The 2010 platform of the Maine State Republican Party is at http:// www.mainegop.com/PlatformMission.aspx. The Canadian Press report "U.S. border sees more sneak into Canada than other way" appeared September 18, 2010. This chapter also draws on Michael Woloschuk, *Family Ties: The Real Story of the McCain Feud* (Toronto: Key Porter, 1995); John DeMont. *Citizens Irving: K.C. Irving and His Legacy* (Toronto: Doubleday, 1991); "Northern Maine Woodlands 2007-2031 Strategic Forest Management Plan, Public Summary," J.D. Irving Limited, June 2010; Marian Botsford Fraser, *Walking the Line* (Toronto and Vancouver: Douglas and McIntyre, 1989); Frank Graham, Jr., "That Mess on the Prestile" (*American Heritage Magazine,* Vol. 21, no. 2, February 1970); Bob Colby, "The Nicest International Incident Imaginable" (*Memories of Maine Magazine,* Aroostook County Edition, Winter 2010); International Boundary Commission Annual Report, 2007; Peter Sullivan, David Bernhard, and Brian Ballantyne, "The Canada-United States boundary:

The next century" (International Boundary Commission Annual Report, 2009); the aforementioned books by Carroll and Scott; and articles in the New Brunswick *Telegraph-Journal*, Downeast.com, *The Bangor Daily News,* and *The New York Times.*

9 :: THE PERSISTENCE OF ATLANTICA

In addition to my own reporting for CBC News, this chapter is based on Statistics Canada, "Cross-border shopping and the loonie: Not what it used to be" (*Canadian Economic Observer,* December 2007, Vol. 20, no. 12) and on Robin Neill, "Historical Atlantica: How the impact of the past will shape our future" (Atlantic Institute of Market Studies, Halifax, 2007). Accounts of early trading links include Caroline St-Louis, *Regard du Massachusetts sur l'Acadie: le Journal de Winthrop, 1630-1649* (Tracadie-Sheila: Editions La Grande Marée, 2009) and N.E.S. Griffiths, *From Migrant to Acadian: A North American Border People 1605-1755* (Montreal and Kingston: McGill-Queen's University Press, 2005). Thomas E. Perley's letter to Samuel Leonard Tilley of February 18, 1858, is from the Tilley Fonds, New Brunswick Museum, F14-11. I also quote the Criminal Intelligence Service-New Brunswick's "Organized Crime: Imprints on New Brunswick Communities" (2006 Public Report) and books by Judd and Craig. "Free Trade in Maine: Four Hundred Miles of Boundary for Smugglers" appeared in *The New York Times,* January 10, 1892, and Sharon Kiley Mack's excellent investigation "Drugs weigh heavily on Maine's poorest area, Washington County" ran in *The Bangor Daily News,* August 20, 2010.

10 :: GIVE ME A BREAK

For a brief history on Forest City, I referred to the classic study of the entire border region by Harold Davis, *An International Community on the St. Croix, 1604-1930* (Orono: University of Maine at Orono, 1950). This chapter also uses Carroll's book, and Jim Burant's essay on James Bucknall Bucknall Estcourt, at the Dictionary of Canadian Biography Online. John Stossel's rant on Forest City, "More Pointless Government Growth," is from *John Stossel's Take* (Fox Business News Web site), March 22, 2010. Jen Lynds's story "Forest City port proposal scaled down" appeared in *The Bangor Daily News*, April 17, 2010. The leaked U.S. Consular document describing the trip by American officials along the border is dated March 14, 2007, and is available at http://www.wikileaks.fi/cable/2007/03/07HALIFAX12.html.

11 :: "WE FRATERNIZE ON THIS ROAD"

The account of the Vanceboro festivities is included in Faye Luppi and Marcella H. Sorg's "Vanceboro, Maine, 1870-1900: A Hinterland Community" (*Maine Historical Society Quarterly*, Vol. 25, no. 2, Fall 1985, pp. 88-113). I also used newspaper articles from the *Bangor Daily Whig and Courier*, October 17-19, 1871, and from *The Colonial Farmer* and *The New York Times*. For the story of the railway battle, I consulted Alan Bailey, *Railways in New Brunswick, 1827-1867* (Fredericton: University of New Brunswick MA Thesis, 1955); C.M. Wallace, "Saint John Boosters and the Railroads in Mid-Nineteenth Century" (*Acadiensis*, Vol. 6 [1976–77], no. l: 71–91); Alice Stewart, "The State of Maine and Canadian Confederation" (*Canadian Historical Review*, Vol. 33, no. 2, June 1952, pp. 148-164); Alfred G. Bailey, "Railways and the Confederation Issue in New Brunswick, 1863-1865" (*Canadian Historical Review*, Vol. 21, no. 4, December 1940); Alfred G. Bailey, "The Basis and Persistence of Opposition to Confederation in New Brunswick" (*Canadian Historical Review*, Vol. 23, no. 4, 1942); Donald Creighton, *John A. Macdonald: The Young Politician* (Toronto: MacMillan Company of Canada, 1965); *Correspondence Respecting the Proposed Union of the British North American Provinces* (London, Her Majesty's Stationery Office, 1867); and J.K. Chapman, *The Career of Arthur Hamilton Gordon, First Lord Stanmore* (Toronto: University of Toronto Press, 1964). Also helpful was David Folster's article "Why McAdam, NB has a such a big railway station" (*Canadian Geographic*, Vol. 102 [April-May 1982], pp. 34-36). I also relied on Davis, Chapman, and MacNutt, and on Anne Marie Murphy, "The Border Towns of NB and Maine," http://www.fosterville. ca; on Lilian Maxwell, '*Round New Brunswick Roads* (Toronto: The Ryerson Press, 1951); and on articles concerning the Cianbro toll-road plan in *The Ellsworth American* and the *Halifax Chronicle-Herald*.

12 :: THE GREAT GAME

In addition to MacNutt and Davis, and reporting by my colleague Robert Jones and myself on the NB Power controversy for CBC News, this chapter uses Philip Lee, "Down by the old mill stream" (New Brunswick *Telegraph-Journal*, February 20, 2010) and William Marshall and William Thompson, *Options Analysis for the New Brunswick Electricity Market and the NB Power Group of Companies* (Fredericton: Province of New Brunswick, December, 2008). Information on focus groups and polling on the sale of NB Power is from reports by Innovative Research Group prepared for the government of New Brunswick and obtained by the author through the provincial *Right to Information Act*.

13 :: COLLISIONS ON THE BAY

This chapter cites news articles from the New Brunswick *Telegraph-Journal, The Bangor Daily News,* and *The Quoddy Tides*; books by Murchie, MacNutt, and Davis; and Richard W. Judd and Christopher S. Beach, *Natural States: The Environmental Imagination in Maine, Oregon and the Nation* (Washington: RFF Press, 2003).

14 :: SAVING CHAMPLAIN

I draw here on two classic works by William Francis Ganong: *Champlain's Island* (Saint John: New Brunswick Museum, 2003) and *A Monograph of the Evolution of the Boundaries of the Province of New Brunswick* (Transactions of the Royal Society of Canada, 1901). I also draw on William Henry Kilby (ed.), *Eastport and Passamaquoddy: A Collection of Historical and Biographical Sketches* (Eastport: Waterfront Research Committee of Eastport, 1982). A gripping and comprehensive biography is *Champlain's Dream* by David Hackett Fischer (Toronto: Vintage Canada, 2009). I also relied on David Folster, *The Chocolate Ganongs of St. Stephen, New Brunswick* (Toronto, MacMillan of Canada, 1990) and Carroll, Davis, MacNutt, and Murchie. Andrew Coyne's perceptive column on Champlain, "Canada is a French country," appeared in *Macleans*, July 19, 2010.

15 :: NEW BRUNSWICK ON THE PENOBSCOT

The rich history of smuggling on Passamaquoddy Bay comes alive in Joshua Smith's *Borderland Smuggling: Patriots, Loyalists, and Illicit Trade in the Northeast, 1783-1820* (Gainesville: University Press of Florida, 2006). I used three fascinating accounts of the British occupation of eastern Maine: John Boileau, *Half-Hearted Enemies: Nova Scotia, New England and the War of 1812* (Halifax: Formac Publishing, 2005); Barry Lohnes, "A New Look at the Invasion of Eastern Maine, 1814" (*Maine Historical Society Quarterly*, Vol. 15, Summer 1974, pp. 4-25); and Lorenzo Sabine, "Moose Island and its Dependencies Four Years under Martial Law," in Kilby. The account of the 1818 handover ceremony is from Sabine and from Wayne Wilcox, "Eastport returned to U.S. under General James Miller" (*Quoddy Tides*, April 9, 2010). The Ganong monograph, MacNutt, Murchie, Carroll, and Davis were all used here as well.

16 :: BELOVED ISOLATION

Jonas Klein's *Beloved Island: Franklin and Eleanor and the Legacy of Campobello* (Forest Vale, Vermont: Paul S. Eriksson Publisher, 2000) helped form the backbone of this chapter. I also used Walter Lowrie, "Roosevelt and the Passamaquoddy Bay Tidal Project" (*The Historian*, Vol. 31, issue 1, pp. 64-89, August 23, 2007); and Stephen Hornsby et. al. (eds), *The Northeastern Borderlands: Four Centuries of Interaction* (Fredericton: Acadiensis Press and the Canadian-American Centre, University of Maine, 1989). "In search of the elusive lousewort," appeared in *Time*, September 19, 1977. Murchie and Davis were again useful, as was LNG coverage in the *Bangor Daily News, St. Croix Courier*, and *Portland Press-Herald*. Tamsin McMahon's "Island Confidential," a thorough investigation of American development schemes on Campobello, appeared in the New Brunswick *Telegraph-Journal* on August 14, 2010. The notion of an Arctic compromise by Stephen Harper is from John Ibbitson, "Arctic policy priority No. 1: settle border disputes" (*The Globe and Mail*, August 20, 2010); and comments from Stephen Harper and Barack Obama on border negotiations are from John Ibbitson, Bill Curry, and Paul Koring, "Beyond the border talks looms a homegrown debate" (*The Globe and Mail*, February 5, 2011).

EPILOGUE :: ÎSLES AUX PERROQUETS

Fraser's book gave some of the recent history of Machias Seal Island; Joan Marshall's *Tides of Change on Grand Manan Island* (Montréal and Kingston: McGill-Queen's University Press, 2008) also touches on the dispute. For the legal arguments, I drew on Denis Roy, *Compromis politique dans la délimitation du plateau continental juridique: Étude du Canada et de la France* (Nantes: doctoral thesis in law, Université de Nantes, 2008); Ted McDorman, *Salt Water Neighbors: International Ocean Law Relations Between the United States and Canada* (Oxford: Oxford University Press, 2009); David H. Gray, "Canada's Unresolved Maritime Boundaries," International Boundary Research Unit (Durham University, U.K.), *Boundary and Security Bulletin*, August 1997; and Department of Fisheries and Oceans, "The Machias Seal Island Lobster Fishery: Backgrounder," June 2004. The January 12, 1865 letter from Arthur Hamilton Gordon about American passport requirements is in the Gordon fonds at the Harriet Irving Library, University of New Brunswick, MG H2a, Box 3, File 14.

INDEX